KNOWLEDGE ORGANIZATION
From Libraries to the Web

KNOWLEDGE ORGANIZATION
From Libraries to the Web

Edited By
K.S. Raghvan
and
A. Neelameghan

Published By

Ess Ess Publications
New Delhi
for

Sarada Ranganathan Endowment for Library Science
Bangalore

Knowledge Organization : From Library to the Web

S.R. Ranganathan's
Five Laws of Library Science

Books are for Use
Every Reader his/her Book
Every Book its Reader
Save the Time of the Reader
Library is a Growing Organism

ISBN: 978-81-7000-718-0

₹ 995/-

First Published 2014

Published by:
Ess Ess Publications
4831/24, Ansari Road,
Darya Ganj,
New Delhi-110 002.
INDIA
Phones: 23260807, 41563444
Fax: 41563334
E-mail: info@essessreference.com
www.essessreference.com

for

Sarada Ranganathan Endowment for Library Science
702, 'Upstairs', 42nd Cross, III Block, Rajajinagar,
Bangalore-560 010
E-mail: srels@dataone.in Phone: 080-23305109

Printed and bound in India at Salasar Imaging Systems.

ACKNOWLEDGEMENT

The Sarada Ranganathan Endowment for Library Science founded by Late Prof. S. R. Ranganathan in 1963 is celebrating its Golden Jubilee this year. This is also the Golden Jubilee year of the journal of the Endowment that was founded by Prof. Ranganathan in 1963 under the title *Library Science with a Slant to Documentation*. Much of classification research done in India after Ranganathan's return to India from Zurich, particularly the work directed at enhancing the General Theory of Classification of Ranganathan and improvements to the *Colon Classification* have appeared as papers in this journal. In the first decade of its publication the papers were almost exclusively on some aspect of Knowledge Organization. The scope of the journal was widened later to include papers on other aspects and consequently the title of the journal was also changed. Today the journal is being published under the title *SRELS Journal of Information Management* and continues to be one of the most sought after channels for publication of research and developmental work carried out in India in different branches of LIS. When the subject of celebrating the Golden Jubilee of the Endowment and the journal came up before the Board of Trustees of the Sarada Ranganathan Endowment for Library Science at a meeting held in 2012 (during the ISKO International Conference at Mysore), it was decided that a special volume/issue of the journal devoted exclusively to Knowledge Organization – an area to which Ranganathan made significant contributions – be brought out. Invitations were sent out to several eminent researchers in the area to contribute research papers for the Golden Jubilee issue/volume and many of them readily responded. We are grateful to all the authors who have contributed research papers to this special issue.

We are also grateful to the Board of Trustees of the Sarada Ranganathan Endowment for Library Science (SRELS) for asking us to edit this special issue/volume. We sincerely thank the staff of SRELS for all the support and cooperation in bringing to fruition the idea that was conceived at the SRELS Board meeting. A special word of thanks to Ms. S.K. Lalitha whose labour of love it was to format all the papers and prepare the print-ready version.

One of the editors, Dr. K. S. Raghavan, would like to place on record his deep sense of gratitude to the support provided under the TEQIP programme (subcomponent 1.2.1) of the World Bank / Government of India research grant to the Centre for Knowledge Analytics and Ontological Engineering (KAnOE) at PES Institute of Technology, Bangalore, India.

The papers included in this volume have been separately published in the *SRELS Journal of Information Management*, 50(6), December 2013, special issue on Knowledge Organization.

CONTENTS

FOREWORD

Sarada Ranganathan Endowment for Library Science (SRELS), founded by Dr. S.R. Ranganathan, renowned Library and Information Scientist, in 1961, is registered as a Charitable Endowment with the Government of India (1963). It is also registered with the Government of Karnataka (2006).

The aims and objectives of the Endowment briefly are:

- To improve the library and information services in India;
- To train library and information service personnel;
- To promote the provision of efficient library and information service; and
- To apply research results to library and information studies.

The Endowment is implementing these objectives by publishing books, reports and the periodical *SRELS Journal of Information Management* and by organizing Workshops, Lectures and Seminars. *SRELS Journal of Information Management* has completed ***50 years*** of publication.

Three series of lectures are organized under the auspices of the Endowment:

1. Sarada Ranganathan Endowment Lectures. (1965-);
2. Dr. S.R. Ranganathan Memorial Lectures. (1973-); and
3. Curzon Co-Seshachalam Endowment Lectures. (2001-).

Knowledge Organization: From Libraries to the Web, edited by K.S. Raghavan and A. Neelameghan, contains 16 articles dealing with various aspects of knowledge organization. The concept of knowledge organization has changed over the years. Today knowledge organization encompasses issues beyond classification, cataloguing and indexing. A variety of factors impact knowledge organization. The papers present contemporary thinking on the subject.

K.N. Prasad
Executive Officer
Sarada Ranganathan Endowment for Library Science

The Facets of Knowledge Organization: An Introduction

K.S. Raghavan

To classify is to put things into meaningful groups. Knowledge Organization is the domain concerned with the ordering of knowledge in a meaningful and logical fashion. I. Dahlberg considered *knowledge* as *what is known* and *organization* as *the activity of constructing something according to a plan*. From the time of Melville Dewey till recently most theorists of knowledge organization and classificationists (to use a term coined by Ranganathan to refer to designers of systems for knowledge organization such as a scheme of classification) have adopted a more or less pragmatic approach largely restricting their discussions to issues relevant to the organization of recorded / documented knowledge. In other words the concern has largely been with knowledge artifacts such as books and other documentary resources. In this sense knowledge organization refers to description of documentary resources in terms of all relevant attributes. This '*documentary resource description-centered approach*' to knowledge organization has dominated much of the thinking in the area since the time of Panizzi, Dewey and Cutter. Another important approach, though very recent, to knowledge organization is the '*use-centric*' approach; i.e. to look at knowledge resources and their organization from the perspective of their potential use.

Knowledge is the term used to represent what is known at any point in time. A significant proportion of knowledge available at any point in time is recorded in artifacts such as books, papers in periodicals, theses and dissertations, digital resources and the like (Explicit knowledge). It should not therefore come as a surprise that the efforts of many theorists and practitioners in the area of Knowledge Organization have been directed towards building better bibliographic tools for more effective control of explicit knowledge. We clearly see two distinct, parallel and complementary streams of research dotting the map of knowledge organization. One stream focused largely on bibliographic artifacts of various kinds and their description as physical entities. The *91 Rules* of Panizzi, the AA code, the

Library of Congress Rules for Descriptive Cataloging, the ICCP (Paris, 1961), the IMCE (Copenhagen, 1969) and the different editions of AACR are all efforts along this. In recent years the efforts along this direction have largely been led by IFLA, national libraries / national bibliographic agencies and professional associations especially in the English language-speaking world and have resulted in FRBR (Functional Requirements of Bibliographic Records), a generalized model of entities of the bibliographic universe. These have been elaborated as the three kinds of bibliographic entities in FRBR– the *work* and its physical manifestations, the individuals and bodies associated with a *work* and / or its physical manifestations, and '*aboutness*' of *works* and / or their physical manifestations. The last one – *aboutness* – was a later addition, added during the IFLA General Conference in New Delhi in 1992. The RDA (Resource Description and Access) could be seen as an implementation of the FRBR model. The second stream focused on tools and techniques for representing the *aboutness* of bibliographic items. This too has a long history beginning with Melville Dewey and Cutter in the last quarter of the 19th Century and enriched by the contributions of Kaiser, Ranganathan & his associates, Mortimer Taube, Calvin Mooers, members of the British Classification Research Group, I. Dahlberg, Hjorland and many others. It was Elaine Svenonius who made a systematic effort to unify these two streams of research. To her the discipline of *Knowledge Organization* is made up of a set of languages and the theory and practice of building such languages[1]. The different kinds of languages that Elaine Svenonius refers to in her book on information organization are, collectively, the various knowledge organization tools to effect the description of information objects to support their representation, identification, search and retrieval. Today *Knowledge Organization* is a much broader area and is by no means limited to *Classification, Indexing and Cataloguing*. There is an international organization (ISKO), quite a few journals that are exclusively devoted to the subject, and many research groups in different countries and universities of the world that are actively engaged in research in the area. Hjorland even suggests that *Knowledge Organization* is related to the theory of *knowledge* per se and has emphasized the need for and importance of taking a broader view of the domain of *Knowledge*

---

1 Svenonius, Elaine. The intellectual foundation of information organization. Cambridge, Mass.: MIT Press, 2000

Organization for developing LIS as a scholarly discipline[1]. The themes of papers in this issue collectively are certainly not exhaustive of the scope of the domain of *Knowledge Organization*; nevertheless they represent a predominant subset of topics of current interest to researchers in the domain. As is to be expected a number of papers relate to Ranganathan's ideas and work.

Smiraglia employs the domain analysis technique to review and map the influence of Ranganathan on research in *Knowledge organization* in the last nearly 30 years. Based on citation analysis of papers indexed in the *Web of Science*, he concludes that Ranganathan's work on *facet analysis* constitutes a primary cluster of influence in the literature of knowledge organization.

A few papers examine specifically the notion of *facets* and categorization – an area that is central to and at the core of much of Ranganathan's writings and thinking on classification. **Widad Mustafa El Hadi** examines the relevance of universal knowledge organization systems for the Web environment and, more particularly the potential of faceted systems for the networked environment. **Vanda Broughton** in an extensive and well documented paper examines the theory of faceted classification critically examining the various schemas of categories including Ranganathan's and Vickery's schemas. The paper also examines the importance of facet analysis as a general research tool, and how it "compares with other content analysis tools as a means of modeling subject domains". **Claudio Gnoli** in his paper *'Facets, levels and semantic factoring'* suggests that use of *semantic factors* (e.g., other *concepts* that occur in the definition of a *concept*) in knowledge organization systems could enhance the value and utility of knowledge organization systems. He argues that it is useful to record the relationships of a concept with its semantic factors. **Fulvio Mazzochi**'s paper examines the similarity Ranganathan's schema of categories and the categories of the Nyaya-Vaisheshika systems of Indian philosophy. He argues that even though most schemas of categories are set in and are influenced by a certain culture, this does not necessarily impact their applicability.

Joseph Tennis looks at the conceptual tools developed by Ranganathan for accommodating new topics including *facets* which are the most commonly known tool constructed by Ranganathan. He suggests that these are only partial solutions to the issues that arise from the changing universe of knowledge. He illustrates the issues with examples indicating the effect of change of semantics of facets over time

Kathryn LaBarre's paper draws from her experience in working on two specific projects aimed at enhancing access to, search and retrieval of two types of cultural heritage resources – films and folktales. She suggests designing systems that use as inputs both an understanding of users' needs and facet analysis.

Knowledge organization is concerned with both *concepts* and *relationships* between concepts both – context independent and context dependent relations. **Green and Bean** examine the close association of syntagmatic relationships with thematic roles and semantic frames. They suggest that the application of semantic frames in the context of knowledge organization has considerable potential.

As is to be expected there are also some papers that look at the challenges and opportunities in the digital Web environment. **Peter Ohly** writes about the challenges for building, what he calls *"new knowledge organization aimed at Semantic Web 3.0"* and the implications for ISKO. **Shepherd and Watters** explore the challenges of knowledge organization in the *Big Data* Environment. Looking at the dimensions *'Big Data'*, they suggest that rather than trying to "manipulate existing knowledge organization models and approaches for the new reality of huge unstructured and heterogeneous real time data sets and unknown user needs, we should redefine knowledge organization for the exploding context of data analytics for Big Data". **Kavi Mahesh and Pallavi Karanth** discuss the limitations of current knowledge organization systems in terms of their ability to support multiple points of view. The paper also examines the gaps in OWL and proposes an extension to OWL to support diverse and multiple points of view in a single knowledge organization system.

Hemalata Iyer and D'Ambrosio look at the potential of a micro-blogging tool, viz., *hashtags* in Twitter for adding value to online library catalogues. The paper suggests that embedding Twitter on the catalog main page and result pages can serve as a social space for users to interact with the community and librarians.

Raghavan and Neelameghan in their paper examine the major contributions of S. R. Ranganathan to knowledge organization and the impact of Ranganathan's ideas on systems of knowledge organization and their relevance for presentation of ideas.

A few papers look at knowledge organization in specific domains or for specific purposes.

Neelameghan and Lalitha in their paper point out the differences between the way in which a set of Tamil classics have been grouped in Ranganathan's *Colon Classification* and the way in which subject specialists have grouped them to suggest the possibility of different kinds of groupings and categorization. The paper illustrates a prototype system built using Greenstone Digital Library software to support search, retrieval and presentation of information objects.

Sugumaran illustrates a methodology for mapping the knowledge in a domain using 'Liquid Rocket Propulsion System' as an example.

Neelameghan in a paper on spatial information systems illustrates with examples, the different categories and types of spatial data and information relevant for socio-economic development planning. The paper focuses on the importance, from the point of view of the planner, of integrating the data and explains how this could be achieved.

CONCLUSION

A review article by I. Dahlberg on *developments in classification* that appeared more than three decades ago in *Advances in Librarianship* began with a sentence: "... no developments since Ranganathan". Looked at purely from a theoretical point of view there is some truth in that statement even when considered in the present context. However, the situation that is obtaining today is vastly different from what it was when Ranganathan and his associates in India and the members of the Classification research Group in U.K. initiated major efforts in the mid 1960s to refine / build KOS to meet the challenges and requirements of MARC and machine-based retrieval. The Internet and the World Wide Web have completely transformed the situation and context in which Knowledge Organization systems have to operate and function. The World Wide Web with its vast unstructured and unorganized repositories has complicated the problems of information retrieval. The Web is unprecedented in many ways: unprecedented in scale, unprecedented in the almost-complete lack of coordination in its creation, unprecedented in the diversity of backgrounds and motives of its participants, and unprecedented in terms of its near complete lack of organization. These are the major environmental changes in which KOS have to operate. The vast quantities of digital information that is available in several formats and genres require KOS that scale up to the needs of the digital environment. The recognition of the importance of the huge volumes of unstructured information (in the form of, e.g., E-mails, blogs, etc) especially in the corporate sector expose the limitations of traditional KOS used in libraries when handling such unstructured information. There is no question that general KOS such as Dewey, LCSH, UDC, Colon and the more specialized vocabularies such as MeSH, *Art & Architecture Thesaurus* will continue to be relevant for handling more structured information resources such as journal articles, conference papers, etc. However, the KO community needs to seriously examine the requirements of knowledge organization systems for the new environment. Knowledge organization, especially in its applied form, has always been purpose-oriented. A variety of factors – language, culture, dimensions and volume of data, user needs and requirements as they obtain in a particular context, the domain of application, available technology, etc – impact knowledge organization. The papers in this volume present contemporary thinking on the subject.

1

Prolegomena to a New Order: A Domain-Analytical Review of the Influence of S.R. Ranganathan on Knowledge Organization*

Richard P. Smiraglia

Domain analytical studies are used in knowledge organization to comprehend the parameters of specific communities. A fruitful but rarely used approach is to examine the theoretical community that is defined by a common core of cited work. Ranganathan's work, especially on facets, has been shown to populate a primary cluster of influence in author co-citation analyses based on the literature of knowledge organization. The basic research question for this study asks what constitutes the ontological community of citers of Ranganathan over time? Evidence from the *Web of Science* shows that Ranganathan's legacy is now shown as leading the knowledge organization domain into new territory.

Keywords: Ranganathan, S.R., Domain analysis, Facets, Co-citation analysis, Web of Science

1 DOMAIN ANALYSIS AND CORE INFLUENCE

Domain analytical studies are used in the field of knowledge organization to comprehend the parameters of specific communities. Domain analyses use a variety of empirical techniques to discover the ontology used in a domain, representing the boundaries of the domain's extension (or external parameters) and its intension (its depth or granularity), as well as the epistemological stances common to the domain as expressed in the research methods employed. Recently I suggested a definition of a domain that encompasses these outcomes (6, p114):

* I would like to thank Ann Graf for assistance in compiling the basic source bibliography used for this analysis. My thanks also to Laura Ridenour for preparing the network visualization in Fig. 4

> A domain is best understood as a unit of analysis for the construction of a KOS. That is, a domain is a group with an ontological base that reveals an underlying teleology, a set of common hypotheses, epistemological consensus on methodological approaches, and social semantics.

Any community can constitute a domain if it meets these requirements, which can be restated more simply as a common vocabulary, objective, methodology, and discourse (usually represented by citation practice).

A variety of approaches have been used in knowledge organization, ranging from qualitative or ethnographic studies [*see* for example 1] to extensive bibliometric analyses [for example, 4 and 5]. A rarely used approach is to examine the theoretical community that is defined by a common cited core work; examples are White [9], in which the identities and images of eight information science pioneers are compared to identify an ontological base, and Smiraglia [3], in which the community of scholarship identified with Patrick Wilson's seminal *Two Kinds of Power* is seen as forming an ideological core in knowledge organization over time.

Several recent domain analyses of knowledge organization have revealed increased influence of core work by iconic Indian classificationist S. R. Ranganathan. Influential in his own lifetime for his introduction of faceted classification in the form of his Colon Classification, as well as for his "Five Laws of Library Science," his work has become the backbone of the 21st century focus on the use of facets. At present facets are enjoying high profile not only for their role in classification but also for the design of search engines and user interfaces. Smiraglia [7 and 8] shows Ranganathan to populate his own cluster of influence in author co-citation analyses based on the literature of knowledge organization. An interesting research question, then, is what constitutes the ontological community of citers of Ranganathan over time?

2 2.0 CITATIONS IN *WEB OF SCIENCE*

For the present bibliometric analysis, all citations to work of S. R. Ranganathan in the Thompson-Reuters *Web of Science* were identified (the University of Wisconsin, Milwaukee's subscription runs from 1985 to the present). 345 cited works were located with 2038 citations to Ranganathan's writing (the mean was 5.9 citations per paper). 44 authors had written at least 2 of the 345 papers; a frequency distribution ofauthor ranked by the number of citations to Ranganathan produced the following table (Table 1).

Table 1: Authors citing Ranganathan in *Web of Science*

Citing Author	# of citations to Ranganathan
SATIJA, MP	10
BEGHTOL, C	8
DAHLBERG, I	7
BISWAS, SC	5
GNOLI, C; POLI, R	5
HJORLAND, B	5
SENGUPTA, IN	5
TENNIS, JOSEPH T.	5
BROUGHTON, V	4
LA BARRE, K	4
CHOWDHURY, GC	3
DEVADASON, F	3
OLSON, HA	3
SWEETLAND, JH	3
WEINBERG, BH	3
BARITE, MG	2
BINWAL, JC	2
BUCKLAND, MK	2
BURKE, M	2
CALDERA SERRANO, JORGE	2
COLE, C	2
COLEMAN, ANITA S.	2
DIAZ, I	2
FUGMANN, R	2
GIESS, M. D.	2
HUSAIN, S	2
INGWERSEN, P	2
ISFANDYARI-MOGHADDAM, ALIREZA	2
IYER, H	2
LEE, HUR-LI	2
LIU, SQ	2
MASSEY-BURZIO, V	2
MIKSA, F	2

Citing Author	# of citations to Ranganathan
NEELAMEGHAN, A	2
NESTEROV, AV	2
PRIETODIAZ, R	2
SACCO, GM	2
SHARMA, RAVI S	2
SLAVIC, AIDA	2
TROTT, BARRY	2
TZITZIKAS, Y	2
UDDIN, MOHAMMAD NASIR	2
VICKERY, A	2
VICKERY, BC	2

There are few surprises on the list, which must be acknowledged to be (in some way) an artifact of *Web of Science* indexing. However, the top segment of the distribution includes core authors from the knowledge organization domain, and the rest of the list includes some authors who might be thought of as contributors both in knowledge organization and information science broadly.

The scope of Ranganathan's influence is truly international. A list of countries of affiliation of citing authors yields the following table (Table 2):

Table 2: Countries of affiliation of authors citing Ranganathan

Countries/Territories	Records	% of 345
USA	115	33.333
ENGLAND	40	11.594
INDIA	35	10.145
CANADA	22	6.377
ITALY	18	5.217
SPAIN	13	3.768
BRAZIL	11	3.188
GERMANY	11	3.188
DENMARK	8	2.319
AUSTRALIA	5	1.449
FRANCE	5	1.449
SCOTLAND	5	1.449
THAILAND	5	1.449
FINLAND	4	1.159
NETHERLANDS	4	1.159
SINGAPORE	4	1.159

Countries/Territories	Records	% of 345
SWEDEN	4	1.159
USSR	4	1.159
BANGLADESH	3	0.870
GREECE	3	0.870
IRAN	3	0.870
IRELAND	3	0.870
NIGERIA	3	0.870
PEOPLES R CHINA	3	0.870
SOUTH AFRICA	3	0.870
NORWAY	2	0.580
URUGUAY	2	0.580

Figure 1 presents a visualization of the data in Table 2.

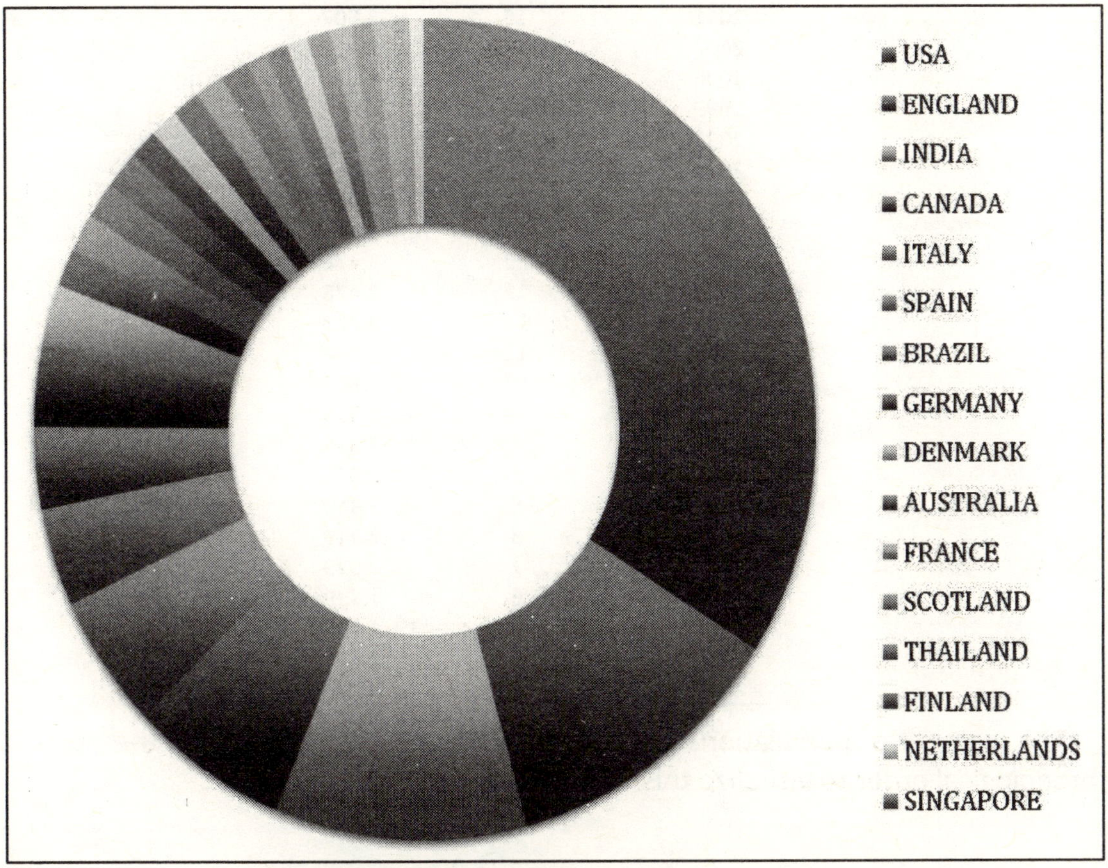

Fig. 1: Geographic distribution of Ranganathan's influence

We can see that one third of the citations are affiliated with authors in the United States, and roughly one-half are affiliated with authors in the U.S., India or England. The next segment of the distribution comes from Europe or Brazil. Overall this is roughly the same shape as the geographic distribution of authors in knowledge organization at large [*see* for example, 7,8].

Years of cited works show a consistent pattern of citation across time; Ranganathan's influence is consistent and strong. The frequency distribution of years of publication appears in Table 3 below.

Table 3: Chronology of citations to Ranganathan

Publication Years	Records	% of 345
2008	28	8.116
1992	26	7.536
2012	22	6.377
2010	21	6.087
2011	19	5.507
2007	18	5.217
2006	16	4.638
1999	15	4.348
2001	15	4.348
2004	15	4.348
2003	14	4.058
1987	12	3.478
1997	12	3.478
2005	12	3.478
2009	12	3.478
1996	11	3.188
2002	10	2.899
1990	8	2.319
1993	8	2.319
1994	8	2.319
1995	8	2.319
1998	8	2.319
1989	7	2.029
1988	6	1.739
1991	6	1.739
2000	6	1.739
2013	2	0.58

The majority of publications are of recent vintage. Figure 2 arrays the years in chronological order to visualize this effect.

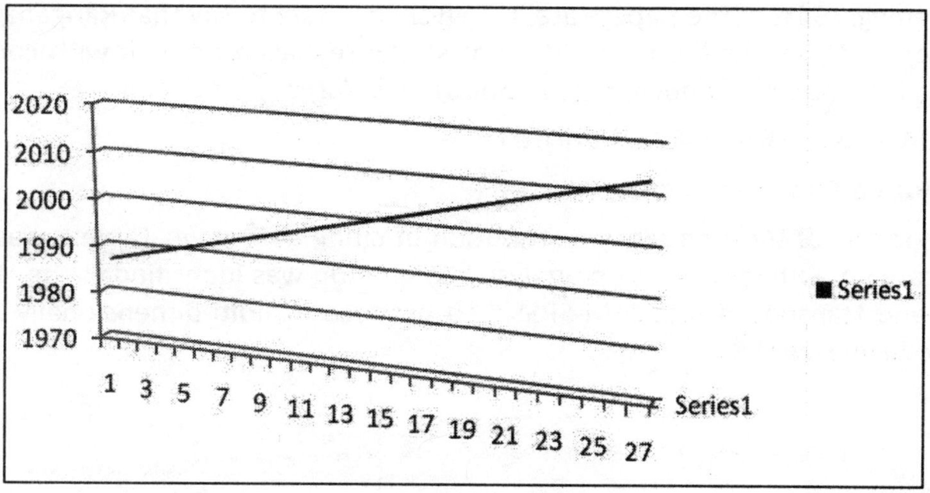

Fig. 2: Years of citations

We see first the limitation of our source, which is an artifact of the *Web of Science* subscription used to compile the basic source bibliography. Publications range from 1985 to the present, thus we see, at least in this study, that Ranganathan's influence is constant over time. There seems to be relatively constant frequency; peaks occur in 1992 and 2008, for example, more or less at both ends of the distribution chronologically.

Forty-one journals are represented; the most productive at the top of the distribution are the eleven journals highlighted in Table 4.

Table 4: Journals citing Ranganathan

Source titles	Records
Knowledge organization	52
Library trends	19
Libri	19
International classification	18
Journal of documentation	18
Journal of the American Society for Information Science and Technology	12
Lecture notes in computer science	11
Journal of librarianship and information science	8
Axiomathes	7
Journal of academic librarianship	7
Perspectivasemciencia da informacao	7

Once again, the shape of this distribution parallels the make up of journal productivity in knowledge organization as a domain. Other metrics available are of less interest—87% o the papers are identified as journal articles and 7.5% as papers in proceedings; 94% of the papers are in English. It is safe to say that Ranganathan's influence, as demonstrated in the present study, reveals a domain with contours similar to the domain of knowledge organization at large.

3 VISUALIZING THE CORE COMMUNITY

3.1 Author Co-Citation Analysis

The top tier of the frequency distribution of citing authors in Table 1 was used to generate an author co-citation analysis. Co-citation was identified in the *Web of Science* and transposed into IBM-SPSS™ to produce a multi-dimensionally scaled map, shown in Figure 3.

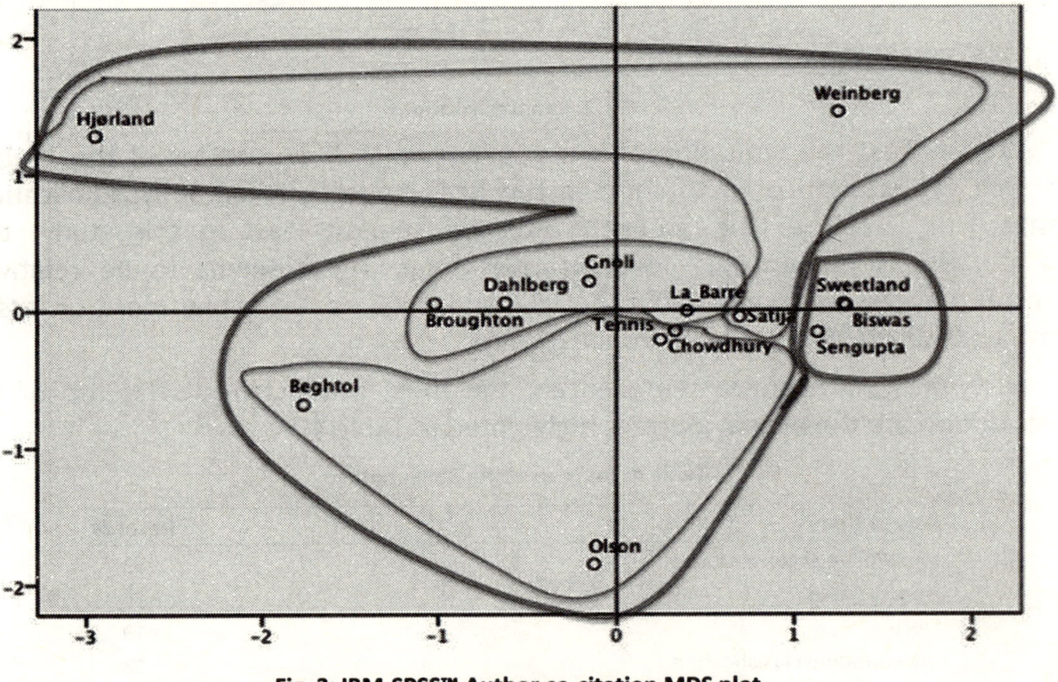

Fig. 3: IBM-SPSS™ Author co-citation MDS plot

It is important to remember that this is a visualization of how these core authors are seen by the entire citing community—presumably the entire knowledge organization domain. The plot shows two distinct regions—a small cluster on the right with the majority of the co-citation taking place in a larger cluster occupying most of the map. Within the large cluster are three smaller distinct sub-clusters. Classic highly-cited authors appear on the outskirts, but the core contains several authors who have written extensively about facets. Thus, it would seem the knowledge organization domain perceives the concept of facets as core, and relates the advance of the concept—a major part of Ranganathan's intellectual legacy—as advanced by this set of authors. Figure 4 is a network visualization of the same data.

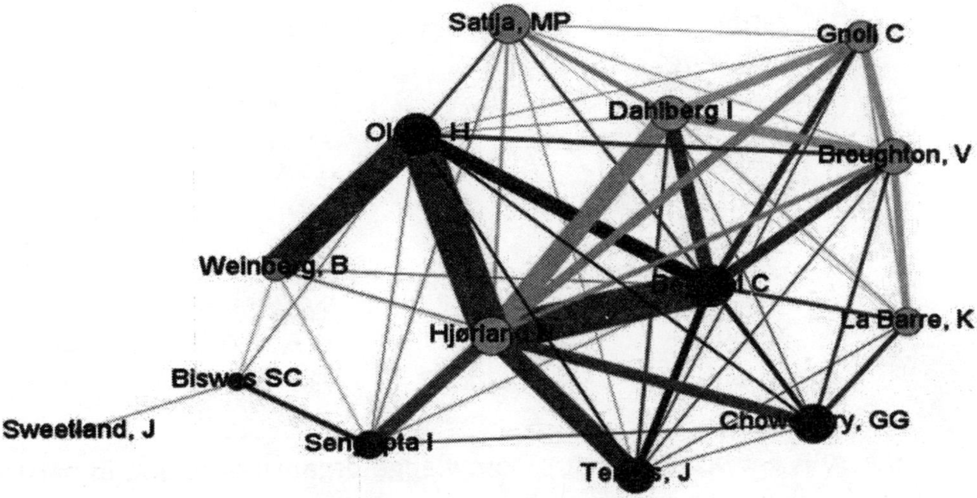

Fig. 4: Author co-citation network visualized using the Force Atlas 2 algorithm in Gephi 0.8.2

This visualization is based on the strength of the co-citation network, the edges blend the colors based on the strength of the association. This time we see something more like a directional plot, with the core intellectual group clustered together at the right. Although the network associations (the number of co-citations) are stronger among the classic authors, the facet core is tightly connected and clearly in a position to lead the domain.

3.2 Co-word Analysis of Title Keywords

The authors in Table 1, who had cited Ranganathan twice or more, contributed 131 papers indexed in *Web of Science*. The titles of those papers were entered into Provalis-WordStat™ software for co-word analysis. A frequency distribution of terms showed the core vocabulary in Table 5 below.

Table 5: Core terms from titles of papers

	Frequency	% Shown
CLASSIFICATION	35	15.00%
INFORMATION	25	10.70%
KNOWLEDGE	24	10.30%
FACETED	14	6.00%

	Frequency	% Shown
ORGANIZATION	14	6.00%
SYSTEM	12	5.10%
RANGANATHAN	11	4.70%
SUBJECT	11	4.70%
THEORY	10	4.30%
LIBRARY	9	3.80%
INDEXING	8	3.40%
NEW	8	3.40%
ANALYSIS	7	3.00%
REPRESENTATION	7	3.00%
RETRIEVAL	7	3.00%
SCIENCE	7	3.00%
STRUCTURE	7	3.00%
BASED	6	2.60%
DOMAIN	6	2.60%
WEB	6	2.60%

The vocabulary is very clearly that of knowledge organization, and in particular of faceted classification with some emphasis on web-based retrieval. Indeed, these core term co-occurrences are demonstrated in the MDS plot in Figure 5.

The visualization is anchored with Ranganathan and information science/ information retrieval in the green cluster at the top, with knowledge organization, faceted classification and domain analysis all clearly represented at the edges. This is a much narrower set of terms—more focused in other words, than usually occur in domain analyses of knowledge organization. That means that a core intellectual base emerges from this study that demonstrates the direct influence of Ranganathan on classification, information retrieval, and knowledge organization.

4 PROLEGOMENA TO A NEW ORDER

Ranganathan's legacy, as represented by contemporary research in facets, is now shown as leading the knowledge organization domain into new territory. The core authors citing Ranganathan in the current four decades clearly acknowledge the influence of his work on today's approaches to both classification and web design. Indeed, all of the knowledge organization domain is expressing the influence of the concept of facets. The term "prolegomena" means a preliminary discussion, and I use it here both metaphorically to describe the legacy of Ranganathan in the knowledge organization domain, but also with reference to his

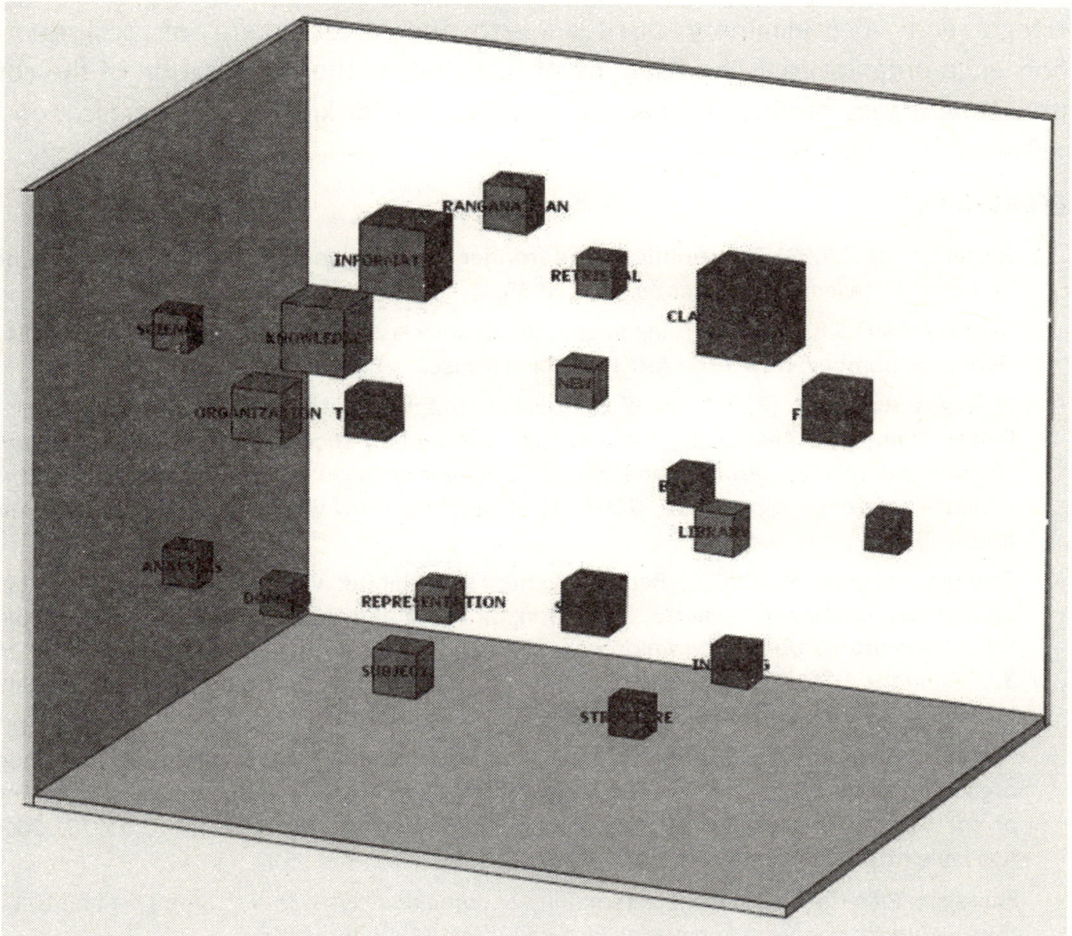

Fig. 5: MDS plot of term co-occurrence

signal work *Prolegomena to Library Classification* (the first edition appeared in 1937, but most citation is to the 1967 third edition [2]). His work was a forerunner of what is now contemporary thought concerning the deconstruction and reconstruction of complexity inherent in enumerative classifications. That is, the *Prolegomena* demonstrates how moving away from the confusion of simple concepts in hierarchical structures, focusing instead on expressing points of view in combination can produce more sophisticated and more precise classification of knowledge. It is exactly this benefit of the faceted approach that is fueling its popularity in both knowledge organization systems and web engineering at the present time. Ranganathan's ideas, then, can be seen as representing a prolegomena—a preliminary discussion—to the present era of progress in knowledge organization. The outcome of this study is the visualization of the core intellectual legacy of Ranganathan as an active part of knowledge organization in the twenty-first century.

REFERENCES

1 Hartel, Jenna. (2003) The serious leisure frontier in library and information science: hobby domains. *Knowledge organization,* 30: 228-38.

2 Ranganathan, S.R. (1967) Prolegomena to library classification.3d ed., assisted by M.P. Gopinath. Bombay; New York: Asia Publishing House.

3 Smiraglia, Richard P. (2007) *Two kinds of power*: insight into the legacy of Patrick Wilson. **In** Dalkir, Kimiz, and Arsenault, Clément eds., *Information sharing in a fragmented world: crossing boundaries: Proceedings of the Canadian Association for Information Science annual conference May 12-15,* 2007. Available http://www.caisacsi.ca/2007proceedings.htm.

4 Smiraglia, Richard P. (2009a) Redefining the "s" in ISMIR: visualizing the evolution of a domain. **In** Rothbauer, Paulette, Stevenson, Siobhan, and Wathen, Nadine eds., *Mapping the 21st century information landscape: borders, bridges and byways: Proceedings of the 37th Annual CAIS/ACSI Conference, May 28-30, 2009, Ottawa, Ontario, Canada*. Available http://www.cais-acsi.ca/search.asp?year=2009.

5 Smiraglia, Richard P. (2009b) Modulation and specialization in North American knowledge organization: visualizing pioneers. **In** Jacob, Elin K., and Kwaśnik, Barbara eds., *Proceedings of the 2d North American Symposium on Knowledge Organization, June 17-18, 2009.* Available http://hdl.handle.net/10150/105092.

6 Smiraglia, Richard P. (2012a). Epistemology of domain analysis. **In** R.P. Smiraglia and H. Lee (Eds.), *Cultural frames of knowledge*. (pp. 111-124). Würzburg :Ergon

7 Smiraglia, Richard P. (2012b) Universes, dimensions, domains, intensions and extensions: knowledge organization for the 21st Century. **In** A. Neelameghan and K.S. Raghavan eds. *Categories, contexts, and relations in knowledge organization: Proceedings of the Twelfth International ISKO Conference, 6-9 August 2012*, Mysore, India. Advances in knowledge organization 13.Würzburg: ErgonVerlag, p. 1-7.

8 Smiraglia, Richard P. (2013) The epistemological dimension of knowledge organization. Keynote address to the *Second Brazilian Conference on Knowledge Organization and Representation*, Rio de Janeiro, Getulio Vargas Foundation, May 27, 28 and 29, 2013

9 White, Howard D. (2003). Authors as citers over time. *Journal of the American Society for Information Science and Technology,* 52: 87-108.

2

Faceted Classifications as a Model for Universal Classifications

Widad Mustafa El Hadi

The pervasive power of digitization causes scientific, educational, economic and cultural communities to change modes of accessing, sharing and disseminating knowledge and leads to a convergence between our cultural heritage, classic culture and technical culture. It is no surprise that some researchers have called for a "digital humanism", pointing out at the force by which new technologies are becoming a sort of 'culture' since they drive us into a new global cultural destiny". Such reflections concern the society as a whole. This paper will examine how knowledge organization meets the growing need to organize digital information. Faceted Classifications will be examined as one of the most adapted knowledge Organization Systems (KOS) for the global information access. One of our objectives will be to understand the reasons underlying its indisputable capacity as a popular tool for global access to information. Thus the main focus of this paper will be to look at the ways in which universal classifications, as language independent concept schemes, can assist humans and computers in structuring and presenting information and formulating queries. We will try through this work to outline some directions for future work and a better understanding of the realm of faceted classification and how its universality is rooted in human cognition.

Keywords: Faceted classification; Facet Analysis; Universal Classification; Digital Environment; Web Environment.

1 BACKGROUND AND RATIONALE: DIGITAL CULTURES AND THE NEED FOR ADVANCED KNOWLEDGE ORGANIZATION SYSTEMS

Digital Culture is defined by Milad Doueihi [12] as a wide range of topics concerning the participation in online culture. This is relevant, as Doueihi pointed out, for information literacy, texts, archiving and storage. The diversity of digital practices and the importance of digital literacy in an increasingly complex textual environment attracted the attention of many authors and is now becoming crucial for KOS and their interoperability. The increasing growth of media leads information professionals to cope with the new needs by developing innovative methods for indexing the ever growing digital contents and to adapt them to new information carriers and repositories. The challenges are how to operate convergence between these different media from two points of views: carriers and contents. The digital carriers are pushing libraries, archives and museums to develop a common universal knowledge space [33, 17]. This trend has been confirmed by the steady growth of new cataloguing standards [9, 6, 1 among many others] and the creation of gateways between KOS [23, 11, among others].

The evolution of the Web, from being purely academic to a variety of commercial, business and social uses coincided with a significant improvement in technology. The Web itself as well as digital libraries and digital repositories of various kinds became essential resources in education, research, and cultural heritage. However, information retrieval in digital libraries is still poorly supported and locating relevant resources has become increasingly difficult as collections grow. To date, most of the efforts in digital environment have been focused on technical issues: architecture, metadata standards, copyright and interoperability that are crucial to the management of digital repositories. Until recently, relatively little effort or expertise has been directed towards matters of semantic content access, semantic interoperability, or knowledge capture and facilitation [34, 35].

2 THE RELEVANCE OF UNIVERSAL BIBLIOGRAPHIC CLASSIFICATIONS IN THE WEB ENVIRONMENTS

We are now witnessing many shifts in knowledge organization as its scope is not limited to organizing books in libraries. For a long time, indexing knowledge contents simply meant applying classification schemes and subject heading lists to printed books. But new media have continuously appeared, whose contents also need to be organized: printed images, magnetic carriers, digital carriers, networked information, etc. [17]. Schemes, such as the popular Universal Decimal Classification (UDC; published in 1904-1907 by Paul Otlet and Henri La Fontaine which expanded the Dewey Decimal Classification of 1876), is still judged as modern by some authors even though it is challenged in practice by search engines [cf. 21].

KOS, such as classification and thesauri are semantically rich terminology tools, traditionally used in library and bibliographic domains to enable information discovery - they are ubiquitous pathways to information in hundreds of thousands of document collections. The full integration of KOS in digital environments will eventually facilitate integrating the large corpora of recorded knowledge in heritage institutions and digitally born Web resources. But even more, KOS can improve access to document contents in digital or hybrid collections and are indispensible in heterogeneous collections of documents (text, images, audio recordings, datasets, etc).

"*Renaissance 2.0*: a journey through the origins of the Web" is the name of an exhibition in the little Belgium city Mons, which received global media attention. Google and the Mundaneum (the archive of Paul Otlet and Henri La Fontaine) partnered to give tribute to the 20th Century 'classifiers of the world' and all their ancestors. It had become quite timely to link traditions of knowledge organization with new digital methods of large scale information processing as they had become visible in search engines, the Wikipedia project, Europeana, and the Web of Knowledge (Web 3.0)[1], [35].

More than fifty years ago, Brian Vickery, a leading member of the British CRG (Classification Research Group) predicted the success of faceted classifications in digital environments.

> "Once upon a time, over 50 years ago, I collaborated in writing an article entitled "the need for a faceted classification as the basis of all methods of information retrieval". A bold, brash claim! Since then we have had thesauri, relational data bases, taxonomies, ontologies, knowledge bases, topic maps, knowledge architectures and more [36]. Yet in many of them we may detect signs of the old facet mole burrowing away. Recently he has been poking his nose a bit more visibly above the surface "Brian Vickery (p. 160)

Other eminent members of the CRG came to the same conclusions:

> "Given that facet analysis has been brought to an advanced state with regard to the categorization and ordering of concepts in a system of classification, we might ask whether it can also be viewed as a more pervasive theory of the organization of knowledge and used to underpin the structure of other kinds of knowledge representation systems. Certainly today there is evidence of the impact of facet analysis on a wide range of conventional indexing tools and on more recent tools developed for retrieval of digital resources" Vanda Broughton [8].

Faceted bibliographic classifications are considered relevant in Web applications. Kathryn La Barre [25] observed that:

---

[1] http://expositions.mundaneum.org/fr/expositions/renaissance2.0-fr

"Information architects seemingly re-discovered a legacy form of information organization and access: faceted analytico-synthetic theory (FAST) consisting of a set of principles and techniques to organize information. This exploration of connections between the intellectual foundations of information organization and current practices of Web design looks to past heritage for guidance and to current practices for evidence", Kathryn La Barre (p. 15-16).

This is how renewed attention has come to be paid in recent years to the work of S.R. Ranganathan, his predecessors and his followers.

The Colon Classification has not become as popular as it might have deserved. It is possible that the global networking, the evolution of virtual libraries, makes researchers of library and information science look for new methods in organizing documents and subjects for networking purposes. We even think that the theory of facet analysis implies ideas which are still to be explored and to be fully utilised in the electronic environment. Ranganathan developed his CC faceted classification 'too early'; the time is still to come to benefit from it as a structured domain language as used in AI (Artificial Intelligence) and expert systems (Hunter 1993) with sophisticated graphic user interfaces (Kuronen, Pekkarinen, [24]: p46).

Ranganathan's legacy goes far beyond his contribution to library science. And even his Five Laws of Library Science can be extended to embrace his faceted classification in global access to information contexts. He developed what has been widely accepted as the definitive statement of ideal library service in his Five Laws of Library Science (1931)

1. *Books are for use.*
2. *Every reader his or her book.*
3. *Every book its reader.*
4. *Save the time of the reader.*
5. *The Library is a growing organism.*

The "free adaptations" of Ranganathan's original *Five Laws of Library Science* to the Web are fairly interesting, whether one looks to Ranganathan's original *Five Laws of Library Science* or to any one of their many new interpretations. One central idea is immediately clear: Libraries and the Web exist to serve people's information needs [32, 24, 10, among many others].

Many authors showed their fascination for Ranganathan's Five Laws by formulating what they call the Five Web Laws (Noruzi, *ibid*). The *Five Laws of the Web* are inspired by the "*Five Laws of Library Science*" which were the basis of all of Ranganathan's practice. These laws lay the foundation for their Web application by defining some minimum requirements. Although they are simply stated, the laws are nevertheless deep and flexible (*ibid*):

1. Web resources are for use.
2. Every user his or her web resource.
3. Every web resource its user.
4. Save the time of the user.
5. The Web is a growing organism.

Clare Beghtol focused on the contribution of S.R. Ranganathan to library science and considered it as even more important than his faceted classification:

> "The contribution of S.R. Ranganathan to librarianship in general is broader than his contribution to library classification facet theory and practice, but the fascination and absorption with which his facet work was greeted have not been equaled in any other area of his contributions. (..) The twenty first century may see an equally valuable way forward using the semantic axis of classification research based in the idea of the semantic warrant of classification systems and the possibility of semantic hospitality in the globalized information systems and services that are emerging [4]. It may be too that further research will reveal possibilities for extending facet theory into the semantic realm and create a fusion of grammar and meaning in classification theory based on facet principles"

The present article[1] is largely inspired by the same approach and looks at the interactions between digital environments, emerging digital cultures and knowledge organization systems (KOS), such as classifications, thesauri and ontologies considered by Hodge [22] as the most advanced type of KOS.The full integration of KOS in digital environments would facilitate integration of the large corpora of recorded knowledge in heritage institutions and digitally generated resources on the Web. Moreover, we will discuss the types of classification that would be suitable for improving global access to information offering high information retrieval capabilities.

---

[1] Previous versions of this paper served as a basis for a DIGIKO research project (Digital Cultures and Universality in KO) we submitted with four partners (France as a pilot, the UK, The Netherlands, and Germany together with an international body of experts). An updated version will be submitted with the same partners. Discussions will be continued in parallel to the *Knowescape* workshop which is supposed to take place in The Hague on October 23rd 2013. The author also wrote two papers dealing with universality in KO [14, 31] and gave a conference at the university of Warsaw on "Digital Cultures and Universality in KO", The 2nd Scientific Conference on Information Science in an Age of Change, Institute of Information and Book Studies, University of Warsaw, 15-16 April 2013, Warsaw

3 THE USE OF FACETED CLASSIFICATIONS IN THE WEB ENVIRONMENTS

Bibliographic classifications have some advantages over other controlled vocabularies such as thesauri, descriptor systems and subject heading lists, in that the notational encoding acts as a control device which is linguistically neutral; retrieval problems such as the proliferation of synonyms, ambiguity of meaning, and other natural language factors are avoided, which makes the exchange of information and cross-searching in a multi-lingual or multinational environment much easier. This offers both a rich terminology and different ways in which concepts can be categorized and related to each other in the universe of knowledge. The faceted classification (FC) is considered as the most adaptable classification for the Web. In the introduction to her PhD dissertation Kathryn La Barre [25] pointed out the timeless relevance of faceted classifications (FC) and facet analysis (FA) as it consists of a set of principles and techniques through which a system of information organization is created. As a result FC is currently used for Web design and commercial websites (*ibid:* 15-16). We will now look more specifically into analytico-synthetic faceted classification and examine the different contributions of theoreticians of universal classifications.

3.1 Potential of Facet Analysis for a Networked Environment: Current Applications of Faceted Classifications and Faceted Interfaces, a Review

Although the features of faceted classification were already known and appreciated even in the early 1980s, recent developments and specially applications in commercial web sites can be traced back to 2000; La Barre wrote [27] "Website designers became aware of the potential and interest of this particular classification". Most of these applications have concentrated on facet structure, and, in the case of commercial applications, used the methodology to build taxonomies based on the different attributes of objects. "Facet classifications have caught the attention of practitioners who create websites and Web applications", as La Barre reported [27], and many research initiatives have demonstrated a variety of approaches and understanding of the facets' importance for the Semantic Web". The most extensive and well documented reviews of faceted classification use are given by La Barre [25]. For her PhD dissertation, she examined two hundred websites in order to look at two basic functions: website searching and navigation [25]. In her findings, basic and advanced search features occurred most frequently. Site examination revealed the integration of search and navigational features in one third of the sites. Interviews with 18 information architects indicated that this is an area of increasing interest and that FAST is considered a viable solution to enhance integration of searching and navigation features on websites. The author continues to publish regularly updates on FAST use in the Web and advocates a better understanding of faceted classification [25, 28, 29, 30].

Popular examples of the use of facets can be found on Amazon, Ebay, and many online shopping sites, as well as some library catalogs and article databases that have been reported in more recent publications [30]. One of the most popular applications is the University of Illinois library faceted searching interface, used for its catalogues. In 2009, the Consortium of Academic and Research Libraries in Illinois (CARLI) designed a customized interface, *VuFind*, for its member libraries. *VuFind* is an open source next generation catalogue interface created at Villanova University (Consortium of Academic Research Libraries in Illinois, 2011) [13].

The FLAMENCO (Flexible information Access using MEtadata), a faceted interface developed as part of Marti Hearst's Bailando project at the University of California School of Information, provides search interface that uses "hierarchical faceted metadata." [26, 27]. One of the popular examples is the Flamenco interface for Nobel Prize Winners[1], and Nobel Prize Winners and Fine Arts ImagesDemos[2]. The facets that are used are gender, affiliation, prize and year, drawn from the textual corpus of individual descriptions by the Castanet algorithm, and then further refined by project researchers.

Another example is the faceted navigation interface of Yelp, a major business review website in the United States. The site is very popular in the Bay Area[3]. The advantages of contextual facets can be described in terms of the theoretical framework for direct manipulation by merging the query-building interface into the item details interface. Contextual facets, as has been suggested by the designers, reduce the cognitive load required from the user to translate his/her goals into input for the faceted navigation interface. Users can also quickly evaluate whether

---

[1] Available at: http://flamenco.berkeley.edu/index.html [retrieved: 21 May 2013].

[2] Available at: http://flamenco.berkeley.edu/demos.html [retrieved: 21 May 2013]

[3] Available at: http:www.yelp.com [retrieved: 21 May 2013].

an attribute displayed on an item's detail page can be incorporated into a query, and then immediately use it to that end. Among the terminology authors, this decreases the *semantic distance* by helping the user to establish whether an interface element will help him/her reach a desired goal, and to decrease articulatory distance by minimizing the required effort to express this goal to the system. To explore how contextual facets might be used, the authors have developed *FacetPatch*, a prototype web browser that can automatically generate faceted navigation interfaces with contextual facets for a collection of WebPages. *FacetPatch* automatically recognizes webpage elements that may be categorical data or metadata and transforms them into contextual facets. *FacetPatch* can generate facets in two different ways. The site is described by the authors as a very popular one in the Bay Area where the research was conducted. Also, the collection of WebPages that make up the site — information and reviews of local restaurants, bars and other businesses — provides a rich set of faceted data that they could use to construct engaging and open-ended tasks (*ibid*).

Faceted classification can be relevant for the humanities as stated by Broughton and Slavic [7] and Slavic [35]. They argued that the need for specific universal classifications is motivated by the nature of the concepts and objects we have to organize. In their articles, Slavic [35] examined the potential of FC for the Humanities. In this domain more often, than in other disciplines, they explained, we will need to look for concepts across heterogeneous information resources (museum objects, images, sounds and texts) which will often force us to reach back into the past and outside the comfort zone of our contemporary language or scripts.

4 THE FACET CONCEPT AS A COGNITIVE UNIVERSAL

In this section the faceted classifications will be described. We will go back to some historical origins and look at the potential of facet analysis for a networked environment. Many authors wrote historical notes and excellent reviews on the origins, expansions and developments of faceted classifications and La Barre wrote a PhD thesis, on the use of faceted classifications for the Web. A special technical issue of "*Axiomathes*" has been edited by Claudio Gnoli in 2008, devoted to facet analysis, in which the contributions of several eminent authors were included.

Clare Beghtol wrote on the universal aspect of this classification [3, 4, 5]. We should also mention the seminal work of the British CRG and its leading members

(Vickery, Broughton, Coates, Slavic, among many others, following the British tradition[1] of FC). The main strength of FC in the global information network is, in addition to their international presence, the fact that it can be deployed as a universal knowledge framework or as a switching language between different more specific vocabularies [7].

One of the more recent articles defines faceted classifications as [the] logical approach to knowledge organization [20]. In his article Hjørland made an extensive historical note on the FC [2] in which he examined the theoretical foundations of the facet-analytic tradition. In this historical note Hjørland accounted for the other traditions linked to the faceted classification and focused on the logical origins in which it is rooted, i.e. in the Aristotelian logic. He made special references to the modern ancestors of faceted classifications such as Paul Otlet, W.C. Berwick Sayers and his best-known student S.R. Ranganathan, the British CRG and to their contributions to the original faceted classification theory:

> S.R. Ranganathan (1892–1972) was an Indian mathematician and library scholar, and, as we saw above, a student of Sayers. Ranganathan also attacked the problems of library classification in an axiomatic way, i.e. to develop a set of basic principles and then to apply these rigorously to the problem at hand. From his background in mathematics (and also his influence from Hindu thought) he was able to develop the axiomatic approach much broader and deeper compared to Sayers. The British Classification Research Group (CRG) developed Ranganathan's work further. The Bliss Bibliographic Classification, 2nd edition (BC2), is also an important product by this group of researchers and it is probably the most theoretically advanced system based on this approach.

It is important to understand why the ideas of "classifiers of the world' are up-to date and relevant in the current Web environments and how a "Faceted semantic web" [26] can be achieved through taking into account the contribution

---

[1] In his paper Birger Hjørland [20] explained the CRG tradition and how it has developed Ranganathan's work; the contribution of Brian Vickery to the development the CRG work, and the impact of Bliss Classification (*ibid*). Hjorland considers Bliss' Bibliographic Classification as being the most theoretically advanced one

[2] "The basic idea of faceted classification (FC) goes – according to Schulte-Albert (1974) – more than 300 years back in time. In the 20th century the Universal Decimal Classification (1905–1907) was an early manifestation of facet classification. It was not, however until the work of W.C. Berwick Sayers (1881–1960) that FC became a research-based approach within the field of knowledge organization. Sayers was an English librarian and researcher who wrote, among other works, *An Introduction to Library Classification* (Sayers, 1918), a book that went through nine editions between its first publication and 1954 . Hjorland [20].

of S.R. Ranganathan and of other faceted classifications linked to this tradition. In the same vein, K. Raghavan (personal communication, 2010), quoted by La Barre [28, p100], outlined the necessity for universals especially in the context of ontologies for the Semantic Web: "digital environments make us increasingly aware of the need for 'universals', is especially resonant in the context of ontologies for the Semantic Web".

To this end we will look at the use of faceted classifications in the Web environments and try to draw, from the literature and applications some hypotheses related to the universals in classifications (3, 4, 5; 25, 26, 28, among many others). The idea is to look at the reasons that made this classification popular and better adapted to web use. The fact that facets are considered as cognitive universals could explain the reasons of their success in many web environments? From LIS tradition, Beghtol [2, 3, 4, 5], Hjørland, [19, 20] and many other linguists who have worked on lexical and semantic universals are relevant to our investigations. Beghtol wrote many articles on the fundamental and original characteristic of faceted classification, pointing out its universality.

> "It has been suggested that the facet concept may be a universal principle of subdivision inherent in human thinking" [4]

Since the main objective of this paper is to focus on the power of faceted classifications and their adaptability to a variety of digital information repositories (Libraries, OPACs, commercial websites), we have to ask ourselves: Can their obvious success in Web environment be explained as due to their fundamental characteristic' i.e. they are cognitively universal? Can we explain their success by the fact that there is an "alphabet of human thought" as Leibnitz posited (Wierzbicka, 1984: 445)? Can this element explain that the facet concept borrowed from Indian culture has turned into a reference for universal classification in global access to information?

5 THE COGNITIVE ASPECT OF THE FACETED CLASSIFICATIONS

In her seminal article, Clare Beghtol [4], pointed out the power of the faceted classification and described its main characteristics and originality in handling information retrieval.

> "Evidence is presented that the facet concept has a claim to be considered as a method of subdivision that is cognitively available to human beings, regardless of language, culture, or academic discipline. The possibility that faceting is a universal method of subdivision

enhances the claim that facet analysis as an unusually useful design principle for information retrieval classifications in any field. This possibility needs further investigation in an age when information access across boundaries is both necessary and possible", Beghtol, [4]: p45)

Since 1995 this author has contributed many articles linking the universality of this classification to its most fundamental feature, i.e. its cognitive aspect. The sets of universal characterizing this classification are described in Beghtol [3, 4 and more recently 5]. According to her, grouping and subdivision is one of the most common universals in classification:

> The cognitive ability to create groups of things and/or ideas appears to be available to all human beings. This strong claim about human cognition has been assumed in many studies in many disciplines and explicitly studied in many others, and this view is apparently seldom challenged. Less studied and presumably less understood is the extent of the universality of the methods that may be used to subdivide these groupings usefully for some explicit purpose. Working on the assumption that semantic and lexical universals are also cognitively universal, Goddard and Wierzbicka [18] studied a large number of languages to discover these kinds of linguistic commonalities. They were able to identify eight categories of semantic and lexical universals across a large number of languages

In her many contributions on universals in classification Beghtol says further

> "(..) The interesting category for our purposes is "Taxonomy and Partonomy: kind of; have parts" It is noteworthy that taxonomy and partonomy are two types of classificatory subdivision of a group, and Goddard and Wierzbicka have apparently felt no need to justify the assumption of the prior existence of the ability to make groups. Taxonomy and partonomy have been studied extensively in a number of fields, and some of their implications for bibliographic classification systems were discussed by Beghtol [3]. Of particular interest here is that it has been shown that subdivision into parts and subdivision into kinds are not mutually exclusive ([3])"

She argues that the facet principle may be cognitively available to all human beings:

> The Evidence that facet principles may be cognitively available to all human beings can be found in the concurrent discovery of the facet principle in two separate disciplines. Louis Guttman in Israel began to use facet principles for social science research, primarily survey research, at about the same time that Ranganathan in India began to use facet principles for bibliographic classification

Thus the conclusion she arrives at in her 2006 article is fundamental for the ongoing research dealing with the nature of faceted classification and goes a long way towards answering some of our questions:

> Ranganathan articulated and developed the facet concept for bibliographic classification systems, and the examples (..) show that he may have used a cognitive universal that can be further exploited in the present era of the globalization of information. In this regard, we might adopt and expand Ranganathan's concept of seminal mnemonics as an explanatory principle that can account for the use of facets in many kinds of research areas and projects. The theoretical basis for seminal mnemonics has been described by Subramanyam (1976) as arising from Hindu thought about the relationship between perception and intuition. As a first step, we may then relate seminal mnemonics to the kinds of symbolic classification explicated by Needham (1979). Both Subramanyam and Needham emphasize the substrata of human consciousness that underlie the perceptual level of human experience. The possibility that we may discover more cognitively available methods of subdivision through the study of seminal mnemonics and symbolic classification strengthens the argument that universal methods of subdivision exist and may not be restricted to taxonomy, partonomy and facet analysis. Study of these universal methods would be appropriate for efforts at creating knowledge organizations across the many boundaries of information retrieval. In addition, these methods are not mutually exclusively and can be used fruitfully to complement each other. These complementarities are also worthy of study.

6 FUTURE RESEARCH DIRECTIONS

We will also look at the contribution of what can be called the "three Facets Classification Schools". In her article "Traditions of facet theory, or a garden of forking paths?" La Barre [28] mentioned the three traditions of faceted classifications and their endeavor in promoting the faceted theory: the British Classification Research Group; the North American Classification Research Study and the Indian Library Research Cycle (LRC). She added, "Broughton and others speak of a British tradition, distinguishing it from that found in the United States. The Indian tradition is considered as more closely linked to the canons of facet theory composed by Ranganathan (*ibid*: 95)". If we look at the contributions of the three schools of thought from the point of view of categories: Ranganathan suggested the PMEST, or the five fundamental categories through which to analyze the information universe: Personality, Matter, Energy, Space, and Time. For its part the CRG School led by Vickery extended them in the following list: Things, entities (naturally occurring, products, mental constructs); Parts, components, structure (organs); Materials, constituents; Attributes (qualities, properties, processes, behavior); Operations (experimental, mental); Operating agents; Place; Condition. The North American School characterized by both theoretical insight (La Barre, 2006, 2010, Hearst, 2003, among many others) and a diversity of applications (Library, OPAC, Commercial web sites, etc.). One of the objectives of our reflection is to see whether the categories suggested by the three schools considered as universal categories will help as a basis for drawing a general theory of FC as an example of universals in classification[1]. Such an investigation would need a thorough examination of universals in semantics drawn from the general framework of universals in linguistics. Universals in classification were one of the questions that La Barre [30] had suggested as a possible area of future theoretical investigations.

In his introduction to *Axiomathes,* Gnoli [16, p128] pointed out the similarities between linguistic universals and classification, saying: "Authors working with verbal systems have found that facet analysis can be related to syntactic concepts in linguistics, like that of deep cases in Fillmore's [15] case grammar: a facet plays a function in subject strings very similar to that played by cases or prepositions in languages, which in turn can be related to cognitive processes (Hutchins 1975; Cheti 1990)". Although investigations in this area by LIS community have not been conclusive[2] the steady uses of facets in the Web make us aware of the need to go back to these investigations.

---

1 La Barre outlined a major difficulty, the variant understandings of the term *facet.* She distinguished two types of variant understandings, one linked to heritage and the other to contemporary use of the term. This results *in* divergences in the use of term by the different communities working on facets. Moreover, she considered a third a broader divergence linked to the nature of the fundamental categories (100). She calls for a concerted work of facet theorist in order to find common ground and regularize term use. This work is essential for researchers to create robust and semantically grounded (faceted) web applications (*ibid*:102)

2 Hjorland mentioned the diferent initiatives related to investigating the facets theory within the linguistic approches of semantic primitives. In his paper, Hjørland [19, p382–384] related the basic philosophy of facet analysis to the philosophy of semantic primitives and to a broader theory of semantics. (..) When a set of elements are discovered or theoretically constructed, they are named in languages, and these languages may subsequently be subject to logical analysis. The important conclusion is that semantic primitives are not something given by a natural language, they are models constructed by specialists in specific domains. (..) It is problematic if FA is based on the view that meanings are given in a language, and that subjects can be constructed by a universal set of semantic primitives given by natural languages He concludes that :. The elements in classification are not given by the logical analysis of the philosopher or the information specialists, but are given by scientific discoveries and theories. This is again the question of the differences between logical divisions and scientific classifications as discussed by Mill (1872). In faceted classification a given document is classified by taking one or more symbols from the appropriate facets and combining them according to certain rules. This combination is called "notational synthesis". The idea is that the same building blocks can be used for all purposes (cf. Meccano). The underlying philosophical assumption is that elements do not change their meaning in different contexts. According to modern theories of meaning, this is a rather problematic assumption.

He says further that "the PRECIS indexing system also drew on Chomsky's generative grammar. Other analogies have been noticed in the social sciences, where Guttman even adopted the same term "facet" without being aware of Ranganathan's work [2]". He argued that Szostak's proposal of analyzing human science theories according to five dimensions goes in a similar direction.

Finally, Gnoli came to the conclusion that:

> "(..) facets are a natural way of analyzing and organizing any kind of concept: for example, an evolution from enumerative to faceted classifications parallel to that of bibliographic tools can be observed in musicology, where faceted alternatives to the classical Hornbostel-Sachs system of musical instruments have been proposed by Dräger (1947) and Hood (1971)" Gnoli, ibid 128)

As Vanda Broughton and Aida Slavic [7] Aida Slavic (34, 35) suggested, KOS, especially universal knowledge classifications, which are currently not sufficiently explored within the digital environments, particularly in the humanities field, may represent an interesting area of research. Wider application of universal knowledge classification in digital humanities may contribute not only to better resource discovery but could also help in improving terminological and research tools for knowledge transfer between humanities and other fields of knowledge. In this respect, our investigations will take on board and make full use of findings that are already available. In addition we will observe and exchange information with current similar research projects[1]. The following past and current projects are of particular relevance to our own research:

- KNOWeSCAPE - The dynamics of information and knowledge landscapes - http://www.cost.eu/domains_actions/mpns/Actions/TD1210;
- The European Library - Connecting Knowledge http://www.theeuropeanlibrary.org/tel4/; Europeana - http://www.europeana.eu/portal/;
- CATCHPlus - http://www.catchplus.nl/;
- STITCH - Semantic Interoperability to access Cultural Heritage http://www.cs.vu.nl/STITCH/; STELLAR - Semantic Technologies Enhancing Links and Linked data for Archaeological Resources, (http://hypermedia.research.glam.ac.uk/kos/STELLAR/);

[1] *Walking through a library remotely,* Andrea Schanrhors, Royal Academy of Arts and science) http://ehumanities.nl/:http://www.dans.knaw.nl/en/content/contact/staff-members/andrea-, Presentation at European Seminar, Ecole Doctorale, 12th April, 2013, Lille, France

- TRSS (Terminology Registry Scoping Study) - http://www.ukoln.ac.uk/projects/trss/;
- STAR (2007-2010) - Semantic Technologies for Archaeological Resources; EnTAG (2009) ENhanced TAGging http://hypermedia.research.glam.ac.uk/kos/entag/;
- KoMoHe (2004-2008) http://www.gesis.org/en/research/external-funding-projects/archive/komohe/; HILT - High Level Thesaurus Project http:// hilt.cdlr.strath.ac.uk/;
- FATKS (2003-2004) Facet Analytical Theory in Managing Knowledge Structure for Humanities http://www.ucl.ac.uk/fatks/; and
- FACET (2000-2003) https://www.comp.glam.ac.uk/~FACET/

7 ACKNOWLEDGEMENTS

The author is deeply grateful for the interesting discussions engaged during the DIGIKO project writing. Special thanks to Aida Slavic, Laurence Favier, Andrea Scharnhorst, Sylvie Davis, Philip Mayer, Fabrice Papy and Peter Stockinger of the DIGIKO project consortium.

REFERENCES

1 Arsenault, C. and Noruzi, A. (2012) Les relations bibliographiques entre une œuvre et une autre œuvre selon le modèle FRBR : la perspective canadienne. In: Dynamisme et Stabilité dans l'organisation des connaissances. Ed. by W. Mustafa El Hadi. Paris: Hermès, p. 105-117.

2 Beghtol, C. (1995) 'Facets' as interdisciplinary undiscovered public knowledge: S.R. Ranganathan in India and L. Guttman in Israel. J Doc 51(3): 94–114

3 Beghtol, C. (2000) A Whole, Its Kinds, and Its Parts. In: Dynamism and Stability in Knowledge, Proceedings of the 6th International ISKO Conference, 10-13 July, Toronto, Canada, p. 313-319. Edited by C. Beghtol, L.C. Howarth, and N. J. Williamson. Würzberg

4 Beghtol, C. (2006) The facet concept as a universal principle of subdivision. In: Raghavan KS, Prasad K.N. (eds) Knowledge organization, information systems and other essays: Professor A. Neelameghan Festschrift. Ess Ess Publications, New Delhi, p. 41–52.

5 Beghtol, C. (2008) From the Universe of Knowledge to the Universe of Concepts: The Structural Revolution in Classification for Information Retrieval. Axiomathes, 18: 131–144.

6 Bourdenet, Ph. (2012) The Catalog resisting the Web: A historical perspective. Knowledge Organization, 39: 276-282.

7 Broughton, V. and Slavic A. (2007) Building a faceted classification for the humanities: principles and procedures. Journal of Documentation, 63: 727–754.

8 Broughton, V. (2008), A Faceted Classification as the Basis of a Faceted Terminology: Conversion of a Classified Structure to Thesaurus Format in the Bliss Bibliographic Classification, 2nd Edition, Axiomathes pp. 193-210

9 Choi, Y. (2012) A Practical Application of FRBR for Organizing Information in Digital Environments, Knowledge Organization, 39: 233-254.

10 David, V. (1999) Ranganathan and the Net: Using facet analysis to search and organise the World Wide Web, Ellis, David;Vasconcelos, Ana, Aslib Proceedings; Jan 1999; 51: 1. ProQuest Central.

11 Dextre Clarke, S. (2011) ISO 25964: a standard in support of KOS interoperability. In: Facets of Knowledge Organization; 4-5 July 2011. Ed. by A. Gilchrist and J. Vernau. London: Emerald, p. 129-134.

12 Doueihi, M. (2011) La grande conversion numérique. Paris: Seuil.

13 Emanuel, J. (2011) Usability of the VuFind next-generation online catalogue. Information Technology & Libraries, 30: 44–52.

14 Favier, L. and Mustafa El Hadi, W. (2012) From text to image: the concept of universality in Knowledge Organization systems designed by Paul Otlet and the International Institute of Bibliography. In: Categories, Contexts and Relations in Knowledge Organization. Proceedings of the 12th International ISKO (International Society of Knowledge Organization) Conference, 6-8 August 2012, Mysore, India. Ed. by A. Neelameghan & K.S. Raghavn Ergon Verlag, p. 220-229.

15 Fillmore C.J. (1968) The case for case. In: Bach E, Harms RT (eds) Universals in linguistic theory. Holt, Rinehart and Winston, New York, p. 1–88

16 Gnoli, C. (2008) Facets: A Fruitful Notion in Many Domains, Axiomathes, 18: 127–130.

17 Gnoli, C. (2011) Keynote address in ISKO-France Conference, Lille 2011. In: Dynamisme et Stabilité dans l'organisation des connaissances. Ed. by W. Mustafa El Hadi. Paris: Hermès, p. 51-66.

18 Goddard, C. and Wiezbicka, A. (1994) Introducing Lexical Primitives. In: Semantic, Goddard and A. Wierzbicka. Amsterdam: John Benjamins.

19 Hjørland, B. (2007) Semantics and knowledge organization. Annual Review of Information Science and Technology, 41: 367–405.

20 Hjørland, B. (2012a) Facet analysis: The logical approach to knowledge organization. Information Processing and Management, 49: 545-557. Available at: http://dx.doi.org/10.1016/j.ipm.2012.10.001

21 Hjørland, B. (2012b) Is classification necessary after Google? Journal of Documentation, 68: 299-317

22 Hodge G., (2000) Systems of Knowledge Organization for Digital Libraries: Beyond Traditional Authority Files, The Digital Library Federation Council on Library and Information Resources http://www.clir.org/pubs/abstract/pub91abst.html

23 Hudon, M. (2012) ISO 25964: vers une nouvelle norme pour l'organisation et l'accès à l'information et aux connaissances. In: Dynamisme et Stabilité dans l'organisation des connaissances. Ed. by W. Mustafa El Hadi. Paris: Hermès, p. 207-219.

24 Kuronen, T.P. Pekkarinen (1999) Ranganathan revisited: a review article, Journal of Librarianship and Information Science, 31: 45.

25 La Barre, K. (2006) The use of faceted analytico-synthetic theory as revealed in the practice of website construction and design. Unpublished dissertation, Indiana University.

26 La Barre, K. (2010a) A Semantic (Faceted) Web? Les Cahiers du Numérique, 6: 103-132.

27 La Barre, K. (2010b) Facet analysis , Annual review of Information Science and Technology, 44: 2010, Medford NJ, Information Today, p. 243-284.

28 La Barre, K. (2011) Traditions of facet theory, or a garden of forking paths? In: Facets of Knowledge Organization, Proceedings of the ISKO-UK Second Biennial Conference, 4th – 5th July, 2011, published by Emerald Books, London, p. 95-105

29 La Barre, K. and Cordeiro, R. (2012) That obscure object of desire: Facets for film access and discovery. In Diane Rasmussen Neal (Ed.) Indexing and Retrieval of Non-text Information. Berlin: DeGruyter Saur. p. 234-262.

30 La Barre, K. (2013) Sepre Avanti? Some reflections on faceted interfaces. In proceedings of UDCC Seminar on Classification and visualization, The Hague, 24-25 October 2013, p. 91-104

31 Mustafa El Hadi, W. (2012) Culture informationnelle, cultures numériques et universalité, Les Cahiers de la SFSIC, 8: 53-58.

32 Noruzi, A. (2004) Application of Ranganathan's Laws to the Web, Webology, 1(2) December.

33 Rayward, B. (1997) http://people.lis.illinois.edu/~wrayward/OriginsofInfoScience.pdf

34 Slavic, A. (2011) Classification revisited: a web of knowledge. In: Innovations in information retrieval: perspectives for theory and practice. Ed. by A. Foster and P. Rafferty P. London: Facet. p. 23-48.

35 Slavic, A. (2013) Classification in knowledge transfer between languages, domains and collections in humanities: from legacy collections to the Web of linked data, Presentation at European Seminar, Ecole Doctorale, 12th April, 2013, Lille, France, forthcoming in Favier & Mustafa El Hadi (ed.) Les Cahiers du numérique, Special Issue on Digital Humanities

36 Vickery, B.C. (2008) Faceted Classification for the Web, Axiomathes, 18(2): 145

3

Faceted Classification as a General Theory for Knowledge Organization

Vanda Broughton

The Classification Research Group manifesto of 1955, 'Faceted classification as the basis of all information retrieval', has been at least in part achieved, and there is much evidence of faceted classification influencing a whole range of modern information retrieval tools. This paper examines the theory underlying faceted classification, how and why it has been taken up so widely, and what benefits it brings to the activity of knowledge organization. The role of facet analysis as a general research tool is also considered, and how it compares with other content analysis tools as a means of modelling subject domains.

Keywords: Faceted classification, facet analysis, categories, knowledge organization

1 INTRODUCTION

In 1955 the recently formed Classification Research Group of the United Kingdom published an article entitled 'Faceted classification as the basis of all information retrieval' [15], which has come to be regarded as the manifesto of the Group, although subsequently there was a divergence between those original members who concentrated largely on faceted classification for knowledge organization in the physical environment, primarily in library collections, and those who had a broader view of the role of classification in general (and faceted classification in particular) as an essential component of retrieval systems of all kinds.The difference in emphases between these two strands of CRG work can be seen in the publications of individual members. Alongside that variation the underlying theory developed collaboratively by the Group can be contrasted with the theory as it was originally posited by S.R. Ranganathan, notably in the understanding of what constitutes a fundamental category.

Today the faceted approach is applied in a large number of indexing, organization, search and browse tools and it is usually interpreted in a looser and more general way with less attention to the fine detail of structures and relationships. Nevertheless most developers are clear about the advantages of a faceted system, and it is possible to determine the conceptual features that are identified as associated with them, primarily the organization of concepts into independent categories or facets, as opposed to their enumeration and pre-coordination in quasi-hierarchies. The structuring of tools, or data, in this way is sometimes referred to as 'facetization' [53,2].

Finally, facet analysis has been identified as useful in a much broader sense in the analysis and management of systems and domains, and some literature exists on its use in specific subject fields and in organization and retrieval of specific formats [3]. It may also be compared with content analysis methodologies in qualitative research as an analytical tool for extracting classificatory structures from large text corpora.

2 CURRENT APPLICATIONS OF FACET ANALYSIS

There is a substantial literature documenting the use of faceted classification, and the occurrence of faceted features both within and without the conventional LIS sphere. General studies include Broughton [11], Adkisson [1],and LaBarre [31]; discussion of the theoretical principles involved can be found in Pollitt [43], Mills [39] and Vickery [62], and there are more specialised discussions of the role of facet analysis in revising bibliographic classification schemes [35], and in constructing thesauri [4,55,10], taxonomies [59], and ontologies [44,50]. The most recent 'new' application of faceting is in the discovery tools to be found in many academic library catalogues, commonly referred to as next generation catalogues, or Catalogue 2.0 [33,36], and which can broadly be described as faceted browsing tools, with interfaces that display a variety of facets to modify or filter search results.This rise in interest in facetization, and the development of faceted systems, can be discerned in the literature, both research and professionally based, with more than 450 papers published in the period from 2010 to date [52].

That the aspirations of the CRG in their 1955 paper have largely been realised is evidenced by this body of work, and the importance of facet analysis is confirmed; indeed Hjorland has referred to it as 'probably the most distinct approach to knowledge organization within Library and Information Science, ... in many ways it has dominated what has been termed "modern classification theory" [28].

3 INTERPRETATIONS OF FACET ANALYSIS

It might be argued that several writers prior to Ranganathan established an approach to organizing information that exhibits 'faceted' features, namely the use of categories for analysis and organization of concepts; Otlet [34], Kaiser [30] and H. E. Bliss [9] all propose systems with a degree of analysis and synthesis explicit in the representation of complex subject content in classmarks. Kaiser identifies *concretes*, *processes* and *place* as categories of indexing terms, while Otlet and LaFontaine in the first edition of UDC in 1905 introduced a whole range of generally applicable auxiliary tables for such categories as place, time, form, language, and point of view, as well as providing a general linking device (the colon) with which any number of notations for concept in the main tables can be combined. Bliss's approach is similar to Otlet's with generally applicable auxiliary tables, subject specific special auxiliaries, and a general linking device, all of which allow some degree of synthesis for complex subjects; however, this is relatively little seen in practice in libraries using Bliss' classification when compared with those using UDC.

Nevertheless, it is generally agreed that the core conceptual basis of facet analysis was laid down by Ranganathan from the 1930s onwards, principally in the *Prolegomena* [25] and the Colon Classification itself [56]. Subsequent theorists developed that theory, and regularly redefined the purpose and objectives of faceted systems, so that several models of faceted classification theory are available.

In her 1998 paper [56] Spiteri makes a detailed comparison of the theory as presented by Ranganathan and the CRG, documenting the differences and presenting a unified model for facet analysis. The contrast between the Ranganathanian approach and the CRG is particularly interesting because the two most substantial statements of faceted classification theory are contained in their works, but neither are especially accessible, on the one hand because of the intractability of the language, and on the other because of the lack of a complete formal statement of the theory.

It is also interesting to note differences in what is seen as the purpose of a faceted classification. Ranganathan writing at the beginning of the machine age, could not have imagined the situation where computers would become freely available locally [25]; so for him the purpose of a faceted classification is very much aimed at the physical organization of materials, and the efficient representation of complex content for browsing and physical retrieval. At the outset the CRG proclaim 'faceted classification as the basis of all information retrieval', but it is clear that what this entails may be variously understood by members of the group. Vickery's position is largely that of 'classification for information retrieval' and most of his writings have machine applications in mind. However, in the 1960s the focus of the CRG as a whole seems to be on a new general classification scheme with a fairly strong physical library dimension [16]; this is followed through in the revision of Bliss's *Bibliographic classification* [5] and the creation of the second edition, BC2 [23]. Soon after this the first work begins on faceted thesauri, primarily by Aitchison [5], although it is some time before this is implemented in a formal manner in the national and international standards [12]. However, Tomlinson and Austin's work under the NATO grant ultimately leads to the PRECIS subject indexing system [7] and generates a CRG review paper by Foskett on the role of classification as a general index language [21]. Here, and in Foskett's article in the *Encyclopedia of Library & Information Science* [23], that it is fairly firmly stated that the underpinning theory of facet analysis is a legitimate foundation for a variety of knowledge organization and retrieval tools, and provides a platform for information exchange on an international basis.

4 RANGANATHAN'S CANONS AND CRG THEORY

There is relatively little in the published work of the CRG that corresponds to the formal and detailed discussion of the nature of concepts and their philosophical understanding as we find it in the *Prolegomena*. Most of the CRG theory is concerned with the design and building of classifications: the nature of categories; allocation of terms to categories or facets; the identification and naming of arrays (sometimes called sub-facets); relationships between terms in facets; the determining of schedule order and citation order; the allocation of notation; and the rules for compounding, firstly in the expression of subject summaries, and then in the building of classmarks.

In his 1970 paper [21] Foskett states that to make a special classification scheme 'one can take a sample of the literature, obtain from it the terms in use, and sort them into categories'. He allows that the 'sequence of facets, sequence of terms in facets, and notation, have to be settled', but that these have always been decided 'on a purely pragmatic basis'.

In reality the CRG did consider some more conceptual questions, notably the order of classes in a general, or multi-disciplinary, classification, through the use of integrative level theory [54]. They also formulated the idea of a standard, or default, citation order, and its associated theory of the dependence of facets as an ordering principle in citation. Schedule inversion and retroactive notation also appear to be CRG introductions; whereas the schedules in CC are laid out in order of the facets as cited and the classmarks derived by application of the facet formula as specified for each class, in a CRG type scheme, for example, BC2, the facets are presented in the inverse of the citation order, and the class notations constructed by combining individual codes in backwards order (that is retroactively) through the class.

5 THE UNDERSTANDING OF CATEGORIES AND FACETS

Crucial to Ranganathan's theory is the notion of the fundamental categories, these being five in number: Personality; Matter; Energy; Space; and Time. But although the use of categories to analyse and accommodate concepts or terms may be what most obviously characterizes a faceted system it is hard to discover any precise definition of what a category is. Foskett observed in 1958 [21] that Ranganathan had 'never given an adequate exposition of the basis of his categories ... (but) adopted them more or less intuitively'. Ranganathan is indeed remarkably constrained on the subject, and discusses them mainly from the viewpoint of their ease of identification [48], which we may take to mean the ease with which concepts can be identified as belonging to one category or another; he provides illustrative examples of concepts belonging to each category, a technique known as ostensive definition. The Oxford English Dictionary [40] defines ostensive definition as '*explanation of the signification of a term by direct demonstration or by indication of an object to which it applies*'. It is commonly used where the concept is very abstract in nature, as in the case of colours the nature of which can be conveyed by pointing out objects of that colour. Wittgenstein puts it thus: *[s]o one might say: the ostensive definition explains the use—the meaning—of the word when the overall role of the word in language is clear* [63]. This is far from the case with the fundamental categories, and it must be considered as a weakness in their use.

The difficulties of even ostensive definition increase as one goes up the order of the fundamental categories; while reasonable examples can be found for Time and Space, things become more awkward with Energy and Matter. Concepts which constitute 'problems', such as disease, once seen as Energy concepts, are to be regarded as part of the Matter category along with materials and properties. Personality Ranganathan regards as insusceptible of definition; it is 'too elusive' and 'ineffable'. Assignment to this category can only be achieved by the Method of Residues, i.e., what is not MEST must necessarily be P.

Ranganathan admits of no more than the five categories, although in practical terms this necessitates the use of rounds and levels in the facet formula, where more than one distinct group of personality, or energy, concepts can be seen to occur. For example in Class D, Engineering the facet formula is D[P]:[P2]:[E], where foci in P are building materials and structures, and in P2 parts of buildings. In J, Agriculture the situation is even more complex with the formula J[P][P2][P3]:[E][2P]:[2E], where P, P2, and P3 are crops defined by function, anatomical part, and species (such as fabric, leaf, sisal, or stimulant, root, chicory); second round facets may be specific to some purpose such as the 2P list of organisms in disease, or the 2E enumeration of specific techniques under propagation.

In the third edition of the *Prolegomena* there is no modification of the fundamental categories, but there is in the discussion of the wall-picture principle (the equivalent of the CRG's principle of dependence of facets) a listing of functional categories that extend the notion of PMEST. As expected they are largely to do with establishing the order of facets, as with the idea that in the cure of diseases, the disease facet must precede the cure. This is still cast within the framework of rounds and levels, but the terminology is very telling, with labels such as whole, part, organ, constituent, and, on a more subtle level, actand, action, actor, tool which can clearly be mapped onto Vickery's patient, operation, agent as described below.

Writing in 1962 de Grolier [17] records that there is no generally accepted definition of category, and that there is general confusion about its meaning. He notes that among other more high level understandings, Foskett regards it as generally synonymous with facet [45], and that Ranganathan's use is very specialised; strikingly he concludes that 'in Ranganathan it seems to be related to a very practical pre-occupation, that of insuring a uniform sequence of the 'facets' under various subjects' [12]. In this respect CC and CRG appear closer together than might immediately be the case, the CRG having given some considerable attention to the business of ordering (through the use of Integrative Level Theory and General Systems Theory), but relatively little to the nature of categories which seem mainly to be derived from analysing the terminology of subjects in a pragmatic manner.

The most significant difference between *Colon classification* and CRG classifications is in the number and nature of the categories employed, and this capacity for variation is what distinguishes subsequent forms of faceted systems up to the present time. The CRG interpretation of fundamental categories is wider and looser than Ranganathan's. In a number of ways it has more in common with European understandings of faceted classification, many of which are described in Grolier's work, and which also use a large number of categories for analysis.

Most familiar of the 'sets' of categories used in analysis by CRG members is that of B.C. Vickery which underlies the standard citation order: thing - kind - part - material - property - patient - process - operation - agent - product - by-product - space - time.The general scope and nature of these categories, or facets, are apparent at a very early stage of CRG activity, with Vickery reporting a slightly modified list at the 1958 International Conference on Scientific Information [28], and providing a case for their philosophical basis as early as 1953 [61]. These categories have a coherent feel to them, with a functional-cum-linguistic approach to the process of categorization; they also represent a fair working model of a system, with the main components of the system well articulated.

Vickery also attempted a comparison with other specifications of categories for retrieval in his 1958 paper with the following (adapted) table of comparisons shown:

Perry [42]	Andrews & Newman [6]	Vickery
Analytic relations	**Modulants**	**Facets**
Class inclusion	Process	Substance, product
Material of composition	Apparatus	Organ or part
Whole-part	Product	Constituent
Process	Starting-material	Property
Agent	Intermediate	Patient
Patient or product	Condition	Action, operation or process
Attributive	Made-from	Agent
Negative	Combination-including	Apparatus

Interestingly, the Introduction to the second edition of Bliss's *Bibliographic classification* (BC2), which contains a substantial statement of the associated theory running to more than a hundred pages, and which is probably the fullest accessible expression of CRG thinking, considers only a limited number of these categories, and deals with them fairly summarily compared to the discussion of facets proper within individual disciplines or subject domains.Those categories chosen appear to be pragmatically derived and variable in nature, in part dependent on the subject domain. The primary facet is '*endproduct*', in contrast to *thing*, *kind*, or *personality*, and it is successively qualified by type, part, material, property, process, operation, agent, place, and time [38].

Nowhere in the BC2 canon is any idea of the fundamental nature of categories. The Introduction to BC2 has only one mention of the fundamental categories (and this in terms of the citation order), and no definition of category, or fundamental category, in the glossary.

It may be observed that the function of the category in CRG work is closer to that of a role indicator, and it is less 'fundamental' than the PMEST categories of the Colon Classification. In CRG analysis a concept may move from one category to another depending on context (although it will always have a primary categorical status in its home discipline). For example, 'straw' is an *entity* in botany, a *by-product* in agriculture, a *material* in construction and the arts, an *agent* in animal husbandry, whereas in Colon Classification it will always have *personality* status. The 'classical' CRG view as exemplified in BC2 has no provision for the representation of relationships; these are implicit in the names of the categories, and in the inter-facet combination (e.g. an agent-operation relationship). In contrast, the view of facets as roles is clearly articulated in the work of one CRG member, Farradane, for whom concepts have no semantic value (they are called 'isolates'), the work of classification relating entirely to the relationships between isolates [19].

The early and mid-twentieth century was a period of considerable interest in the construction of indexing and retrieval systems, and most of them exhibit structural and functional characteristics similar to those discussed above; indexing tools of various kinds were produced in the United Kingdom (where the emphasis was strongly classificatory), the United States, Canada, and most European countries, as well as the Soviet Union, India, China and Japan. For the most part these were aimed at specialist environments, and their purposes quite varied. Literature in a range of academic disciplines such as chemistry, technology, atomic energy, sociology of religion, archaeology and mythology is addressed, as well as particular formats including patent literature and museum objects; there is overlap with work on the representation of relationships in linguistics, and in the construction of artificial languages.

Many tools devised in the 1950s and 1960s describe themselves as 'coding' systems or devices, and were intended to indicate the subject content of documents through the use of codes representing not only topic, but also roles and relationships.

In nearly all of these systems, designed as they are for specific contexts, there is a mixture of subject groupings, relationship indicators, and general categories, and on occasion, other elements of bibliographic description. For example, Holstrom's proposal for indexing business and technical literature has a list of relationships including: action, corporate name, equipment, geographical name, personal name, quality, substance, and title of a publication on the topic [29] such an approach is not dissimilar to the modern discovery tool described below.

De Grolier discusses a number of systems, including those produced by the CRG, which span a period roughly from the origins of the UDC until 1960, immediately prior to publication. In many of these indexing languages the distinction between a category and a role indicator is blurred, as indeed it is in the CRG work. In his own analysis of relationships in the UDC represented by the colon symbol de Grolier names five basic types of relationship: appurtenance; process; dependence; orientation; and comparison. Subject to these relationships he lists some conceptual groups that we might interpret as categories, such as parts, organs, components, constituents, properties, attributes, actions (on and affected by), origin, and condition. His own analysis of Ranganathan's fundamental categories regards them as 'an a posteriori standardization of a purely practical method'; in particular 'personality has no theoretical value', 'the concept [of energy] is vague, conceived after the event'.

In 1958 Perry and Kent's *Semantic code dictionary* [60], intended for the coding of abstracts in metallurgical literature, shows a typical two level structure with a separate list of relationship indicators subordinate to some more general categories. They propose a classification for the semantic code, which at the broad level consists of: general concepts; relationships; states; processes; substances; and objects. A more detailed classification for relationships subordinates these to some general categories of materials, properties, processes and conditions, and elsewhere Vickery [60] has noted the presence of analytic relations for: class inclusion, material of composition, whole-part, process, agent, patient or product, attributive, and negative, as being extremely close to his own thinking.

Perhaps the most interesting examples from a contemporary point of view are those in the French tradition, notably Robert Pagès and Jean-Claude Gardin. Pagès' system [41] is specifically referred to as a 'coded analysis', perhaps the first occasion on which the ideas of coding and analysis have been explicitly brought together. In combination with a lexicon containing twenty-two categories of subject oriented content, the code consists of an extremely complex systematization of 'syntactical relationships'; the lexicon also exhibits some of the general categories we have come to expect, including processes, properties, operations, phenomena, space and time.

Gardin [26,24,18,25] presents the richest and most compelling examples of coded analysis. His earliest work is on analytical codes for archaeological material, both its documentation and the objects themselves, and addresses Bronze Age metal tools, vases, and ornamentation. He distinguishes the morphological and syntactical elements of coding (categories and relationships) which have previously often both been present in the same parts of the classificatory structure. His linguistically based categories which he calls declensions (subject, object, qualificatory, action, instrumental, locative) in the field of iconography show a strong resemblance to Vickery's thing, patient, property, operation, agent, place, confirming the validity of these general categories as a means of data structuring.

More unusually, as well as the analytical coding of objects, itself an innovation at the time, Gardin applies his techniques to textual content in a manner very similar to modern qualitative data analysis methodologies. His first study sample was that of Mesopotamian tablets, which was followed by a conceptual analysis of the Quran. From that he derived five hundred concepts, which were then aggregated into six large subject related categories, building a classificatory structure from first principles. Unlike previous exercises in analysis Gardin did not use any *a priori* group of categories or classificatory codes to manage the text, but extracted his concepts and categories on a strictly empirical basis. A subsequent analysis of myths had the aim of classifying the structure of the myth, and to permit a comparison of structural models, and finally to constitute a universal grammar of myths, and a catalogue of fundamental representations, or mythemes. These activities of modelling and classification building 'from the ground up' are so striking, that it is surprising to find so little reference to them in more recent work.

6 MODERN USES OF THE FACETED APPROACH

Few online examples of faceting employ any kind of complex classificatory structure or controlled vocabulary; most employ categories as a way of structuring the search interface, where they function as a browsing, and sometimes, filtering tool. The categories or facets are presented for use as a source of search terms, either alone or in combination; alternatively facets may be brought in to qualify, and hence narrow, an existing search.

E-commerce applications are typical and represent the simplest example of faceted tools; the categories are normally limited to properties of the entity being marketed, and, by the standards of LIS classifications, contain only one 'facet', that of the entity organized into arrays by various principles, or characteristics, of division. The prototype e-commerce faceted system, Peter Meerholz's classification of wine [37], consisted of a series of arrays, or subfacets of wine: colour; region; grape variety. Later versions often added style (light and fruity, for example) and/or price, but remained within the entities facet. Very similar approaches can be found currently on most sites selling clothes or shoes [20] with the interface displaying choices of gender, age group, size, colour, function, and style; occasionally these can become very complex with more than a dozen types of attributes displayed.

The recently introduced 'discovery tools' now frequently encountered as a search application in online academic catalogues represent a hybrid interpretation of faceting. Usually referred to as having faceted browse functions these packages present a complex interface; the initial search results, achieved by keyword searching, are presented as a central frame with left and right hand frames containing various 'facets' from which terms can be selected to filter and refine the search. The facets include may include *author*, *date of publication*, *format*, *location*, and *language* as well as *subject* per se, and content related facets such as *period* or *place* (although this may not be distinguished from *place of publication*), rather like Holstrom's system described above. The facets in this case seem to be related to the fields in the catalogue database, and the content is drawn from the bibliographic data in that database (and in some cases from external databases). Some systems include a 'thesaurus' of associated terms, but again these do not come from a controlled vocabulary but are derived from the text of the bibliographic records in the database on the basis of co-occurrence of terms.

It seems that it is essentially the use of categories to accommodate terms or concepts that defines a system as faceted. Systems outside the conventional library or information management environments seldom involve any theory for the definition or ordering of terms, which is largely done on a pragmatic basis. But the allocation of terms to categories, the lack of pre-coordination of terms, and the avoidance of 'hierarchies' of cross-facet compounded terms, seem to be the principal features.

It seems that Foskett may well have seen this future when he wrote that it 'does not seem necessary to keep within the limits of these [i.e. Ranganathan's] fundamental categories to use the technique of facet analysis, and it is not always helpful to do so'. [47]. Current interpretations of the faceted model are characterised by the use of categories for structuring data, but the choice of those categories are closely related to the domain, the nature of the terminology, and the needs and interests of users, rather than to any general philosophical or linguistic principles.

7 FACET ANALYSIS AND SYSTEMS THEORY

At an early stage of development Austin makes the connection between a faceted system and general systems theory: 'A system is a set of objects (sub-systems) together with relationships between them and their attributes. Since a system never occurs without an environment, a characterisation ... is incomplete without reference to the total system.' Austin's 1969 paper [8] also makes reference to the idea of a 'root concept' comparable to the 'root definitions' of soft systems theory. As Foskett points out [22] General Systems Theory may be used to operate in conjunction with integrative level theory to provide frameworks within which first subject analysis (ILT), and then ordering (GST) can be carried out consistently, but the use of GST involved the introduction of 'active'and 'passive' systems.

This leads to a more complex set of 'categories' in the resulting indexing language, consisting of the conventional categories (such as *entities*, *properties* and *activities*) combined with operators which establish the relationships between the individual concepts and the containing system or systems. These relationships, which indicate active nature, passive nature, activities and interactions within and between the systems and their environment, changes in the system, and classes defined by attributes, can be listed as follows:

1. Properties of system;
2. Second system (environment);
3. Activities and interactions not involving change;
4. Active subsystem;
5. Passive subsystem;
6. Interactions within system;
7. Second system (environment);

8. Interactions involving change of system; and
9. Attribute defining a sub-class.

We have already noted the similarity of Vickery's fundamental categories to the components of a system, and a cursory inspection of systems theory, particularly of soft systems methodology, reinforces that impression. Soft systems methodology has the same objective of building models from what are termed 'root definitions'; these are constructed by 'consciously considering the elements of the mnemonic CATWOE. [14].

The standard 'categories' represented by the acronym CATWOE can, as before, be seen to correspond closely to the categories used in faceted systems:

Soft systems elements	Facet categories
C = customers	patients
A = actors	agents
T = transformations	actions/operations
W = weltanshauung (world view)	discipline
O = owner	entity/organization
E = environmental constraints	properties/context

Similar thinking is common to a wider group of disciplines including systems analysis, systems engineering and operational research [13].

8 FACET ANALYSIS AS A CODING TOOL

A number of publications in the early days of faceted classification speak of its role as a coding tool; Ranganathan's own publication [49] refers to both classification and coding as relevant to search, and de Grolier's study of categories [12] speaks of their role in both classification and coding.

The latter is careful in his definition of coding, and one must allow that the understanding of it may have changed over time; it does in any event precede the current use of coding to mean the representation of document content in machine readable formats. Generally he takes a 'code' to mean 'a system of conventional signs which permit faithful translation between unevenly developed groups of signs or symbols [12]; this may include natural and artificial languages, classificatory structures, and, in the narrowest sense, of machine understandable codes used in information retrieval. Based on the glossary and index document circulated at the Dorking Conference [46] he finally settles on the definition of code as 'a system of symbols for the representation of information and rules governing their combination'.

The variety of categories identified in various classifications and indexing languages suggest that faceted classification is as much an analytical tool for the identification of categories as it is a modelling tool for the structuring of domains and the construction of specific knowledge organization systems. Although categories belong to the conceptual aspect of the domain (Ranganathan's *idea plane*), the categories identified arise from a detailed examination of the vocabulary in the domain (the *verbal plane*), and it is difficult in practice to separate the two at the primary stage of analysis. In most of the cases provided by de Grolier, the conceptual nature of the categories is not discussed but they appear rather to have been derived on a pragmatic basis as a result of analysis of vocabulary.

There is too a symbiotic relationship between text and categories in that the text may be examined to determine categories (as is the case with grounded theory) and, inversely, the categories may be used as an analytical tool upon the text for the grouping and ordering of terms into a structured domain (as is the case for the building of faceted KOSs).

In this respect facet analysis has some features in common with other content analysis tools, although most of these are more recent in development than facet analysis. Today the concept of coding in information work generally implies the use of mark-up languages to represent both structure and content in web sites and their constituent text; text encoding is also a familiar activity, and the TEI (Text Encoding Initiative) [58] provides a standard for categories and codes used to facilitate textual analysis of digital text.

Alternatively, coding as a means to content analysis is now a very common qualitative methodology in social science and humanities research, where it is seen as an important technique for the qualitative analysis of data in the form of texts, derived from interviews, observations, or field notes, as well as more formal document types. Unlike most of the coding methods used in information retrieval and documentation, coding of textual content uses lexical labels to denote content. The coding is an intellectual exercise, but may be managed electronically, and results in the codes being entered into a frame to the right of the text itself at the appropriate point. As in the case of the subject analysis of document content for classification and indexing, the coding is interpretive and conceptual, i.e. the wording of the codes may differ from the wording of the text.

The framework used for coding is remarkably similar to that used in faceted structures, with a mixture of categories, relationships, and topical content. Lofland et al. [32] note that social behaviour occurs within four co-ordinates, 'the intersection of one or more *actors*, engaging in one or more *activities*, at a particular *time* in a specific *place*'. Within the specific context of social interactions they identify units of social behaviour: cultural practices, episodes, encounters, roles and types, personal relationships, groups, organizations, habitats, subcultures/lifestyles (which define persons), and these look very similar to the what one might expect as facets and sub-facets (or arrays) in a faceted classification of the field.

One purpose of coding is to identify patterns and structures in the documents under analysis, and to establish links between content elements; such patterns may include: similarity, difference, frequency, sequence, correspondence, and causation [51]. More significantly coding may generate categories [49], as in the case of Harry, Sturges and Klinger's study of minorities in special education programmes [27] where the identification of codes for materials, computers and textbooks, generated the category *resources*; in the same study emergent categories were teacher *skills*, subdivided into instructional and management skills. Saldana [49] provides examples of more complex structures, where categories have self-assembled into a classificatory structure, in a way very closely aligned with Gardin's work on myth, and in much the same way that classificationists may assemble terms into facets and arrays, and hence into a complete knowledge organization system. The process tends to be iterative, with second and third levelsof coding and categorization, as is frequently the case when building documentary classifications. Other parallels between the two methodologies include the use of notions such as code mapping or code landscaping where the process of categorization exposes structures and relationships, or reveals structures alternative to those expected. Such maps can manifest themselves in the form of operational model diagrams [49], reminiscent of concept maps or topic maps, and which mirror the use of classification as a domain modelling tool. Ultimately the modelling process may result in theory generation, as is the objective of grounded theory as an analytico-synthetic methodology.

Grounded theory is the one coding methodology that has been formally compared with facet analysis, in a 1998 article by Susan Leigh Star [57]. Some similarities between faceted classification and grounded theory are commented on by Star, although her study is largely of the similar contexts in which the two arose, and her examination does not go very far in looking at the detailed methodology.

Star regards faceted classification as '*a movement away from a flat proliferation of particular aspects of a field of knowledge towards a synthetic representation that includes basic (both abstract and concrete) categories. These latter, crucially, remain open to revision*', a view which accords well with that taken in this paper. She also comments that '*both grounded theory and faceted classification began as reform movements .... These are unusual in that this reform did not consist of abandoning the attempt to formalize and systematize*'. Of Ranganathan it might be said that his was one of the earliest attempts in classification to establish a formal and systematic basis to organizing systems. But there are closer, and more important, similarities between facet analysis and coding methods that are perhaps only more recently apparent. She does, however, line up facet analysis with '*other analytical tools [as] ... a means of managing large bodies of text*' [4].

9 CONCLUSIONS

Faceted knowledge organization systems are widespread, but differ considerably, particularly in the complexity of their structure, and the provision for syntax and synthesis. Classification and indexing languages are usually highly organized with complex structuring, ordering, and combinatorial principles; online applications may use very much simpler systems with less regard for the expression of relationships and nothing much in the way of rules for synthesis.

What all faceted systems have in common is the idea of categorical organization of concepts, as opposed to enumeration and pre-coordination in hierarchies; the simplicity and logic of this approach is what makes it particularly attractive for mechanized retrieval. The nature of categories may vary greatly, although work by Ranganathan, Vickery, other CRG members, and documentalists internationally show a commonality of thought, with a general consensus around functional categories of the kind proposed by Vickery.

Some of this work is very close in its underlying thinking both to systems methodology as a modelling tool, and to more recent methods of qualitative data analysis through the coding of textual content. Similarities occur in the detailed examination of terminology, the identification of concepts, the use of categories to contain concepts, and the building of classificatory structures from the bottom up. Although grounded theory in particular proceeds from the basis of no *a priori* classification, the techniques and established categories of facet analysis may provide a useful starting point for other text analysts.

REFERENCES

1 Adkisson, H.P. (2005) Web design practices: use of faceted classification. Retrieved from www.webdesignpractices.com/navigation/facets.html

2 Agostini, Alessandro; Devika P. Madalli and A.R.D. Prasad. (2011) Faceted Approach To Diverse Query Processing. *DiversiWeb 2011*. 17. (Accessed at http://ceur-ws.org/Vol-762/paper4.pdf)

3 Agostini, Alessandro; Devika P. Madalli and A.R.D. Prasad. (2011) Facet-based opinion retrieval from blogs. *Information Processing and Management*, 46(1): 71-88.

4 Aitchison Jean. (1986) A classification as a source for a thesaurus: The Bibliographic Classification of H. E. Bliss as a source of thesaurus terms and structure. Journal of documentation, 42(3): 160-181.

5 Aitchison,J.; Gomershall, I. and Ireland, R. (1969) Thesaurofacet: a thesaurus and faceted classification for engineering and related subjects. Whetstone, Leicester : English Electric Company (Book).

6 Andrews, D.D. and Newman, S.M. (1956) Storage and retrieval of contents of technical literature, non-chemical information, 15 May 1956, US Patent Office, Research and Development Report (Report)

7 Austin Derek. (1984) PRECIS: a manual of concept analysis and subject indexing 2nd ed. London: The British Library Bibliographic Services Division (Book).

8 Austin, D. (1969) Prospects for a new general classification. *Journal of Librarianship and Information Science,* 1: 149-169,

9 Bliss, H.E. (1940/1953) A bibliographic classification, extended by systematic auxiliary schedules for composite specification and notation, New York: Wilson (Book)

10 Broughton, V. (2008) A faceted classification as the basis of a faceted terminology: conversion of a classified structure to thesaurus format in the Bliss Bibliographic Classification, 2nd Edition." *Axiomathes,* 18(2): 193-210

11 Broughton, V. (2006) The need for faceted classification as the basis of all information retrieval. *Aslib Proceedings* 58(2): 49-72

12 BS 8723-2. (2005) Structured vocabularies for information retrieval. Part 2: Thesauri. 2005, London: British Standards Institution (Book).

13 Checkland, P.B. (1981) Systems thinking, systems practice. Wiley, Chichester (Book).

14 Checkland, P.B. (1989) Soft systems methodology. *Human systems management*, 8(4): 273-289.

15 Classification Research Group. (1955) The need for a faceted classification as the basis for all methods of information retrieval. *Library Association Record*, 57(7): 262-268.

16 Classification Research Group. (1964) Some problems of a general classification scheme. Report of a conference held in London June 1963, London (Book)

17 de Grolier, E.A. (1962) Study of general categories applicable to classification and coding in documentation, Paris: Unesco (Book), p.15

18 Digard, F. *et al.* (1975) Répertoireanalytique des cylindresorientauxpubliésdans les sources bibliographiqueséparses (3 vols.). Editions du Centre *National de la RechercheScientifique*, Paris (Book).

19 Farradane, J.E.L. (1950) A scientific theory of classification and indexing. *Journal of Documentation*, 6: 83-99.

20 For example the Hotter Shoe website: http://www.hottershoes.com/en/info/Women

21 Foskett, D.J. (1958) The construction of a faceted classification. **In** Proceedings of the International Conference on Scientific Information, 1959 Washington, DC: National Academy of Sciences (Conference proceedings) 53-74.

22 Foskett, D.J. (1970) Classification for a general index language: a review of recent research by the Classification Research Group. London: Library Association (Book), p.39.

23 Foskett, D.J. (1971) The Classification Research Group 1952-1968. **In** Kent, A. & Lancour, H. (Eds.), *Encyclopedia of library and information Science*, 5: 141-145. New York: Marcel Dekker (Book).

24 Gardin, J.C. On the coding of geometrical shapes and other representations with reference to archaeological documents. *ICSI* E: 889-901

25 Gardin, J.C. (1958) Four codes for the description of artefacts. *American anthropologist*, 60(2): 335-7.

26 Gardin, J.C.; Chevalier, J.; Christophe, J. and Salomé, M.R. (1976) Code pour l'analyse des formes de poteries. CNRS, Paris (Book).

27 Harry, B.; Sturges, K.M. and Klingner, J.K. (2005) Mapping the process: an exemplar of process and challenge in grounded theory analysis. *Educational researcher*, 34(2): 3-13.

28 Hjørland, B. (2013) Facet analysis: the logical approach to knowledge organization. *Information Processing and Management*, 49(2): 545-557.

29 Holstrom, J.E. (1951) Facts, files and action in business and public affairs. Vol. 2, London: Chapman & Hall (Book) p.70-83.

30 Kaiser, J. (1911) Systematic indexing, London: Pitman (Book)

31 La Barre, K. (2006) The use of faceted analytico-synthetic theory in the practice of website construction and design. Unpublished dissertation. Indiana University. Retrieved from https://netfiles.uiuc.edu/klabarre/www/LaBarre_FAST.pdf

32 Lofland, J.; Snow, D.; Anderson, L. and Lofland, L.H. (2006) Analyzing social settings: a guide to qualitative observation and analysis (4th ed.), Belmont, CA: Thomson Wadsworth (Book).

33 M. Breeding. (2007) Next generation library catalogs, *Library technology reports*, 43(4): 5-14.

34 Manuel du Repertoire BibliographiqueUniversel, Brussels: IIB, 1905-1907 (Book)

35 McIlwaine, I.C. and Williamson, N.J. (1994) A feasibility study on the restructuring of the Universal Decimal Classification into a full-faceted classification system. **In** Albrechtsen, H &Oernager, S. (Eds.), *Proceedings of the Third International Society for Knowledge Organization (ISKO) Conference: Knowledge organization and quality management, Copenhagen, Denmark, 20-24 Jun 94* (Advances in Knowledge Organization Vol. 4, pp. 406-13) 1994Frankfurt/Main: INDEKS. (Conference proceedings)

36 Mercun, T. and Zumer, M. (2008) New generation of catalogues for the new generation of users: A comparison of six library catalogues. *Program: Electronic Library and Information Systems,* 42(3): 243-261.

37 Merholz, Peter Innovation in classification. 23.09.2001 www.peterme.com/archives/00000063.html

38 Mills J. and Broughton, V. (1977) Bliss bibliographic classification, 2nd ed., London: Butterworth (later Munich: Bowker Saur; Saur) (Book) p.40.

39 Mills, J. (2004) Faceted classification and logical division in information retrieval." *Library Trends,* 52(3): 541-70

40 Oxford English Dictionary. http://www.oed.com.

41 Pagès, Robert. Introduction à l'analysecodée: une technique documentaire en psychologiesociale et sciences humaines, *Recherchessociologiques, 1955,* (2): 55-66; 1956(3) 65-76.

42 Perry, J.W.; Kent, A. and Berry, M.M. (1956) Machine literature searching, Interscience: New York (Book).

43 Pollitt, A.S.; M.P. Smith and P. Braekevelt. (1996) View-based searching systems: a new paradigm for information retrieval based on faceted classification and indexing using mutually constraining knowledge-based rules. **In** C. Johnson & M. Dunlop (Eds.), *Information retrieval and human computer interaction (Proceedings of the joint workshop of the information retrieval and human computer interaction specialist groups of the British Computer Society)* GIST Technical Report G96-2, Glasgow University. Glasgow: Glasgow University, 73-77 (Conference proceedings)

44 Prieto-Diaz, R. A faceted approach to building ontologies. Submitted to the *21st International Conference on Conceptual Modeling, Tampere, Finland, October 7-11, 2002* Retrieved from https://users.cs.jmu.edu/prietorx/public/RubenPubs%5B1%5D.html (Conference proceedings)

45 Proceedings of the International Study Conference on Classification for Information Retrieval. (1958) Held at Beatrice Webb House, Dorking, England, 13th-17th May 1957. London: Aslib (Conference proceedings), p.115

46 Proceedings of the International Study. (1958) Conference on Classification for Information Retrieval held at Beatrice, Webb House, Dorking, England, 13th-17th May 1957. London: *Aslib* (Conference proceedings).

47 Ranganathan, S.R. (1960) Colon classification: Basic classification (6th ed.). London: Asia Publishing House.

48 Ranganathan, S.R. (1967) Prolegomena to library classification 3rd edition. (*Ranganathan Series in Library Science*, 20). London: Asia Publishing House (Book), 399f.

49 Ranganathan, S.R. (1950) Classification, coding and machinery for search. Paris, France: Unesco (Book).

50 Rodriguez-Castro, B.; Glaser, H. and Carr, L. How to reuse a faceted classification and put it on the semantic web. **In**: *The 9th International Semantic Web Conference (ISWC), November 2010, Shanghai, China_* (Conference proceedings)

51 Saladana, J. (2013) The coding manual for qualitative researchers. London: Sage(Book), p.6

52 Search results from Library and information science abstracts (Database). http://www.proquest.com/en-US/catalogs/databases/detail/lisa-set-c.shtml

53 Slavic, A. (2009) The Round Table: 'UDC editorial perspectives' a report. *Extensions and corrections to the UDC*, 31: 19

54 Spiteri, L. (1995) The Classification Research Group and the theory of integrative levels. *Katharine Sharp Review*, 1.

55 Spiteri, L.F. (1997) The use of facet analysis in information retrieval thesauri: an examination of selected guidelines for thesaurus construction. *Cataloging and Classification Quarterly*, 25(1): 21-39.

56 Spiteri, Louise. (1998) A simplified model for facet analysis. *Canadian journal of library and information science* 23: 1-30 (April-July)

57 Star, Susan Leigh. (1998) Grounded classification: grounded theory and faceted classification. *Library trends*, 47(2): 218-232.

58 Text encoding initiative. http://www.tei-c.org/index.xml

59 Tzitzakas Y. et al. (2004) An algebraic approach for specifying compound terms in faceted taxonomies. *InInformation Modelling and Knowledge Bases XV, Proceedings of EJC'03 67–87.* IOS Press (Conference proceedings)

60 Vickery, B. C. (1959) Subject analysis for information retrieval. **In** *Proceedings of the International Conference on Scientific Information, 1958,* Washington, DC: National Academy of Sciences (Conference proceedings) p. 41-52

61 Vickery, B.C. (1953) Systematic subject indexing. *Journal of Documentation*, 9(1): 48-57.

62 Vickery, B.C. (2008) Faceted classification for the web. *Axiomathes*, 18(2): 145-160. DOI:10.1007/s10516-007-9025-9

63 Wittgenstein, Ludwig. (1953) Philosophical Investigations, Oxford: Blackwell, §30.

4

Facets, Levels and Semantic Factoring

C. Gnoli

Knowledge organization systems (KOS) can be constructed on the basis of three main kinds of relationships: classical hierarchies; facets; and concepts related in some other relevant way. Among related concepts, of special interest are semantic factors, that is concepts occurring in the definition of a term or class. In an evolutionary perspective, factors can combine, leading to the emergence of a new class of phenomena at a higher integrative level. Recording factors in the schedules of a KOS can make it more sound in ontological terms, and allow for additional functionalities in its application to information retrieval, like query expansion. Some aspects and problems of this are discussed, including of the extent of the semantic network to be considered for each search, and fuzzy relationships with concepts concurring to the definition of terms or classes. Examples are provided from UDC, ILC, and the ISO standard for thesaurus interoperability. It is concluded that facets and semantic factors should be reconsidered as powerful components in KOS development, as well as in KOS representation in the context of the Semantic Web.

KEYWORDS: Concept definition, Facet analysis, Integrative levels, Knowledge organization systems, Prototype theory, Relationships

1 INTRODUCTION: SEMANTIC FACTORING IN A KOS

The variety of conceptual tools allowing people to index and retrieve the subject content of documents is known nowadays by the collective term of *knowledge organization systems (KOS)*. This includes, among many types of tools, keywords and tags, subject heading lists, taxonomies, thesauri, classification schemes, classauri, and ontologies.

According to Dahlberg [1], the basic units of a KOS are concepts. These are connected to each other by semantic relationships, such as genus-species, whole-part, class-instance, entity-property, action-agent, etc. Together, concepts and relationships between them form a semantic network (a graph in mathematical terms). The nodes of the network can be labeled by either verbal terms or notational symbols, depending on the KOS type.

The exact relationships that can be established between a particular concept and others depend on the meanings that are summarized in its term or symbol. Indeed, a concept is "a knowledge unit synthesizing the characteristics of a stated item of reference by a term or a name" [1, p. 17]. As the concept labeled by the term `girl` synthesizes the characteristics of being human, young, and female, it can be connected in the semantic network with other concepts expressing humanity, expressing youth, and expressing femininity.

In the classical Aristotelian approach, all the characteristics of a concept can be specified in an explicit definition: "a girl is a young female human". This can be recorded in a KOS by establishing a genus-species relationship between the term `girls` and the term `humans` (girls are a type of humans).

The remaining characteristics of the definition are not always recorded in KOSs. However, they can be. In a thesaurus, RT relationships can be established between `girls` and `youth`, as well as between `girls` and `females`. In a classification enriched with thesaurus-like relationships, also called a classaurus [2], the class of girls, as a subclass of humans, can be provided with the additional information that it is connected with the classes of youth and of females, situated somewhere else in the scheme.

Youth and females are *semantic factors* of girls, as they are implied in the definition of girls even if not treated as their broader class in this particular KOS (of course a different KOS could treat, e.g., `women` as a subclass of `humans`, and `girls` as a subclass of `women`; thesauri often have node labels such as "humans by gender" for such purposes). Indeed, the ISO standard for thesauri observes that in RTs "one of the terms is often a necessary component in any explanation or definition of the other; the term `birds`, for example, forms a necessary part of the explanation of `ornithology`" [3, 10.3.1].

Semantic factoring is variously treated in the literature on knowledge organization [e.g. 4, p. 256-260]. A recent case is the plan to build a Basic Concepts Classification by notation for primitive concepts connected with symbols for causal links [5]. A question arising in such projects is how far should semantic analysis proceed. Linguists adopting the Natural Semantic Metalanguage approach have identified a set of 64 semantic primitives whose combinations should be able to express the meanings of any natural language [6]. However, if applied to knowledge organization, this approach would produce very long and complex phrases or classmarks to index even a simple document.

In this paper, I will discuss the ways and usefulness of recording the relationships of a concept with its semantic factors. To this purpose, I will consider especially the case of faceted classifications, as a type of KOS being relevant for its power and expressiveness. Facets are a KOS device well-known in Indian information science, as they were explicitly described and introduced in classification on a regular basis by S.R. Ranganathan.

2 CLASSES AS CRYSTALLIZED COMBINATIONS OF FACETS

In the perspective of this paper, facets can be seen as specifications of a combination of characteristics of a class. (I am adopting the term *facet* as it is used in its classification tradition, initiated by Ranganathan. In the tradition of thesauri, on the other hand, "facets" are usually meant to be the categorial top terms of each hierarchy, such as `materials` or `activities`, hence they are not subordinated to any particular class [7]; the syntactic relationships provided by facets in classification are then provided by "roles". These appear to be just different terms for the same basic conceptual structures.)

In bibliographic classifications, facets are usually applied to a disciplinary class: thus, youth and femininity can be treated as facets of the class of sociology. However, just like classifications of disciplines, classifications of phenomena can also be developed (some then call them *taxonomies*, especially when used by scientists rather than by information professionals: the taxonomy of plants, of soils, of languages, of musical instruments, etc.). In the latter case, we can have a class of people instead of a class of sociology; while youth and femininity can be facets of people rather than facets of sociology [8]:

people, of age: young, of gender: female

A class of phenomena can have properties of any kind, like "people working in India" or "people wearing a hat". These can be expressed by a *freely faceted* syntax [9], which uses facet relationships to connect any class with any other. However, some facets (such as age and gender in our example) occur more regularly in combination with a given class, and are more relevant to specify the essential characteristics of that class. They then become part of the *facet formula* of the class: as people are supposed to always have some age and some gender, notation provides appropriate facet indicators for them, to be used each time that they are specified in subject matter.

Especially relevant can be some particular combinations of characteristics. These combinations usually identify a concept, and they often also get a name in natural language, like *girls*. In other words, they are a crystallization of a particular combination of facets into a new class. In a classification, they can be represented as a subclass of the original class:

people
    girls (type of: people) (semantic factors: youth; femininity)

The information that girls are a subclass of people can be included in their notational symbol, e.g. because it has the same letters or digits as people plus an additional one. Notice that, on the other hand, the semantic relationships with youth and with femininity, which were explicit in the faceted combination, are not expressed anymore in the notation for the synthesized subclass. If they are to be recorded, this has to be done in a special field of the schedules' database devoted to semantic factors. This will allow users to track the relationship when needed.

Deciding whether a given combination of characteristics deserves to be crystallized into a subclass, or has to be expressed only by an occasional combination of facets, is not always obvious. Let us consider the following example:

Romance languages
    French
    French spoken by bakers
    French spoken in Orléans
    Québecois
    Occitan

It is quite clear that French spoken by bakers is just an occasional combination, that can be expressed by a free composition of facets. At the other end of the series, Occitan (spoken in Southern France) is well known to be a language in its own right, hence will deserve to be a subclass of Romance languages, a sister class of French.

However, what about the other two concepts? Is the French dialect spoken in Orléans different enough from standard French to be considered as a separate class, or at least as a special subclass of French? Probably not, in which case it can be expressed just by a combination of facets, including a Space facet as a part of the facet formula of languages:

French, spoken in: Orléans

As for Québecois (French as spoken in Canada), it does have some distinctive features making it a relevant variety of French, although these are probably not different enough from standard French to make it a fully different language.

We thus have a gradation of diversities that can be expressed in different ways: occasional free combination of concepts (French spoken by bakers), combination of concepts provided in the facet formula (French spoken in Orléans), distintinctive subclass (Québecois), and sister class (Occitan):

Romance languages
  French
    French, spoken by: bakers
    French, spoken in: Orléans
    Québecois (semantic factor: Canada)
  Occitan

Similar questions arise when developing KOSs in other domains, like plants, or religions: is a certain faith different enough from the mainstream religion (e.g., Christianity) to be treated as an independent confession (e.g., Universal Unitarianism), or is it just a sect (e.g., Quakerism), or even an occasional variety of the standard religion (Christianity in Nigeria)? [10]

3 ONTOLOGICAL ASPECTS

In the terms of ontology – the branch of philosophy investigating the kinds of existing entities – the relationship between Québecois and Canada can be described as one of *existential dependence*: in order to make sense, the concept of Québecois implies the previous existence of the concept of Canada. That is, Canada is part of the definition of Québecois.

Although concepts deserving a separate class, rather than a combination of facets, are usually identified in an intuitive way, one can wonder whether they can be identified by more formal principles. This, indeed, could give KOSs a better foundation from the viewpoint of ontology.

Concepts like "religions of ancient Egypt" or "architecture for railways", although their captions may look like compounds at a first glance, are treated as independent classes in the Universal Decimal Classification (UDC) on the basis of the principle that the result of the combination of their factors is "the thing in itself": that is, they form a well-identifiable class, rather than just an occasional combination of facets like in "religions of modern France" (as there is no religion that can be defined as peculiar to modern France more than of other regions) or "architecture for blond people" (as blond people are not supposed to have architectural needs different from those of other people).

Some interesting considerations in this direction have been expressed by Austin [11] while developing a general classification of phenomena based on the theory of integrative levels. In that draft system, one main class is 'chemical elements'. Another main class is 'chemical compounds', like iron sulphide, which are formed as *integrates* of elements. However, not all juxtapositions of elements give rise to a genuine integrate. Mixtures of iron filings and sulphur are only an *aggregate* of elements, not giving rise to an integrate. Only integrates, in which "components can no longer be recognized", deserve to be considered as a new level, hence to be represented as a separate main class [11].

Thus, on the scale of a whole general classification, a list of main classes can be identified in a series of integrative levels: chemical elements, gas clouds, stars, planets, crystals, paracrystals, living entities, etc. Each of them can be seen as dependent on the previous ones, although showing new emergent properties that make it a separate class of phenomena:

...
chemical elements
gas clouds (semantic factor: chemical elements)
stars (semantic factor: gas clouds)
...

In many cases, existential dependence can be easily interpreted in an evolutionary framework: the integrate can be considered to have emerged by some synergy of pre-existing phenomena that has given birth to a new class of phenomena with novel properties. Stars emerge from gas clouds, but have additional properties like luminosity and thermonuclear fusion. It is indeed these properties that make stars deserving to be considered as an autonomous class of objects, at a new integrative level.

In a general KOS based on an emergent evolutionary ontology [12], existential dependence of a class (or term) on others can then be recorded as semantic factors [13-14]. The whole KOS will thus become a network structured according to two basic kinds of relationships: the genus-species relationship, connecting each class with its subclasses, and the dependence relationship, connecting each class with higher-level classes that emerged from it (that is, emerged from synergies between it and other phenomena). A third major kind of relationships can be provided by facets [15].

Dependence relationships between main classes, such as chemical elements and stars, can be relevant for visualizing the macrostructure of the system; on the other hand, dependence between more specific classes, like between iron and Iron Age, can be especially useful in suggesting relevant connections between phenomena scattered in very different places of the scheme (chemical elements and human history in this example).

4 RETRIEVAL ASPECTS

This architecture opens interesting possibilities for information retrieval, as a user can be enabled to navigate the KOS both towards narrower classes (from iron to its isotopes), and towards dependent classes (from iron to pyrite or to Iron Age).

Links of a class with others that are its semantic factors, e.g. of "religions of Ancient Egypt" with "Ancient Egypt", are recorded in the authority file of UDC. This has the potential of making them exploitable for information retrieval; in practice, however, this is rarely implemented, as it also requires this kind of information to be loaded in OPACs and bibliographies using UDC, and their users to be provided with an appropriate search function.

A question arose in the Discussion List for UDC Editors [`udc-development @udcc.org`] on June 17-18, 2013, concerning the possibility of representing the common auxiliaries for "fathers" and "mothers" as a faceted combination of "parents" plus "male" or "female", rather than as subclasses of the auxiliary `-055.52` for "parents". This was rejected, mainly on the basis of practical considerations: users are expected to search for any document dealing with mothers (probably in combination with some other concept) but not for any document dealing generically with females, including female trees or female dolphins.

The idea of query expansion in searching has been discussed especially as an application of thesauri [16-17]. The semantic network of a thesaurus, consisting of BT/NTs and of RTs, can be exploited to automatically connect a search term as input by the user with broader, narrower or related terms, and to retrieve additional results matching the latter ones. It is a matter of choice whether expansion should be the default option, or should be selected by the user as a special search mode; one possibility is to make it automatic only when the exact search yields few or no results.

A crucial point in deciding between these options is probably the kind of relationships used for query expansion. Narrower terms in a thesaurus (or subclasses in a classification) are usually relevant for a search, thus many systems include them in the results by default. Broader terms (or broader classes) can be useful especially when the user has started from too specific a concept, or when the specific search yields few hits: indeed, more general documents will often include some sections dealing with the specific subject searched.

Related terms or classes may be relevant for a search or not; this is difficult to predict, as in most KOSs the exact nature of the associative relation is not recorded. This becomes especially problematic when several relationships in a chain are used: indeed, a concept related to another which in turn is related to the search term may lead to a very different semantic field, thus producing weird results as compared to the original choice. For this reason, it is believed that only one step should generally be used in query expansion via RTs, or that subtypes of RT could be specified [16].

Existential dependence, as it has been described above, is a particular kind of associative relation. Compared with unspecified RT, it is more explicit. Indeed, many RT relationships like that between `stars` and `night` are not cases of existential dependence. Furthermore, dependence is not symmetrical: while stars depend on gas clouds for their existence, gas clouds do not depend on stars. On the other hand, dependence does have the property of transitivity: if stars depend on gas clouds and these in turn depend on chemical elements, then stars depend on chemical elements.

These considerations suggest that testing query expansion based on dependence relationships can produce interesting results. Cases suitable for performing this include the domains that involve combinations of spatio-temporal concepts. These, indeed, require a careful modeling of conceptual relationships [18]. Archaeological concepts like "Wales Bronze Age" depend on combinations of a territory (Wales) with a time range: notice that Bronze Age will cover different time ranges in different regions, according to how prehistorical technologies have developed in them. Similar considerations are valid for palaeontological subdivisions.

Another domain where spatio-temporal combinations are relevant are administrative-governmental units. Although based on land features with such "natural borders" as seas and mountain ranges, they do not always match these: one and the same valley can be divided between two different countries, states or regions, sometimes producing real-life problems in e.g. the exploitation of water flowing in one country / state but originating from another. The Amu Darya watershed, now divided between several former-USSR states, is a well-known case [19]. Other subdivisions, like those of religious administration (dioceses in the Christian church) or telephone area codes, can divide the same territory in ways different from the political divisions. Also, subdivisions change in time. One same place will belong to different administrations at different times; and a given political entity can rise, expand, restrict, merge, or be dissolved, thus changing its extension at different times [18].

A political subdivision can be defined as existentially depending on the combination of the corresponding land portion and a time range. Recording these relationships will allow for applications of query expansion: a search for the land can also retrieve political subdivisions having included it in various time ranges; or a search for a year in history can yield all political units existing at that time (that is, work as a historical atlas).

Recording of semantic factors can be performed in different KOS types, such as thesauri, ontologies, or classification schemes. One difference between these is that classifications are capable of managing meaningful orders between concepts, by means of their notation; verbal systems based on thesauri can manage the citation order of terms within a subject string, though not the order of terms belonging to the same array in the schedules; and ontologies usually do not address sorting problems at all, although in principle their means of expression would permit them to manage any order. While order can be irrelevant to retrieve a concept connected to another, for which the existence of some recorded relationship is enough, it can become relevant for the presentation of large lists for browsing or as the results of a search.

In this respect, the citation order between the different semantic factors of a concept can also be considered. If the factors are simply listed one after the other, those having a greater "weight" in the definition of the concept should be listed first, in agreement with the principle that in a subject string what acts as a base theme should precede what is only a particular theme [20].

If, on the other hand, factors are expressed as a faceted combination, like in "humans, of gender: female, of age: young", a standard citation order of facets can be adopted (the gender facet can be requested as the first one, followed by the age facet). Again, this order can be modified if the concept implies a greater emphasis on a facet than on another (a "rookie" is especially a new guy, beside being usually a young one, so time of arrival can be cited before age). This has connections with the question of what concepts are most relevant in the definition of a prototype class [next section].

If semantic factors are considered already while constructing the KOS, their filing order can be used even to establish the filing order of the resulting classes. Thus the filing order of the classes

x (semantic factors: A, D)
x' (semantic factors: D, A, B)
x'' (semantic factors: B, C)

will be $x < x'' < x'$, because of their respective first-cited factors. This can recommend the choice of symbols expressing their established order, e.g.

x = L
x'' = M
x' = N

These principles are especially relevant in a general levels-based classification, where the first classes will be low-level phenomena (atoms, molecules, cells etc.) while the last classes will be high-level phenomena (societies, cultures, economic systems etc.). Indeed, in order to decide whether a high-level class should file before or after another, e.g. whether political systems should file before or after economic systems, their existential dependence on certain lower-level classes can be examined.

5 FUZZY SEMANTIC FACTORING

While identifying semantic factors of a concept is often possible, defining a set of factors covering its meaning in a complete way can prove much more difficult. Not all concepts have as precise meanings as "young female human" or "atom with ten protons and ten electrons". Szostak and Gnoli [21] drafted a classification of types of social theories, allowing each theory to be represented as a combination of five facets: classical political economy is then defined as a "theory of individuals as agents, performing an active action, as moved by rationality, producing a new equilibrium, in a highly generalizable way". While this technique has advantages, it leaves the question open whether any theory can be expressed in a satisfying way as a combination of these, or other, facets: Admittedly, "in some cases classification is rendered difficult by the vagueness with which certain theories are expressed, or by ambiguity in how a particular theory is interpreted by different theorists" [21, p. 208]. Clearly there are domains, especially in the human sciences, where concepts are intrinsically vague.

This problem can be addressed if one accepts that semantic factoring can include fuzzy relationships. The existence of such relationships is in agreement with the theory of prototypes [22], according to which a concept has a core typical definition rather than having precise borders, as classical Aristotelian logic would assume. Thus there can be a typical Burmese cat, showing all the characteristics typical of Burmese cats, as well as other cats that are only Burmese-like, as they have only some of those characteristics. Classes are then gradations of distance from a prototype, rather than containers with waterproof borders.

To provide a possible link for information retrieval, it will still be useful that a fuzzy relationship is recorded, together with the additional information that it is a partial or approximate one. This will offer links to concepts in other regions of the semantic network that combine in some way to shape the meaning of a class. A dialect spoken in Sicily can be a variant of southern Italian (belonging to Romance languages) but with some influences of Arabic (belonging to the very different Semitic languages); the music performed by a contemporary folk player can be basically traditional music, but with some touch of jazz. In some searching situations, the relationships with Arabic and with jazz can prove useful.

Fuzzy relationships have not been addressed often in knowledge organization. Facets for expressing resemblance of a class to another, and for degrees of intensionality are included in the Integrative Levels Classification [23], although not tested in a systematic way yet. Symbols for these facets, each followed by its verbal meaning, are listed below:

88X similar to *x*

X89a not *x*
X89e not too much *x*
X89g almost *x*, about *x*
X89n scarcely *x*, barely *x*
X89o little *x*, a bit *x*
X89q quite *x*
X89s definitely *x*, just *x*
X89t typical *x*, stereotype of *x*
X89v very *x*, extremely *x*

Similar questions are addressed in the growing work aimed at the representation of mapping between concepts belonging to different KOSs – a key problem in the perspective of the Semantic Web. It is good news that the recent ISO standard for mapping between thesauri [24-25] admits both "exact equivalence" and "inexact equivalence" (e.g. `lawns` ~EQ `turf`), and includes the possibility that a concept is mapped with the combination of two others in a different thesaurus (e.g. `inland waterways` EQ `rivers` | `canals`).

6 CONCLUSIONS

As shown by our examples and references, semantic factoring has been repeatedly considered and experimented with in knowledge organization research. Recording semantic factors clearly demands an additional effort in terms of development and maintenance of a KOS and its user interfaces. This has been rarely implemented beside the stage of research tests until now. Admittedly, such light KOSs as taxonomies for website menus may not justify its cost. However, more sophisticated ones like faceted classifications, classauri or ontologies may be improved in worthwhile ways by recording semantic factors.

This is even more promising in the new perspective of Linked Data and the Semantic Web, aimed at promoting the automatic discovery of connections between data from different sources. While developers of standards for the Semantic Web, such as OWL or SKOS, have focused on hierarchical relationships until now, more work is needed to leverage other kinds of relationships, such as facets and semantic factors, between data in available knowledge bases.

We have outlined how semantic factoring could be integrated with facet analysis and classical hierarchies to produce powerful general systems. If these three basic kinds of relationships are recorded consistently in a KOS, it becomes only a matter of convenience to decide which applications have to exploit each of them, either by default or as an additional option, for browsing, searching, query expansion, or sorted display of results.

7 ACKNOWLEDGMENTS

The author is grateful to Douglas Tudhope and Ceri Binding (University of South Wales) for stimulating discussions on relationships in connection with query expansion; to Aida Slavic (UDC Consortium) for clarification of principles of class definition and combination in UDC; and to Koraljka Golub, Rick Szostak, and

Leonard Will for insightful suggestions and comments on a previous version of this paper.

REFERENCES

1. Dahlberg, I. (1978) Ontical structures and universal classification, Sarada Ranganathan Endowment for Library Science, Bangalore, Manipal Power Press, 1-64.
2. Bhattacharyya, G. (1982) Classaurus: its fundamentals, design and use, **In** Universal classification: subject analysis and ordering systems: proceeding of the 4th International Study Conference on Classification Research - 6th Annual Conference of Gesellshaft für Klassifikation, Augsburg, 28 June–2 July 1982, I Dahlberg ed., Indeks, Frankfurt 1982, 1: 139-148.
3. ISO DIS 25964-2: Information and documentation. Thesauri and interoperability with other vocabularies. Part 1: Thesauri for information retrieval, International Organization for Standardization, Geneva 2011.
4. Soergel, D. (1985) Organizing information: principles of data base and retrieval systems, Academic Press, Orlando.
5. Szostak, R. (2011) Complex concepts into basic concepts, *Journal of the American Society for Information Science and Technology*, 62(11): 2247-2265.
6. Goddard, C. (2002) A Wierzbicka, *Meaning and universal grammar: theory and empirical findings*, 2 v., John Benjamins, Amsterdam-Philadelphia.
7. Will, L. Rigorous facet analysis as the basis for constructing knowledge organization schemes of all kinds, **In** *Knowledge organization: pushing the boundaries: ISKO UK biennial conference, 8th-9th July 2013, London.* http://iskouk.org/conf2013/papers/WillPaper.pdf
8. Gnoli, C. (2006) The meaning of facets in nondisciplinary classifications, **In** Knowledge organization for a global learning society: proceedings of the Ninth international ISKO conference, July 4th-7th, 2006, Vienna, G Budin - C Swertz - K Mitgutsch eds., Ergon, Würzburg, 11-18.
9. Austin, D. (1976) The CRG research into a freely faceted scheme, **In** *Classification in the 1970s: a second look*, A Maltby ed., Bingley, London, 158-194.
10. Gnoli, C. (2012) Per una demarcazione ontologica dei concetti nell'organizzazione della conoscenza [For an ontological demarcation of concepts in knowledge organization], **In** *Prospettive ontologiche: proceedings of the conference held in Trento on 8-10 November 2012*, R Poli ed., Morcelliana, Brescia in press.
11. Austin, D. (1969) The theory of integrative levels reconsidered as the basis of a general classification, in Classification Research Group, *Classification and information control*, Library Association, London, 81-95.
12. Blitz, D. (1992) Emergent evolution: qualitative novelty and the levels of reality, Kluwer, Dordrecht-Boston-London.

13. Foskett, D.J. (1961) Classification and integrative levels, **In** *The Sayers memorial volume*, DJ Foskett - BI Palmer eds., Library Association, London 1961, p. 136-150, republished **In** *Theory of subject analysis*, LM Chan - PA Richmond - E Svenonius, eds., Libraries Unlimited, Littleton 1985, p. 210-220.
14. Gnoli, C.; Bosch, M. and Mazzocchi, F. (2007) A new relationship for multidisciplinary knowledge organization systems: dependence, **In** *La interdisciplinariedad y la transdisciplinariedad en la organización del conoscimiento científico: actas del VIII Congreso ISKO-España: León, 18, 19 y 20 de Abril de 2007*, B Rodríguez Bravo - ML Alvite Díez eds., Universidad de León, León, 399-409.
15. Gnoli, C. (2010) Levels, types, facets: three structuring principles for KO, **In** Paradigms and conceptual systems in knowledge organization: proceedings Eleventh International ISKO conference, August 23-26, 2010, Rome, C Gnoli - F Mazzocchi eds., Ergon, Würzburg, 129-137.
16. Tudhope, D.; Alani, H. and Jones, C. (2001) Augmenting thesaurus relationships: possibilities for retrieval, *Journal of Digital Information*, 1(8), http://journals.tdl.org/jodi/article/view/181/160
17. Tudhope, D.; Binding, C.; Blocks, D. and Cunliffe, D. (2006) Query expansion via conceptual distance in thesaurus indexed collections, *Journal of Documentation*, 62(4): 509-533.
18. Lopez-Pellicer, F.J.; Lacasta, J.; Florczyk, A.; Nogueras-Iso, J. and Zarazaga-Soria, F.J. (2012) An ontology for the representation of spatiotemporal jurisdictional domains in information retrieval systems, *International Journal of Geographical Information Science*, 26(4): 579-597.
19. Rakhmatullaev, S.; Huneau, F.; Kazbekov, J.; Le Coustumer, P.; Jumanov, J.; El Oifi, B.; Motelica-Heino, M. and Hrkal, Z. (2010) Groundwater resources use and management in the Amu Darya River Basin (Central Asia), *Environmental Earth Sciences*, 59(6): 1183-1193.
20. Cheti, A. (1996) Testo e contesto nell'analisi concettuale dei documenti [Text and context in the conceptual analysis of documents], **In** *Il linguaggio della biblioteca: scritti in onore di Diego Maltese*, M Guerrini ed., Editrice Bibliografica, Milano, 833-855.
21. Szostak, R. and Gnoli, C. (2008) Classifying by phenomena, theories and methods: examples with focused social science theories, **In** *Culture and identity in knowledge organization: Proceedings of the Tenth International ISKO Conference, 5-8 August 2008, Montréal*, C Arsénault and JT Tennis eds., Ergon, Würzburg, 203-209.
22. Rosch, E. and Lloyd, B.L. eds. (1978) Cognition and categorization, Erlbaum, Hillsdale.
23. Integrative Levels Classification: research project, ISKO Italia, http://www.iskoi.org/ilc/ 2004-.
24. Dextre Clarke, S. Types of mapping recommended in ISO 25964, and the question of reciprocity, *9th European NKOS Workshop, Glasgow, 9-10 September 2010*.
25. ISO DIS 25964-2: Information and documentation. Thesauri and interoperability with other vocabularies. Part 2: Interoperability with other vocabularies, International Organization for Standardization, Geneva 2013.

5

Ranganathan's Universe of Knowledge and Categorical Thinking

Fulvio Mazzocchi

This paper examines Ranganathan's idea of the 'universe of knowledge' and highlights how his search for a new approach to classification (beyond the enumerative model) was influenced by this idea. It then scrutinizes Ranganathan's approach in the light of the cultural background in which it developed. In particular, his PMEST is looked at against the background of the Indian philosophical tradition, comparing it with the Vaisesika categorial systems. Finally, the role of categorial systems as a cognitive means is analyzed. Certain basic categories have surfaced within the Indo-European linguistic and cultural frame in different ages and latitudes. The fact that they are somehow 'culturally constructed' does not undermine their role of establishing the meaningful domain of discourse of a cultural tradition.

Keywords: Ranganathan, S.R., Fundamental categories, Facet analysis, Indian philosophy, Vaisesika hilosophy

1 INTRODUCTION

It has been argued that if any classification system or theory is to be fully understood it should be regarded as part of a specific socio-cultural and philosophical framework [32,14,26]. This implies that an inquiry into their foundations needs to include also an analysis of the underlying ontological and epistemological questions. Shiyali Ramamrita Ranganathan's ideas about classification are not an exception. In this paper it is asserted that these ideas were influenced significantly by the Indian philosophical tradition, in which together with metaphysical thinking schools of logic and dialectics sprung up too. Some authors have stressed the kinship with the *Nyaya-Vaisesika* system [1]. Indeed, Colon Classification embeds elements of the Hindu worldview, such as the idea of transitoriness in respect to the ceaseless transformation of the universe and above all the inclination to analyze existence into fundamental categories.

2 RANGANATHAN'S UNIVERSE OF KNOWLEDGE

To investigate the nature of knowledge and its dynamics is of paramount importance for library science scholars and classification theorists, since the 'world' in which they are supposed to operate is made up of such items. Ranganathan's 'universe of knowledge' is the universe of subjects (as an analogy of what occurs in chemistry, three types of subjects are distinguished: basic, compound and complex). This universe is described in terms of a complex, dynamic multi-dimensional space. It is a "dynamical continuum" which is "turbulently growing at every moment" and made up of "infinity of points" [33]. Being a mathematician, a certain correlation between mathematics and classification theory is noticeable. For example, the idea of infinity with which Ranganathan describes the universe of subjects has been compared by analogy to the infinite set theory developed by the mathematician Georg Cantor in the late 19th and early 20th Centuries [16].

The question is how to handle this dynamic complexity for practical purposes. Ranganathan was aware that we are living in an age typified by an increasing proliferation of subjects. New discoveries constantly occur and there is a social and intellectual interest for an advancement of research activity. He criticized the shortcomings of enumerative (classification) systems such as the Dewey Decimal Classification and Library of Congress Classification. These systems attempt to enumerate all possible subjects in a given domain within a fixed set of predetermined classes. However they encounter many problems in dealing with the dynamic aspect of knowledge. Their functional value would be greater if the 'universe of knowledge' corresponded to a closed system, but it is open and dynamic; new items are continuously added, resulting in the nonstop need for new classes to be created: "new branches may stem from any of its infinity of points at any time; they are unknowable at present. They cannot therefore be enumerated here and now; nor can they be anticipated, their filiations can be determined only after they appear" (Ranganathan 1951, p.87ff).

In response to this, Ranganathan searched for a novel flexible approach based on a "sound resilient foundation" and capable of coping with continuous change in knowledge:

> If a scheme for classification forms an essential element to be built into a document finding system, the helpfulness of the document-finding system will depend upon the efficiency of the scheme for classification in keeping step with the incessant growth of the Universe of Subjects and also with the variation, from time to time, of the subject approach of readers. To secure this efficiency, the scheme for classification should be based on a dynamic theory of classification (Ranganathan 1970, Vol. 7, p. 99, in Ranganathan 1964 -1971)

These ideas are coupled with the belief in the situadeness or artificiality of any (unilateral) classification. "There is no unique system of natural classification even for the universe of knowledge in abstract" [Ranganathan 1964, Vol. 1, p.3, in 35]. In any grouping of subjects a factor of convention is implied. There is no single way, for example, to decide if the discipline of Biochemistry belongs to Chemistry or Biology or Medicine. "Only God can make a classification true to the needs of all readers at all times" [Ranganathan 1968, Vol. 5, p.296, in 35]. Nowadays many would argue that classification is socially and culturally biased [32,26] or that even within the same cultural tradition the social value and the spatial order of subjects can change through time [39].

On the one hand, Ranganathan believed that the structure of knowledge exhibits a kind of underlying unity, and a classification has to display this structure hierarchically. On the other hand, he acknowledged that the universe of subjects is multidimensional and that any classification involves a linearization of this multidimensionality, i.e. "transforming a multi-dimensional space into a uni-dimensional one" [Ranganathan 1964, Vol. 1, p.19, in 35]. Classification should be able to include multidimensionality within itself:

> The terms Like and Unlike are in respect of a single attribute or a complex of attributes...Classification in this primitive sense should have originated with the primitive man. It is practised very early in childhood. It may be done on the basis of a single characteristic to begin with. But, with the evolution and the development of the cortex of the brain, the single characteristic has been giving place to a characteristic - complex; the complex itself has been steadily increasing in complexity" [Ranganathan 1964, Vol. 1, p. 3, in 35].

3 RANGANATHAN'S CATEGORIAL SYSTEM

The Colon Classification is a general scheme which "aims to classify by discipline all subjects and all forms of documents" [39], and was designed by Ranganathan as a type of faceted classification. A classification scheme has to comprise a set of (minimal) elements which can be freely combined to match the needs of any particular subject, and then applied in a transdisciplinary manner. Such elements function as building blocks just like a Meccano Set. Indeed, it was his first encounter with a Meccano Set in a London toy shop that triggered in Ranganathan a breakthrough and the consequent decision that a classification scheme should function like it. This idea is embodied in the analytic-synthetic methodology, where 'analysis' consists of breaking down subjects into their elemental concepts, and 'synthesis' is the process of recombining such concepts into subject strings. The flexibility of Colon Classification, as a result of his dynamic theory of classification, is compared by Ranganathan to that of the trunk of an elephant which has at the same time the strength to eradicate a tree with ease and the ability to pick out a single grain with equal ease [Ranganathan 1968, Vol. 5, p. 6, in 35]. At the same time, this is combined with the presumption that there are "five and only five fundamental categories in the universe of knowledge" which lead him to believe that such (mutually exclusive) categories establish necessary and sufficient conditions to express, in reason of their combination, all possible subjects. Not only existing knowledge but any possible knowledge is covered by them, including newly discovered one [34,36].

The five fundamental categories, included in the fourth edition of Colon Classification, are named *Personality*, *Matter*, *Energy*, *Space* and *Time* (PMEST). Such categories are however not easily definable. This is particularly true for *Personality*, which is used to express the distinguishing features of an object. Being difficult to describe it in positive terms, it becomes recognizable only by elimination: "After separating out the manifestation of time, space energy and matter in a subject the residue will often turn out to be personality" [34, p83]. *Personality* can be seen as the substratum making possible the application of all the other categories.

Matter is used to specify all relevant features of an object, not concerning in fact exclusively physical composition. It can be further divided into three subcategories: *Matter Material, Matter Property* and *Matter Method.* The first two concern respectively the physical composition (e.g., marble in a marble statue) and the properties (e.g., permeability as a physical property of soil) that can be related to an object. *Matter method* is used in relation to methods (e.g. physical and biological methods). For some authors, nonetheless, this subcategory should be considered as a specification of *Energy* [21].

Energy represents the dynamic aspects (action) occurring with respect to an object. The Classification Research Group will divide it into two to distinguish spontaneous events (processes) from man-induced ones (operations).

Space and *Time* indicate respectively the geographic area and the period associated with an object.

4 INFLUENCES ON RANGANATHAN'S THOUGHT

Ranganathan was an exponent of the facet classification (FC) tradition which he shares with W.C. Berwick Sayers [40] and the British Classification Research Group (formed in 1952). In his *An Introduction to Library Classification* (1918), Sayers delineated the approach of FC, emphasizing the need for library classification to have a rational foundation in term of a logical basis, and advanced a methodology in terms of canons and axioms. Miksa [27, p64] says that in relating FC to logic Sayers meant by the latter the classical logic following Aristotle's philosophical ideas (and approach to categorization):

> The most striking correlation that he made in this respect was to adopt definitions, relationships, and operations that arose from Aristotle's five predicables – i.e., genus, species, difference, property, and accident. Sayers' use of these ideas included describing the process of classificatory division that of 'genus et differentiam'.

Ranganathan was an Indian library scholar and the most notable student of Sayers from whom he inherited the search for a rational foundation of library classification. As mentioned earlier, he was also a mathematician and such a background reinforced his attitude to deal with classification in an axiomatic way, even surpassing Sayers in this task. He thought that a general theory of classification should be based on a few general normative principles or axioms and include "laws of Library Science, postulates, canons and principles for classification" [Ranganathan 1971, Vol. 8, p. 101, in 35]. Ranganathan is believed to have continued the logical approach to classification [27,16] and to have worked within the frame of the (Western) rationalist tradition. One of the chief assumptions of rationalism is that (empirical) reality only appears complicated. Beneath it, a univocal (e.g., mathematical as in Descartes) order exists, which can be discovered by rational investigation. In the same tradition, the idea of some basic elemental items (or primitives) to be combined rationally to obtain more complex things is not uncommon. For example, the German philosopher and mathematician Leibniz (1646 - 1716) aimed at discovering primitive notions and the rules for their composition from which all complex notions could be obtained. FC partly follows the same principles of logical division on which traditional classifications have been based [43][1]. The latter are mostly constructed in terms of the genus-species relation, which led to the creation of fixed hierarchical (tree-styled) structures [37]. At the same time, it differs significantly in that it adopts a more flexible approach based on a minimal set of fundamental categories which can be combined in multiple ways to produce compound subjects, ensuring that "every type of relation between terms and between subjects may be expressed" [44, p46]. As mentioned earlier, in Ranganathan's view this is the only possible way to cope with the complexity and dynamism of contemporary knowledge. Furthermore, another (often undermined) aspect needs to be taken into consideration. Miksa [27, p67], argued that the Indian scholar aimed to

> discover the very nature and order of things, an order based on principles which are eternal, unchanging, and all-encompassing. There is virtually no area of Ranganathan's work and personal life in which this quest for discovering the inner or essential order behind the visible world is absent.

He [27, p73] goes on to argue that Ranganathan's use of faceted structure of subjects could have represented "his need to find more order and regularity, in the realm of subjects, than actually exist". Yet this inclination may depend on a different reason in respect to his presumed adhesion to a Western rationalist (or reductionist) view.

It is important in fact to consider the influence of Hindu thought on Ranganathan's theories and view of reality. There is evidence of such an influence in many of his writings.

For example, coming back to his idea of 'infinity' of knowledge, he wrote (Ranganathan 1964, Vol. 1, p. 15, in 35):

---

[1] "The essence of facet analysis is the sorting of terms in a given field of knowledge into homogeneous, mutually exclusive facets, each derived from the parent universe by a single characteristic of division. We may look upon these facets as groups of terms derived by taking each term and defining it, per genus et differentiam, with respect to its parent class" [43, p12] .

> The number of items of knowledge - past, present, and future taken together tends to infinity. According to a Vedic statement[2] if infinity is taken away from infinity, then infinity itself will be left as residue. This represents the intuitive grasp of a certain experience by the seers of yore.

And in respect to the classification of knowledge, he asserted [Ranganathan 1965, Vol. 2, p. 3, in 35]:

> The Vedic Scheme of Classes postulates four Main Classes of knowledge - Dharma, Artha, Kama and Moksha. These main classes correspond roughly and successively to our modern partially comprehensive classes:
>
> Religio-Social Sciences with Law as an auxiliary (= Dharma);
>
> Economic-Political Sciences with Natural Sciences as auxiliaries (= Artha);
>
> Creative or Fine Arts including Literature and Linguistics and Psychology as auxiliaries (= Kama); and
>
> Spiritual Experience with Logic, Epistemology and Metaphysics as distant intellectual auxiliaries mediating between intellectual and trans-intellectual experiences (= Moksha).

In effect, many authors like, for example, Adhikary and Nandi [1], have stressed how the way Colon Classification depicts reality should be seen as an expression of a Hindu worldview. It seems difficult to fully understand Ranganathan's thought if it is taken out of this context. This concerns also Ranganathan's argument for a basic set of categories. There is in fact a strict resemblance between PMEST and classical Hindu categorial system which is worth investigating more thoroughly. As already stated in previous papers [24,25], what needs to be searched are not the signs of a direct relationship. And yet, it would be important exploring a different angle for

---

[2] At the very beginning of the *Isha Upanishad* is stated:

Om
Purnamadah Purnamidam
Purnat Purnamudachyat
Purnasya Purnamadaya
Purnameva Vashishyat
Om shanti, shanti, shanti

One of translation of this verses is:

Om
That is infinite, this is infinite;
From That infinite this infinite comes.
From That infinite, this infinite removed or added;
Infinite remains infinite,
Om. Peace! Peace! Peace!

interpreting Ranganathan's thought with regard to the tradition of his own country. Bearing this in mind, in the following section a comparison is made between the *Vaisesika* categorial system and Ranganathan's PMEST [3].

4.1 The Relationship between PMEST and Hindu Thought

One of the characteristic features of the Indian philosophical tradition is the spread of categorial thought. Most classical Indian metaphysicians analyzed existence in fundamental kinds or categories [29]. Although different terms are used for such a purpose, such as *artha, padartha, tattva, prameya, jneya, visaya, vastu, sat, bhava* [22], categories are thought to supply a definitive listing and classification of all the kinds of things existing in the world. The use of categories, which is common to many different philosophical schools, concerns also other domains such as logic, linguistics and aesthetics. It could hence be argued that it is an intrinsic part of the Indian philosophical style of thinking.

Vaisesika is one of the *darsanas* (the verbal root of the Sanskrit term *darsana* is *drish,* whose chief meaning is 'to see'), i.e. Hinduism's six orthodox or classical systems of thought. These are all grounded in the Vedas and accept their authority as revealed scriptures. In fact although the Supreme Reality (*Brahman*) is one, there are however six basic viewpoints to portray it: *Nyaya* deals with logic and the means to achieve true knowledge. *Sankhya* considers the fundamental principles underlying the manifestation of the universe. *Yoga* focuses on the means by which direct knowledge of *Brahman* is obtained. *Purva-Mimamsa* is concerned with describing the correct ways of performing Vedic rituals. *Vedanta* is devoted to the investigation of the ultimate nature of *Brahman.*

Vaisesika can be regarded as a kind of physical philosophy, whose focus is the analytical portrayal of sensible reality. Things are described in their individual and concrete manifestations. A restricted set of basic categories are believed to be the constitutive elements of the universe (ontological primitives), under which all the different types of existent can be subsumed [22]. The founding text of this system is the *Vaisesikasutra* which is attributed to Kanada[4]. The exact date of its

[3] Other authors have highlighted the resemblance (or a possible derivation of the former from the latter) between Ranganathan and Aristotle's categories (30,11).

compilation is disputed: for some it goes back to the 4th Century B.C., whereas others set it in and around the 1st Century A.D. [3].

The Sanskrit term that is normally rendered as category is *padartha.* The etymological analysis of the term reveals that *padartha* is the *artha* (meaning) of a *pada* (word), or 'what is referred by the words'. The term *padartha* by extension could also be interpreted in a metaphysical sense to refer to the most general kinds of things [29].

In the original version of *Vaisesikasutra,* however, the term *padartha* was not used but rather *artha,* from the verb root *arth* meaning 'to request the sense, to point out' [13]. 'Meaning of a word', 'thing', 'object', 'purpose', and 'aim' are among the other meanings attributed to a*rtha* which is therefore more distant from the concept of category than *padartha.* The latter was introduced afterwards by Prasastapada, who was the author of *Padarthadharma-sangraha* and lived in approximately around 991 A.D. The *Padarthadharma-sangraha* is one of the most influential commentaries of *Vaisesikasutra*, in which a number of modifications and adaptations in respect to the Kanada's original version were introduced[5].

The original nucleus of categories in the *Vaisesikasutra* is compounded by *dravya, guna* and *karma.*

---

[4] As frequently occurs in the Indian tradition, the name of the author does not correspond to a single individual. Rather it has a symbolical value and represents a school of thought or a lineage

[5] The number of the categories would be extended by Prasastapada to six, and subsequently by Sivaditya to seven in his

Sapta-padarthi

Dravya (substance)

Guna (quality)

Karma (action)

Samanya (generality)

Vishesa (particularity)

Samavaya (inherence)

Abhava (non existence)

All the added categories basically concern relationships: *Samanya* corresponds to the generic characteristic that resides in all the members of a class. An individual is a member of that class only by virtue of possessing it. *Visheha* (from which the term *Vaisesika* derives) relates to *particularity,* that is the 'distinctive character' typifying substances, and by which they can be differentiated from each other. *Samavaya,* labeled as *inherence,* concerns the relationship between inseparables, i.e. things that cannot both exist separately from each other: for example quality and action with substance, or universal and particular, eternal substance and particularity, and whole and parts. The last category, *abhava,* is *non-existence* (from the verb root *bhu*: 'to become, exist', and 'a' = not), being conceived in privative terms as opposed to *bhava* (*existence*) which is covered by the other six categories

Table 1: *Vaisesikasutra* categories in Kanada's version

Dravya (substance)
Guna (quality)
Karma (action)

The most fundamental category is *dravya,* which in Western terms is frequently referred to as *substance*. *Dravya* is explained as the locus of qualities and actions and as "that in which the effect inheres" [29, p44], i.e. the material or inherence cause of effect. *Dravya* is not manifest and perceptible as such, but becomes so in the sensible world solely through its attributes (*guna-s* and *karma-s*). These are the modes of substance but to exist they need the latter as their common substratum.

Guna, the second category, might be understood as *quality,* having however a broader meaning compared to Aristotle's idea of *quality*. The *guna-s* are those (inherent) features of things (or *dravya-s*) which are stable and permanent, typifying them in a static sense [18].

Karma, the third category, could be seen as *action* (from the verb root kr: 'to act, do, make'). It corresponds to the dynamic aspects of substance, and then to motion. The latter inheres to substance and is the direct and immediate cause of conjunction and disjunction.

The importance of these basic categories is proved also by the spread of their usage, which is not restrained to *Vaisesika* but rather occurs in several philosophical systems of the Indian tradition. For example, in *Prabhakara Mimamsa, Bhatta Mimamsa,* and *Dvaita Vedanta* [13]. *Dravya* and *guna* are used by Jainism too to refer respectively to substance and its fundamental attributes [41].

These are also the categories which are relevant for a comparison with Ranganathan's PMEST. Their likeness with the first three PMEST categories is plainly clear.

Table 2: mapping between *Vaisesikasutra* original categories and Ranganathan's PMEST.

Dravya (substance	*Personality*
Guna (quality)	*Matter (properties)*
Karma (action)	*Energy*

Similarities are more evident between *guna* and *Matter property* an alternative mapping between *Vaisesika* and Ranganathan's categories was proposed by Adikhary and Nandi [1]:

Table 3: mapping between PMEST and *Vaisesika* categories by Adhikary and Nandi [1]. *Dika* and *kala* in *Vaisesika* system are subtypes of *dravya*

Personality	*Samanya* (generality) and *Vishesa* (particularity)
Matter-material	*Dravya* (substance) and *Abhava* (non existence)
Matter-properties	*Guna* (quality)
Matter-method	*Samavaya* (inherence)
Energy	*Karma* (action)
Space	*Dika* (space)
Time	*Kala* (time)

Nevertheless some elements of such a proposal are rather controversial. The most evident lapse is the conflation of *dravya* (together with *abhava*) and *Matter-material* (which relates exclusively to the physical composition of an object) causing a restriction of the meaning of *dravya*. However the latter is perhaps the most important category of the *Vaisesika* system. It is a highly complex notion in which all (living and non-living) entities are included: "those who, like the Vaisesikas, admit *dravya* as a category must, in addition, recognize it as the most fundamental category. For, entities belonging to the other categorial kinds, in some way or other, depend on *dravya-s,* and cannot be without either inhering in, or in some other manner being related to, a *dravya.* All others rest upon *dravya-s"* Mohanty [29, p44].

Furthermore the way in which *dravya* is often defined has clear analogies with Ranganathan's definition of *Personality*: "Substance is a distinct genus, but a positive definition can only ascribe to it either the possession of qualities or action" [18, p182].

5 CATEGORIES AS BASIC COGNITIVE MEANS [6]

Ranganathan identified five basic categories. The Classification Research Group, who followed his theory and method developing his work further, provided,

[6] There is no doubt that the LIS concept of categories is not same as the philosophical one. In the Western philosophical tradition, Aristotle and Kant provided two different paradigms of categorial thinking. Aristotle's categories correspond to the ultimate determinations of (sensible) reality, being reflected at the logical level to the most general concepts, and having also a linguistic-grammatical significance. Kant operated a radical shift of view. His categories are, in fact, a priori forms of the human intellect, which apply to things with respect to the conditions under which these become experienceable and knowable. However with regards to the theory of classification categories are seen as "relevant instruments of analysis and organization of objects" [4, p5]. On the one hand this is true but on the other hand, in the light of certain approaches, such as those of Ranganathan and Dahlberg, the two aspects go hand in hand. They extrapolated the idea of category from philosophy to knowledge organization, positing that the practical role of a categorical system depends on its philosophical basis (and presumed ontological reality).

however, a longer list, expanding their number to thirteen: *object, kind, part, property, material, process, operation, agent, patient, product, by-product, space, time* (44,6). Hjørland [16] assumes that the expansion of the number of categories can be seen as a sign of the fact that a pre-established or fixed set of categories is not given, and for him this represents a "loosening of the rationalist view". However, despite the change in number, their nature is basically unvaried. These general categories, by means of their combinatorial properties, are still seen as providing necessary and sufficient tools to analyze the vocabulary of almost any field of knowledge, although other general categories may still exist [5].

In Hjørland's view [15,16], the philosophical background of facet analysis (FA) should be put in relation to an account of language based on the theory of semantic primitives. Semantic primitives represent words that 'cannot be defined further': since it is not possible to define all words some primitive words have to exist which are not defined and represent a finite set of indecomposable meanings [12]. "The idea is that the same building blocks can be used for all purposes (cf. Meccano)", asserts Hjørland [16, p554]. And he continues: "*The underlying philosophical assumption is that elements do not change their meaning in different contexts.* According to modern theories of meaning, this is a rather problematic assumption".

A number of problems are highlighted in relation to this approach. One is the static and aprioristic view underlying it:

> While it is correct that it may be easier to combine existing elements to form new classes and thus easier to place new subjects in faceted systems, it does not follow that it is possible for FC to represent all new subjects as combinations of existing elements (...) New conceptual structures therefore require new concepts and classification systems, and this is true for enumerative classification as well as FC [16, p548].

In Hjørland's opinion, any set of categories is not discovered or given by a natural language. Rather it is 'pragmatically constructed'. This costruction (and the use of such categories in any process of 'analysis' and 'synthesis') is not something that can be done solely on the basis of logic, but should instead rely on empirical knowledge. The latter is provided by specialists of the different fields of knowledge:

> It is problematic if FA is based on the view that meanings are given in a language, and that subjects can be constructed by a universal set of semantic primitives given by natural languages. The decomposing of complex concepts into primitive concepts (and the synthesis of primitive concepts into complex concepts) cannot be done without

> considering the specific subject knowledge (...). The decomposing of complex concepts into primitive concepts cannot simply be done by a priori, conceptual analysis. But when a given set of elements is provided from outside, it may be used in classification, and new discoveries may be classified as new combinations of elements from the set– as long as the set is considered in accordance with the scientific theory on which it is based (often there are conflicting scientific views). The elements in classification are not given by the logical analysis of the philosopher or the information specialists, but are given by scientific discoveries and theories. This is again the question of the differences between logical divisions and scientific classifications as discussed by Mill [28] [16, p554].

Hjørland reframes the issue in terms of the rationalism-empiricism debate. However the analysis of Ranganathan's thought cannot be restrained within the limits of this debate because it involves conceptual elements which are extraneous to the Western tradition. Besides we risk overlooking another important question, namely the possible cognitive role of foundational items which is beyond the rationalism-empiricism debate.

The dynamic process of knowledge development implies the transformation of concepts, vocabularies, methods, etc. As argued by Thomas Kuhn [20], in the history of scientific knowledge this can correspond to a 'revolution', i.e. a paradigm shift in which a new theoretical view of the world is established. However this does not mean that everything is put under discussion. For example, scientific revolutions do not impair the fundamental epistemic principles of science (e.g. observation, induction and deduction). There are certain 'deep' levels of assumptions which are less exposed to transformation (and are instead used to assess the sense of it) [7]. This may be applied to semantic (and general cultural) planes too.

A restricted number of fundamental categories which are comparable with those of the *Vaisesika* system and also with PMEST have reappeared within the Indo-European linguistic and cultural setting in different ages and regions. Albeit in different forms, fundamental categories like *substance*, *attribute* and *action* have represented the common ground for many top conceptual structures, and continue to surface in some form also in knowledge organization schemes [17].

[7] This does not mean that they cannot change but a process of change at this level is very rare and when it occurs is often associated with epochal social transformation

A correspondence between these categories and the structure of language is presumed too, for example, between the three basic *Vaisesika* categories and the lexical categories of noun, adjective and verb [10,2] [8].

Dahlberg [9] used similar categories to order Aristotle's (*see* table 4). In her view, the former can be considered as *Ur-categories*, i.e. the ultimate (and universal) logical foundation: any conceptual structure, although developed in different cultures or associated to different linguistic frameworks, would necessarily culminate in them. Differences would concern only their lexicalization.

Table 4: The ten categories of Aristotle ordered by four supercategories (or *Ur-categories*) in Dahlberg's view (1978): the category of substance or *Ousia* is divided into Principles, Material Objects and Immaterial Objects.

Entities (*Ousia*, 'substance' or 'essence')
Principles
Material objects
Immaterial objects
Properties
Quantity (*Poson*, 'how much')
Quality (*Poion*, 'what sort')
Relation (*Pros ti*, 'related to what')
Activities
Operation or Action (*Poiein*, 'doing')
State (*Ekhein*, 'having')
Process or Affection (*Paskhein*, 'undergoing')
Dimensions
Time (*Pote*, 'when')
Position (*Keisthai*, 'being situated')
Space (*Pou*, 'where')

At the same time, mappings between *Vaisesika* and Aristotle's categorial systems have been proposed too (*see* table 5).

[8] Trendelenburg [42] thought that Aristotle's categories relate to the structures inherent in language, for example, the subject-predicate distinction is reflected in the distinction between *substance* and all other categories

Table 5: Nakamura's [31] mapping of *Vaisesika* categories with Aristotle's ones (modified version: only correspondences including categories from Kanada and Prasastapada's versions of *Vaisesika* are shown)

Substance	*Ousia*	*Dravya*
Quantity	*Poson*	*Guna*
Quality	*Poion*	
Relation	*Pros ti*	*Samanya*
		Vishesa
		Samavaya
Action	*Poiein*	*Karma*
State	*Ekhein*	
Affection	*Paskhein*	
Time	*Pote*	
Position	*Keisthai*	
Space	*Pou*	
		Abhava

The issue arising here is whether such basic categories possess a psychological basis[9], and if some cognitive functions can be assigned to them, perhaps restraining the field to the Indo-European world and linguistic family.

Categories can be conceived as constructive grounds of knowledge [19]. In many cultures they have played an essential role as they reflect the kind of 'interface' for the interaction between the (external) world and the (internal) mental structures a particular society has developed. Their value of meaning is the most basic and general. For this reason, they are able to connect the member of a community sharing a certain 'language game' [46].

In my opinion, following for example Ceruti [8], in order to understand the role of genuine categorial systems two different (and complementary) aspects should be taken into consideration: i) their origin and ii) their (cognitive) function. On the one hand, categories originate empirically in a culturally and historically-biased

[9] Primitives are also seen as manifesting themselves in the structure of language, not being nonetheless part of the representational level. They would inhere to a deeper level, as patterns underlying the perceptual and conceptual systems around which basis human experience is built [see e.g. 45].

context; this supports the case for the categorial pluralism thesis (there is no single legitimate categorical system). On the other hand, they operate as (cultural-historical) apriori, establishing the distinction between sense and nonsense and the preconditions to select experience and make it 'possible'. This implies that the way in which a cultural or knowledge system is predisposed to investigate the world depends on the categories it employs. For such a reason, the influence of the latter is deep and far-reaching. As argued by the philosopher Cassirer [7, p117-118]:

> The object, as an object of knowledge, as an object of appearance, is not determined 'in itself', but rather its determination grows progressively with the productivity of the mind. The direction of this productivity - the categories, which in this endevour are determinative and operative (...).

To embrace as a foundation something that cannot be justified belongs to, since the emergence of 'philosophy', the Western idea of rationality as a means to avoid a *regressio ad infinitum* [38]. However the motivation of such an occurrence could pertain to a deeper level and be transculturally relevant.

The need for a foundation, such as a categorial system, might reside in how our 'life form' [46] functions at the cognitive level. No proofs of its 'ontological reality' are given. However to exercise its role, any foundation needs to be assumed *as if* it was 'real' and 'true', and placed even before the distinction between logical and empirical.

Kwan [23] highlights how once integrated into a language, a categorial system, like the one we are speaking of, becomes a central part of a particular cultural tradition. The assumptions and values inherent in such a system are embodied in the collective subconsciousness of the members of that language community. As a result, systems of categories act as foundational items which exercise tacitly an enduring influence through the ages. This should be related also to an intrinsic psychological mechanism for in order to function as fundamental cognitive tools, categories need to be obscured [8]. Categories operate as a stable ground on which everything else is constructed, and yet hidden and barely discernible (until some philosophical or other intellectual enterprise renders them explicit).

There is always the risk of naturalizing categories. However in different cultural settings alternative categorial systems have been developed. Any human community has to adapt to its world. The way in which experience is structured has to guarantee a success in such a task. Categorial systems play a fundamental role in this and their multiplicity reflects the diversity of cognitive paths humans have experienced: different 'fitting' representations of reality and ways of classifying it are possible [*see* e.g. 26].

6 CONCLUSIONS

This article has explored Ranganathan's idea of the 'universe of knowledge', which is depicted as a complex and dynamic multidimensional space. It has highlighted how this view influenced significantly the search for a new (faceted) approach to classification beyond the limits and rigidity of enumerative models. In order to fully understand it, Ranganathan's approach has to be contextualized in the light of the Indian philosophical tradition. Accordingly, resemblances between PMEST and *Vaisesika* categorial systems have been discussed. Finally, categorial systems could function as cognitive tools. Whereas the analysis is limited to the Indo-European linguistic and cultural frame, the need of a 'foundational base' like a categorial system may be inscribed in the cognitive organization of the human life form.

REFERENCES

1 Adhikary, Madhabmohan and Nandi, Amitava. (2003) Ideas of Ranganathan's classification theory pervaded by Oriental philosophy. *SRELS Journal of Information Management,* 40: 275-284.

2 Ambuel, David. (1998) Ontology in Indian philosophy. **In:** Craig, Edward, ed., *Routledge Encyclopedia of Philosophy.* London: Routledge, p.118-127.

3 Arena, Leonardo V. (1987) Il Vaisesika Sutra di Kanada: introduzione, testo, traduzione, commento, lessico. Urbino: Quattroventi.

4 Barite, Mario G. (2000). The Notion of 'Category'. Its implications in subject Analysis and in the construction and evaluation of indexing languages. *Knowledge Organization,* 27(1/2): 4-10.

5 Broughton, Vanda. (2001) Faceted classification as a basis for knowledge organization in a digital environment: The Bliss Bibliographic Classification as a model for vocabulary management and the creation of multi-dimensional knowledge structures. *The New Review of Hypermedia and Multimedia* 7: 67–102.

6 Broughton, Vanda. (2004) Essential classification, London: Facet.

7 Cassirer, Ernst. (1923) Die Kantischen Elemente in Wilhelm von Humboldts Sprachphilosophie. **In** *Festschrift für Paul Hensel.* Göttingen: Ohag-Greiz i.V, p.105-127.

8 Ceruti, Mauro. (1994) Constraints and possibilities: the knowledge of evolution and the evolution of knowledge. Lausanne: Gordon and Breach.

9 Dahlberg, Ingetraut. (1978). Ontical structures and universal classification. Bangalore: Sarada Rangathanan Endowment for Library Science.

10 Faddegon, Barend. (1918) The Vaicesika-System: described with the help of the oldest texts. Amsterdam: Johannes Müller.

11 Glazier, Jack D. and Glazier, Rhonda R. (2003) Cultural roots of modern classification. **In**: Frías, José Antonio and Travieso, Críspulo, eds. *Tendencias de Investigación en Organización del Conocimiento: 4° Coloquio Internacional de Ciencias de la Documentación: 6° Congreso del Capitulo Español de ISKO: Salamanca: 5-7 mayo 2003,* Salamanca: Universidad de Salamanca, p. 211-215.

12 Goddard, Cliff. (1994) Semantic theory and semantic universals. **In**: Goddard, Cliff and Wierzbicka, Anna, eds. *Semantic and lexical Universals.* Amsterdam: John Benjamins Publishing Company, p. 7-30.

13 Grimes, John, A. (1996) Concise dictionary of Indian philosophy. Albany, NY: State University of New York Press.

14 Hjørland, Birger. (2003) Fundamental of knowledge organization. *Knowledge Organization,* 30: 87-111.

15 Hjørland, Birger. (2007) Semantics and knowledge organization. *Annual Review of Information Science and Technology,* 41: 367–405.

16 Hjørland, Birger. (2013) Facet analysis: The logical approach to knowledge organization. *Information Processing & Management*, 49: 545–557.

17 Iyer, Hemalata. (1995) Classificatory structures. Concepts, relations and representations. Würzburg: ErgonVerlag.

18 Keith, Arthur B. (1977) (originally published 1921). Indian logic and atomism: an exposition of the Nyaya and Vaisesika system. New Delhi: Oriental Books Reprint Corp.

19 Körner, Stephan. (1970) Categorial frameworks. Oxford, UK: Basil Blackwell.

20 Kuhn, Thomas S. (1962) The structure of scientific revolutions (1st ed.). Chicago, IL: University of Chicago Press.

21 Kumar, Krishnan. (1974) Theory of classification, 14th rev. New Delhi: Vikas Publishing House Pvt Ltd.

22 Kumar, Shashiprabha. (2009) The concept of categories in Vaisesika philosophy. **In** *Shivdasani Conference 2009 'Thinking Inside the Box: The Concept of a Category in Indian Philosophy'*, Oxford University, UK. Available http://www.ocvhs.com/research/shivdasani-conference-2009.

23 Kwan, Tze-wan. (1995) The doctrine of categories and the topology of concern. *Annalecta Husserliana,* 46: 243-302.

24 Mazzocchi, Fulvio and Gnoli, Claudio. (2006) Il Vaisesika e le categorie di Ranganathan. *AIDA Informazioni,* 24(3-4): 17-28.

25 Mazzocchi, Fulvio and Gnoli, Claudio. (2010). S.R. Ranganathan's PMEST categories: analyzing their philosophical background and cognitive function. *Information Studies,* 16: 133-147.

26 Mazzocchi, Fulvio. (2013) Images of thought and their relation to classification. The tree and the net. *Knowledge Organization,*. 6: in press.

27 Miksa, Francis L. (1998) The DDC, the universe of knowledge, and the post-modern library. Albany, NY: Forest Press.

28 Mill, John Stuart. (1872) A system of logic, ratiocinative and inductive: Being a connected view of the principles of evidence and the methods of scientific investigation. In two volumes. 8th ed. London: Longmans, Green, Reader, and Dyer.

29 Mohanty, Jitendra Nath. (2000) Classical Indian philosophy. Lanham, ML: Rowman & Littlefield.

30 Moss, R. (1964) Categories and relations: origins of two classification theories. *American Documentation,* 15: 296–301.

31 Nakamura, Hajime. (1992) A comparative history of ideas. Delhi: Motilal Banarsidass.

32 Olson, Hope A. (2002) Classification and universality: application and construction. *Semiotica, 139*: 377-391.

33 Ranganathan, Shiyali Ramamrita. (1951) Philosophy of library classification. Copenhagen: Munksgaard.

34 Ranganathan, Shiyali Ramamrita. (1952) Elements of classification. 3rd ed. Bombay: Asia Publishing House.

35 Ranganathan, Shiyali Ramamrita. (1964 – 1971) [Works published in] *Library Science with a slant to Documentation.* Available http://arizona.openrepository.com/arizona/bitstream/10150/105050/20/memor_ft.pdf

36 Ranganathan, Shiyali Ramamrita. (1967) *Prolegomena to Library Classification.* Bangalore: Sarada Ranganathan Endowment for Library Science.

37 Robinson, Lyn and Maguire, Mike. (2010) The rhizome and the tree: changing metaphors for information organisation. *Journal of Documentation,* 66: 604-613.

38 Sankey, Howard. (2011) Epistemic relativism and the problem of the criterion. *Studies in History and Philosophy of Science Part A,* 42: 562-570.

39 Satija, Mohinder P. and Singh, Jagtar. (2010) Colon Classification. **In** *Encyclopedia of Library and Information Science. Third Edition.* New York: Taylor and Francis.

40 Sayers, William Charles Berwick. (1918). An introduction to library classification. London: Grafton and Co.

41 Shah, Pravin K. (1993). Six universal substances (Dravyas or Entities). Available <http://www.ibiblio.org/jainism/database/JAINEDU/6dravya.doc>.

42 Trendelenburg, Adolf. (1846) Geschichte der Kategorienlehre, Berlin: Verlag von G. Bethge.

43 Vickery, Brian C. (1960) Faceted classification: a guide to the construction and use of special schemes. London: ASLIB.

44 Vickery, Brian C. (1966) Faceted classification schemes. New Brunswick, NJ: Graduate School of Library Science at Rutgers University.

45 Violi, Patrizia. (2001) *Meaning and experience.* Bloomington, In: Indiana University Press.

46 Wittgenstein, Ludwig. (1958) Philosophical investigations. 2nd edition. Oxford, UK: Blackwell.

6

Facets as a Viewpoint Framework: Enhancing Connections in Search and Discovery

Kathryn La Barre

For this Golden Jubilee of *SRELS*, it is appropriate to revisit the contributions of S.R. Ranganathan to library and information science (LIS), a field long concerned with providing optimal access to cultural heritage resources. Serious obstacles to this goal remain. This paper will discuss ongoing work to address the difficulties in creating effective access for two types of cultural heritage materials – films and folktales – that draws from the facet analytical approach developed by Ranganathan. Chief among the lessons that will be discussed is the abiding positive valence of frames of reference, viewpoints and context as guideposts during searching for both groups of users in these projects.

Keywords: Facet analysis; Frames; Viewpoints as facets; Films; Folktales

1 OVERVIEW

This discussion will center upon the role that facets can play in enhancing access to complex cultural heritage resources located in digital repositories. The lens for this discussion will focus upon evaluating the lessons learned in two projects: *Films and Facets* [9] and *Folktales and Facets* [10]. Both projects used facet analysis as the centerpiece for user-focused and task-focused approaches as a way to better understand the needs of librarians, scholars and storytellers working with folktales *(Folktales and Facets)* and casual film enthusiasts *(Films and Facets)*.

The two methods used in these projects are task and facet analysis. Task analysis focuses upon the task as a basic unit of analysis. A task may consist of any discrete information seeking activity necessary to complete a goal. This method uses a variety of techniques commonly associated with user-centered interface design and commonly used to investigate human information seeking processes

[2,22]. The facet analytical approach used in both projects draws from Brian Vickery's definition of the approach as the "sorting of terms in a given field into homogeneous mutually exclusive facets each derived from the parent universe by a single characteristic of division" [23]. The following steps are central (1) Define the subject field (2) Examine materials that reflect user interests (3) Develop a list of characteristics, concepts or categories (4) Sort these terms into facets.

Through a combination of these two methods, the research design for both projects sought to provide insights into both the information activities of people looking for folktales and films, as well as to provide greater understanding of the structural and functional affordances of current access systems for these types of material. At a time of rapidly changing codes and standards that seek to reflect the changing expectations of our users we find ourselves at a junction of disruptive solutions that fail more often than they succeed. Far too often, system designers rely on expediency rather than empirical study to inform the creation of new discovery and access systems. This work is offered as a counterpoint and a possible model for more deeply grounded design practices that take into account user needs, and integrate the facet analytical approach.

2 FRAMES AND VIEWPOINTS

The value systems of those with access to power and those far removed from such access cannot be the same. The viewpoint of the privileged is unlike that of the underprivileged [1, p. 268].

Chief among the lessons from both studies is the abiding positive valence of frames of reference, viewpoints and context as guideposts during searching for both groups of users in these projects. Here, frames and views or viewpoints represent those ideas or assumptions that determine how a resource might be approached, perceived or understood.

2.1 Frames and Aboutness

Frames, a familiar concept to many LIS researchers, are structures that divide knowledge into 'stereotyped situations' that can be connected together to form a complete idea [14]. Here, frames represent a set of ideas, conditions or assumptions about the entities that exist in the world, and about the relations between them, and the knowledge we have about these entities and relations. Frames attempt to lay bare the simple fact that these ideas, conditions or assumptions often determine the perception or understanding of the person experiencing these aspects of the universe. Minsky's most famous description of a frame describes the stereotypical understanding of what the different aspects or components might be of a birthday party or celebration– or in the present case, a Golden Jubilee, and how we might describe it in order to capture or reflect the most essential aspects. These include the person (or entity) for whom the celebration is given, where the celebration is most typically located (a home, for example), the fact that gifts or honors are often given (as in the case of this paper) to honor the celebrant, the fact that a list of the gifts is often made so that people giving a gift can be acknowledged in some way – often through a written note or some other form of acknowledgement.

The concept of framing is integral to the ways in which the user groups in *Folktales and Facets* interacted with cultural heritage materials. Frames also served as the greatest source of disconnect because search systems did not provide these users with the means to search according to context or viewpoint. For example, the casual film enthusiast group in *Films and Facets* sought a variety of frames, or views of films, including descriptions of subject or theme, and devices to refer them to various associated or connected items. These were among the most highly desired system features, but these aspects were rarely provided in contemporary search and discovery systems.

Providing optimal access to information resources in ways that enhance associations and connectedness is part of the long trajectory of Hope Olson's research agenda that builds upon Fairthorne [4] and Maron's [13] three types of aboutness: subjective (S-about), objective(O-about) and retrieval focused(R-about). In advancing awareness of the critical need for connectedness in access systems, Olson deeply situates her work in feminist theory as the locus of system design into which awareness of context and social and cultural differences can be more fully integrated into search and discovery.

Folktales and Facets and *Films and Facets* seek to further this tradition by building upon Olson's [17] observations of the need to integrate four '*traces of connectedness*' in existing systems for information access and discovery. These traces consist of (1) associative relationships as embedded in thesauri and subject headings, (2) the existence of facets and synthetic devices in subject access systems, (3) the entity relationship model of FRBR, and (4) structures which support collaborative tagging practices. These four areas, or 'traces of connectedness' are identified as especially fruitful approaches that may well enhance access to information resources.

2.2 Viewpoint and Aboutness in the Multiverse

Clear themes of the need to enhance aboutness and connectedness emerge from the results from both the *Folktales* and the *Films*projects, especially with regard to the *viewpoint* facet. Facet analysis in both projects validated the utility and usefulness of this facet, which relates to the worldview, ethnic origins, ethical concerns or possible methodological approaches to a given item. Examples of *viewpoint* include theoretical scholarly understandings of a story as well as the folklore tradition (such as structuralist or anthropological) from which an interpretation or adaptation of a story has been drawn. This information frequently appears in textual annotations, notes, and prefatory material added to published folktales by authors, editors and tellers.

Viewpoint also encompasses whether or not a storyteller can recount a tale from a different culture without express permission. Both scholar and storyteller informants in the *Folktales and Facets* project expressed interest in being able to search by *viewpoint* as best supporting their information seeking needs for information about attribution and representation, particularly in the case of Native American tales. Highly salient considerations are among the following: 'Under what circumstances is it appropriate to tell these stories?' Does the answer change if a story exists in print, having been published by a Native American author, or if the teller receives permission from the original teller, or under circumstances in which the teller gives enough history and context for the tale, even if no permission was obtained? [10].

Awareness of *viewpoint* can also extend to the circumstances of the time of year during which a tale can be told, and to whom. Some stories may be known as winter tales – not to be told in other seasons, or may be intended for a particular audience not for the ears of anyone who might hear. Olson's observations about the prospects for connectedness through the use of switching languages, metathesauri and other approaches that help better situate and map such syntagmatic relationships are a key part of the future directions for both research projects.

Rapid increases in the availability of digital cultural resources foreground a number of serious concerns about multiculturalism, appropriation and representation. Smiraglia and van den Heuvel [20] present one path forward through this difficult territory for researchers in the form of their *Knowledge Collider* project. As part of this project, they posit that contemporary Knowledge Organization (KO) needs to replace the regnant metaphor of our domain as the 'universe of knowledge' with a more dynamic and interactive understanding of the 'multiverse of knowledge'. The first mention of the notion of a multiverse is credited to William James [7], "Visible nature is all plasticity and indifference, a multiverse, as one might call it, and not a universe."

The importance of adopting the multiverse as the metaphor for KO is further developed in Lee and Smiraglia's [11] discussions of dimensionality, in which an entity viewed from within or across different dimensions will have different characteristics and different contextual boundaries. Smiraglia continues to remind us of the salience of the multiverse concept as a way tobroaden and diversify the discourse of KO byforcing us to pay greater attention to the role epistemology and culture. As part of these discussions, Smiraglia often highlights Otlet's development of the Universal Decimal Classification as a fruitful path towards creating access to and understanding of the 'multiverse of knowledge'. Though Smiraglia places Ranganathan as one of the group of knowledge organization theorists with a unitary view of the universe of knowledge – often citing the 1957 version of the *Prolegomena* (p. 100) - the truth is more nuanced [18].

Ranganathan's seminal paper, *The Hidden Roots of Classification* [19] and the 1957 [15] edition of *Prolegomena* offer clear indications that his understanding of reality is not that of a unitary universe, but rather one which accords with a multiverse of knowledge. Ranganathan's own roots as a South Indian Brahmin born in the Tanjavoor District of Tamil Nadu [8] added profound depth to his understanding of the complexities of the multiverse, whether corporeal, philosophical, or spiritual. In this article, Ranganathan discusses his own epistemology of the multidimensionality of the universe of subjects in the form of the 'two-fold infinity' inherent in the design of classification systems, and also in terms of the diversity of reader interests. Ranganathan's epistemology sought to accommodate past, present and unknown future knowledge. This has resulted in a long history of effectiveness in creating access for the turbulent and dynamic multiverse of users and ideas. This author is in agreement with Smiraglia and others, that faceted classification, whether from the perspective advanced by the UDC or as conceived by Ranganathan, permits the assignment of multiple characteristics, which can be ordered in dynamic ways, according to the needs of the searcher. The facet analytical approach embedded in the theory of faceted classification proved ideal for both research projects under discussion especially since both the UDC and the Colon Classification provide devices to account for *viewpoint*, or *bias* – as it is labeled in the Colon Classification.

3 SUNKEN WORKS AND THE MULTIVERSE: A CONUNDRUM

To sharpen the reader's understanding of the role of *viewpoint* in the current research, and as embedded in the model being proposed by this paper, the concept of the *sunken work* is offered. A *sunken work* may occur in the form of a written recollection of an oral tale located in a colonialist narrative – such as a report sent to a mercantile company or in the form of a missionary's diary. In this way, a composite, or multi-layered work is formed and the oral tale assumes existence as a bibliographically dependent or hosted work. These dependent works, according to Nicholas [16, p.189-190], are often scattered and lost to history, in archives and other repositories until they are rediscovered serendipitously. Nicholas describes the necessity of accounting for the *sunken works* in the context of a set of necessary and sufficient considerations for written instantiations of oral narratives, such as folktales, that are not currently well represented by bibliographic access forms or contemporary search and discovery systems. Nicholas provides an acute set of complementary observations in light of the fact that within the oral tradition, each time a tale is told, the audience experiences a new version of a tale, reliant upon the source material the teller draws upon, and also upon the common memory and experience of the audience, and also upon the worldview and experience of each individual audience member. A teller relies upon this store of common memory and knowledge of previously told versions of a story even while introducing new variations of plot, of character, and title (p. 180). Our current systems of access fail to adequately note and represent such variations, even though they constitute the heart of the oral narrative experience. Nicholas' notion of the necessity of finding ways to surface the *sunken work* is central to the *viewpoint* facet as well, as it supports this vital user task, and serves to enhance connectedness in ways that can overcome the weakness of present systems.

The documentary, Coming to light: Edward S. Curtis and the North American Indians,

Makepeace [12], provides a deeply layered example of a *sunken work*. In this film, we learn about Edward S. Curtis, an early photographer who embarked on a project from 1896 until 1930 to record the rapidly disappearing culture of the First Nations people in North America. During his lifetime, he captured 40,000 images, and created some early motion pictures and wax recordings of tales and songs. His work culminated in a twenty volume encyclopedic set of images interspersed with text, and a rich trove of ethnographic materials [3]. Known to his subjects as 'Shadow Catcher', Curtis created a body of work that remains deeply controversial and mired in a colonialist narrative. Curtis' work continues to draw anger from contemporary First Nations people who assert that Curtis had no right to create and disseminate audio and visual images of vulnerable subjects and cultures.

In 1904, Curtis set out to capture the profoundly sacred Navajo Tł'éé'jí (Yei'Bi'Chei) Ceremony. Lasting for multiple nights during the winter, the ceremony is one in which masked *dancers* personify the gods in order to restore balance and harmony to the universe. Forbidden to film the actual proceedings, Curtis hired three tribal members to stage the ceremony at a different time of the year. He paid these individuals to create the required ritual objects such as masks, because the masks were buried each year until the proper time for the ceremony. They also created weavings and other ritual objects because tradition required other ceremonial aspects to be created anew for each ceremony. In so doing, Curtis became famous for being the first white man to create an ethnographic record of this ceremony, a feat attempted by many others during the previous twenty years. He toured with this film in an attempt to raise money for his extended photographic venture. The three men Curtis hired were later arrested for this serious violation of tribal conventions, and also punished by the US Military for participating in rituals forbidden by the government of the United States.

Many First Nations people provide narration for the *Coming to light* documentary, among them Navajo tribal member Avery Denny. He and other narrators are unhappy with the documentarian, herself a First Nations person, and the fact that the movie will further disseminate images of their ancestors that should instead, be laid to rest. Denny tells the documentary crew that filming or taking photographs of any Navajo ceremony means that by the process of capture, the ceremony is disrupted and the healing nature of the ceremony destroyed. As Denny watches the film made by Curtis in 1904, he observes in a bemused fashion, that the men perform only a small part of the Tł'éé'jí (Yei'Bi'Chei), not as expected but in a secularized way that retains the power of the ritual. He points out that the dancers hold ritual objects such as rattles, in the left – not right – hand. Denny observes that each part of the performed dance is done backwards. In so doing these men kept the most sacred parts to themselves, thereby obscuring or retaining the power of the ceremony, while at the same time giving the Western world a glimpse into a culture on the verge of extinction. Finding ways to represent this kind of inside out, deeply layered or nested set of viewpoints, which include those of resistance, of colonial intent, of ethnographic record - is an aspect of access not currently offered by search systems, but is one highly valued by researchers.

4 CROWDSOURCING CONNECTEDNESS

Folklorists and storytellers are also frequently frustrated by the limitations of the traditional library and archival systems which seek to provide access to folktales through special classifications or type and motif indexes [10]. One such example of this approach can be found in *Thompson's motif-index of folk literature* [21]. In order to overcome these failures and frustrations, folklorists often resort to a variety of approaches, from the compilation of bibliographies to reliance upon collegial networks of scholars to help them make connections between and among works in a manner closely akin to crowdsourcing. The rapidity and complexity of these conversations is well illustrated by the *h-folk* discussion network, which "supports international conversation on research, teaching, policy, and historiography in the fields of folklore and ethnology". Excerpts from a ten-day discussion thread begun by David Hopkin, tutor and lecturer in modern European history at Hertford College in Oxford, are offered as an example of Olson's crowdsourced forms connectedness referenced earlier. With the subject: the child (children) in search of a remedy (for their mother), a long discussion among an international cast of list subscribers began in reply to Hopkin's [6] posting:

> A recent article contains the transcript of a family narrative (1982) by the Hebridean Mary Manson entitled, 'The story of the bottle of medicine'. It concerns the narrator's mother and cousin travelling in search of a remedy for the heroine's cousin, and the various adventures the two young women had on the way. The basic plotline is reminiscent of other stories ... such as the one told to Paul Sébillot by the 14 year-old cabin boy Joseph Macé in Saint-Cast (Brittany) in 1880 *('L'Enfant qui va chercher des remèdes', Contes des paysans et des pêcheurs)*.... the opera Brundibar, (based on a Czech folktale by Hoffmeister and Krása).

Hopkin continued:

> 'Is 'The Child[ren] in search of a remedy [for their mother]' in fact an international tale type?' Is it listed in Aarne-Thompson-Uther? Do folklorists know of other examples? I'd be grateful for any indications.

One list member responded:

> A recent article contains the transcript of a family narrative (1982) by the Hebridean Mary Manson entitled 'The story of the bottle of medicine'. It concerns the narrator's mother and cousin travelling in search of a remedy for the heroine's cousin, and the various adventures the two young women had on the way. The basic plotline is reminiscent of other stories ... such as the one told to Paul Sébillot by the 14 year-old cabinboy Joseph Macé in Saint-Cast (Brittany) in 1880 ('L'Enfant qui va chercher des remèdes', Contes des paysans et des pêcheurs).... the opera Brundibar, (based on a Czech folktale by Hoffmeister and Krása)

Another responded:

> "I hadn't thought of this tale in terms of ATU551 [the index term assigned to the tale type – child in search of a remedy], but then neither had the compilers of the French folktale catalogue.

Another extends the discussion to include other possible tale types:

> This looks like a case of the indeterminate nature of 'tale type', given the large number of related plots listed by H.-J. Uther (I:321). As you are interested in distant as well as closeresemblances, I point to tales 4.08 and 4.301 in my Malagasy TaleIndex (FFC no. 231). The one was printed in the first collection of
>
> Malagasy folktales, L. Dahle's Specimens of Malagasy Folk-lore (1877). The other, as its number indicates, is pretty much a version of ATU301. A third tale, no. 5.21 in my index, isn't much closer, but if youhave a chance to read my summary (unfortunately not on line), you'llsee the vague resemblance.

One Czech scholar corrected one suggestion – and extends understanding of another tale in the process:

> [A]s far as I know, there's no Czech folk tale being retold in Brundibar (at least, no such tale is registered in the catalogue of the Czechfairy-tales by Vaclav Tille).
>
> I was looking into some Czech sources and I found something about thehistory of the opera (http://is.muni.cz/th/361153/ff_b/Bakalarka_final_sshbelzp.pdf; *see* pages 8 and 9). The piece was written on demand, for acompetition given by the Ministry of education. Jan Krasa, the composer, remembers, he and the author of the libretto Adolf Hoffmeister wanted to deal with the real problems of the time (read: to write something against the war and Hitler), but at the same moment – because of the theme of the competition – they had to write something for children and – furthermore – something what would fitto the genre of opera.
>
> It may be, the characteristic features you mentioned, or at least someof them, were the authors' own inventions and adaptations of the common type (the "Bumblebee" was a caricatured picture of Hitler, the voice contest between the children and the "Bumblebee" was here

because of the genre of opera, and sick mother because the king wouldbe to abstract, too "fairy" for what they wanted to speak about).

Yet another poster suggests that Hopkin should review a recent paper by Patrick Ryan "The Well of D'yerree-in-Dowan": Manifestations of Grimm's "The Water of Life" in Irish Folklore and Literature' recently published by Gramarye (May 2013). The last person responding to Hopkins request noted, "I can see some connections...the story 'feels' different from the versions of ATU551 with which I'm familiar ...might there be others lurking?" This person suggested other motifs from Thompson's motif index to review including, 'Quest assigned by father H.1331.1' and 'Quest for miraculous remedy H 1324'.

The variety of connections revealed in this brief thread included those, which expand, narrow, refocus, and refine the initial query. One points to the inevitable development of variationsso central to the enterprise of oral narratives, and especially to the fraught nature of the act of capturing the oral narrative in written form. Others point to extant literature or current discussions, providing leads at a different level in the scholarly network. Some point to related inquiries or discussions, or suggest other indexes that assign other tale and motif types to similar narratives. In a few days, the scholar posting the initial query received a rich set of suggestions that point to the aboutness and the connectedness of the tale he has in hand with others in literature throughout history and across the world. These kinds of conversations happen regularly on this list, and throughout the literature of this domain. Tracing this rich history in ways that plumb the depths of the uncovered connections and result in maps of the terrain is the next direction for the projects *Folktales and Films.*

5 CONCLUSION: ABOUTNESS, CONNECTEDNESS AND VIEWPOINT (OR BIAS)

This paper proposes a model that takes into account the critical role of aboutness and enhanced connectedness among complex cultural heritage resources such as films and folktales in ways that could inform the development of more culturally aware systems of organization and access. The chief lesson discussed here is the abiding positive valence of frames of reference, viewpoints and context as guideposts during searching for both groups of users in these projects, aspects which could be well supported if the *viewpoint* facet is integrated into system design.

This line of research also suggests that connections, like the deeply nested layers of viewpoint in Curtis' film, and those uncovered by the folklorists on *h-net* [5] may lend themselves to interfaces which assist researchers in visualizing the multiverse. By embedding deep awareness of social and cultural differences, such systems can provide support for navigation across multicultural and multidisciplinary domains in ways that preserve context and enhance access for those traditionally underprivileged by discovery and access systems more often designed for the privileged.

Connecting conversations among researchers who see the value of creating systems that help researchers visualize aboutness and connectedness is another key part of the current research. These conversations are ongoing among researchers who will attend the next UDC seminar "Classification & Visualization: Interfaces to Knowledge" at the Koninklijke Bibliotheek in The Hague, on 24-25 October 2013. The objective of this conference is to explore cutting edge advances and techniques in the visualization of knowledge across various fields of application and their potential impact on developments in traditional bibliographic and documentary classifications. This group will discuss models and metaphors, like the ones discussed in this paper that bridge historical and technological perspectives and may well provide support for navigating the rich connections to be found in the multiverse of knowledge.

6 ACKNOWLEDGMENTS

Funding for the project FACETS and FOLKTALES came from a grant from the OCLC/ALISE Library and Information Science Research Grant Program. Other support for this project came from the Graduate School of Library and Information Science and the Center for Informatics Research on Science and Scholarship at the University of Illinois. Funding for the project FACETS and FILMS came from the Universidade Federal Fluminense (UFF), Niterói, Brasil and from a grant by the Brazilian Government Research Committees (CAPES/ CNPQ). Additional support was granted by the Graduate School of Library and Information Science at the

University of Illinois at Urbana-Champaign. My attendance at the upcoming International UDC Seminar 2013 and the COST workshop will be generously funded by the UDC Consortium and the MPNS COST Action TD1210 funded project KNOWeSCAPE: Analyzing the dynamics of information and knowledge landscapes. Special thanks to Andrea Scharnhorst and Aida Slavic.

REFERENCES

1 Aung Sang Suu Kyi. (1995). Freedom from fear. London: Penguin Books.

2 Crandall, B., Klein, G.A. and Hoffman, R.R. (2006) Working minds: A practitioner's guide to cognitive task analysis. Cambridge, MA: MIT Press.

3 Curtis, E. S. and Hodge, F.W. (1907-1930). The North American Indian: Being a series of volumes picturing and describing the Indians of the United States, and Alaska. Seattle, Washington, E.S. Curtis. Cambridge, USA: The University Press.

4 Fairthorne, R. A. (1969). Content analysis, specification and control. *Annual Review of Information Science and Technology*, 4: 73-109.

5 h-net Discussion Network. Available: http://www.h-net.org/~folk/

6 Hopkin, D. (2013) Query: the child (children) in search of a remedy (for their mother). Written May 14, 2013 on h-net Available: http://h-net.msu.edu/cgi-bin/ logbrowse.pl?trx=vx&list=h-folk&month=1305&week=b&msg=xA/S5EU46XE53sH TkkYATg&user=&pw=

7 James, W. (1895) Is Life Worth Living? *International Journal of Ethics*, 6(10): 245-56.

8 Kent, A. (1978) Shiyali Ramamrita Ranganathan. *Encyclopedia of Library and Information Science*, Ed. by Allen Kent v. 25, p. 118. New York: Marcel Dekker.

9 La Barre, K. and Cordeiro, R. (2012) That obscure object of desire: Facets for film access and discovery. **In** Diane Rasmussen Neal (Ed.) *Indexing and Retrieval of Non-text Information.* Berlin: DeGruyter Saur. p. 234-262.

10 La Barre, K. and Tilley, C. (2012) The elusive tale: Leveraging the study of information seeking and knowledge organization to improve access to and discovery of folktales. *Journal of the American Society for Information Science and Technology, 63*(4): 687-701.

11 Lee, H. and Smiraglia, R. (2012) Cultural frames of knowledge. Würzburg, DE: Ergon Verlag.

12 Makepeace, A. (Director). (2000) Coming to light: Edward S. Curtis and the North American Indians. [DVD]. United States: Makepeace Productions/Bullfrog films.

13 Maron, M. E. (1977) On indexing, retrieval and the meaning of about. *Journal of the American Society for Information Science*, 28(1): 38-43.

14 Minsky, M. (1974) A Framework for Representing Knowledge. MIT-AI Laboratory Memo 306. Reprinted **In** *The Psychology of Computer Vision*, P. Winston (Ed.), McGraw-Hill, 1975. http://web.media.mit.edu/~minsky/papers/Frames/frames.html

15 Neelamegham, A. (compiled) (1957) S.R. Ranganathan's postulates and normative principles: Applications in specialized database design, indexing and retrieval, 1-42, Bangalore, India: Sarada Ranganathan Endowment for Library Science. Retrieved September 28, from http://dlist.sir.arizona.edu/1108/02/ postuchapter1.pdf

16 Nicolas, Y. (2005) Folklore Requirements for Bibliographic Records: Oral Traditions and FRBR . *Cataloging and Classification Quarterly,* 39(3-4): 179-195. Available at http://dx.doi.org/ 10.1300/J104v39n03_11.

17 Olson, Hope A. (2007) How we construct subjects: A Feminist analysis. *Library Trends, 56*(3): 509-541.

18 Ranganathan, S.R. (1957) Prolegomena to Library Classification. (2nd Ed.). London: The Library Association.

19 Ranganathan, S. R. (1967) Hidden roots of classification. *Information Storage and Retrieval.* 3(1): 45-77. Also available: Paper presented at *the Symposium of Relational Factors in Classification,* College Park, MD, USA.

20 Smiraglia, R. and van den Heuvel, C. (April/May 2011). Idea Collider: From a Theory of Knowledge Organization to a Theory of Knowledge Interaction. *Bulletin of the American Society for Information Science and Technology,* 37(4): 43 – 47.

21 Thompson, S. (1955–1958). Motif-index of folk literature. *A classification of narrative elements in folktales, ballads, myths, fables, mediaevalromances, exempla, fabliaux, jest-books and local legends [6 vols.]* Bloomington, **In**: Indiana University Press.

22 Vakkari, P. (2003). Task-based information searching. *Annual Review of Information Science and Technology,* 37: 413–464.

23 Vickery, B. (1960). Faceted classification: A guide to construction and use of special schemes. London: Aslib.

7

A Kaleidoscope Perspective: Change in the Semantics and Structure of Facets and Isolates in Analytico-Synthetic Classification

Joseph T. Tennis

Examines the limitations of the *dynamic theory of classification* in accommodating the changes and rapid growth of new topics in the universe of knowledge. Change in an analytico-synthetic scheme for classification is much more a web of connections and mapping these changes is a complex process. Suggests that there is need for exploration of this complexity for both improving systems, and revisiting our theory

Keywords: Analytico-Synthetic classification, Colon Classification, Classification theory

Shiyali Ramamrita Ranganathan, often considered the founder of library science in India, is known for many innovations with regard to conceptualizing library services and systems. Not the least of his contributions is the commitment to developing a *dynamic theory of classification* [4]. This theory surfaces in the early twentieth century due to that fact that libraries and documentation centers were trying to accommodate the increased production of publications on established as well as new topics.

Accommodating the rapid increase in the number of new topics gives rise to new conceptual tools that classificationists now draw on. Facets are the most commonly known tool constructed by Ranganathan, but there are others – and there is a large and rich body of literature that describes these tools dating from 1927 to the posthumously published texts in the 1980s.

In this paper we outline the purpose, design requirements, and assumptions of these conceptual tools, but then highlight how dynamic theory of classification is a partial solution to the issue of the changing universe of knowledge. The main lacuna in the dynamic theory of classification is changing denotation of facets and isolates – that is the effect of time on the semantics of facets.

For example the facet ELECTRICAL ENGINEERING appeared in the 1930s in the Colon Classification. We cannot expect the meaning to have persisted unchanged from then to today. Given this we would also expect to find a different body of literature collocated under this facet in 1930 compared with today. This is further complicated by the addition of facets to the scheme, which may or may not have been considered part of the meaning of a previously used facet. The intention of facet analysis and schemes for classification that are fully analytico-synthetic is that the classificationist is only adding new facets and isolates. However the reality of this is only borne out if we fully apprehend the extant semantics in the scheme. Further, we can only verify our understanding of facet semantics when we look at the collection of texts fixed under that facet-cum-class. Given this we have a number of relationships to consider when we consider change in schemes for classification built on a dynamic theory of classification. This paper lays out some of those considerations and constructs a kaleidoscope perspective on facets over time in analytico-synthetic schemes.

1 KINDS OF CHANGE IN CLASSIFICATION SCHEMES IN GENERAL

Change is inevitable for classification schemes. And the particular characteristics of classification schemes means we have to account for change in particular ways. For our purposes in this paper, classification schemes are a general class of knowledge organization system that is a mutually exclusive, jointly exhaustive listing of classes arranged in a hierarchical and systemic order, where the further down the hierarchy we find classes that are of greater intension and lesser extension than those above, and where in each rank in the hierarchy classes are listed in a meaningful and systematic order of first-in-the-rank, second-in-the-rank, third, and so on – all at the same level of intension and extension. This is a formal definition, and is not always adhered to in practice, but it will serve as our starting point when discussing what changes in classification schemes. That is, we have to assume this structure when we consider the ramifications of change on semantics in classification schemes.

There are three major kinds of change that surface when we examine revisions to classification schemes. These types are (1) structural change, (2) word-use change, and (3) textual change. We can use EUGENICS as an example since it has undergone much change in the Dewey Decimal Classification system, first surfacing in 1911 as a biological science and now no longer placed there, but rather in a range of disciplines. Historically, EUGENICS is the betterment of the human race through scientific and policy-based practices like measurement, purification, and sterilization. And because of the nature of this concept and the literatures associated with it, it serves as a good example for discussing scheme change – semantics and structure.

Structural change affects the relationships represented in the classification scheme. It also affects how users navigate in the scheme. Structural change can happen in at least five ways. We can (a) add a new facet, (b) change synonym structure (e.g., use EUGENICS to lead to both GENETICS and PSYCHOLOGY), (c) change equivalence structures (e.g., USE and/or USED FOR), (d) assign a facet to another part of the scheme or hierarchy, and (e) add or delete an associative relationship (viz. RT).

Word-use change does not affect how users navigate in the scheme. Word-use change is adding or replacing words linked to a digit in a scheme. For example the classificationist might (a) use a new word with a digit, (b) add a synonym (e.g., replace GENETICS with EUGENICS), (c) formally change a definition of a facet or isolate.

The final form of change in classification schemes is textual change. These are changes in the relationships, over time, between the facets or isolates in the scheme and the texts described by those facets and isolates. There are two primary forms of textual changes. The first is textual warrant change and the second is document-set change. The former, textual warrant change is the change of the texts used to create the facet or isolate and its relationships to other facets and isolates in the scheme. The second change is document-set change. This is the change alluded to in my ELECTRICAL ENGINEERING example above. The meaning of this facet can be interpreted through which texts are referenced by it. We can assume that those texts have changed over time.

We can see effects of this on classifying documents in recent studies of the DDC [8]. What we do not know is how this might affect faceted and analytico-synthetic schemes in ways that are different from enumerative schemes.

2 KINDS OF CHANGE IN SCHEMES FOR CLASSIFICATION THAT ARE FULLY ANALYTICO-SYNTHETIC

Elsewhere I have discussed some of the problems with change in an analytico-synthetic scheme for classification [7]. Here I will do it in the context of the conceptual tools used in the most refined theory for dynamic classification.

Ranganathan's thoughts on how best to design a scheme for classification that could accommodate change evolved over time. At the end of his career he calls his theory and the schemes for classification built from it, analytico-synthetic. Facets are part of this theory, but they are not the only part. If we can accommodate new subjects in what Ranganathan calls a filiatory sequence by breaking apart subjects we have ot have a meaningful way of recombining those pieces. This is where the postulates and principles come into play in faceted classification that makes it analytico-synthetic. This latter kind of classification is guided by a set of principles on how facets should be sequenced and therefore how to accommodate new subjects as the universe of knowledge grows.

The interesting research question that surfaces here lies at the intersection of the principles and the structure of the facets and isolates. As mentioned above, the semantics of a single facet are assumed at a particular time. So that ELECTRICAL ENGINEERINGand EUGENICScarry with them particular meaning in the 1920s and that is different from the meaning in the 2010s. Thus the interesting research question that surfaces in the context of analytico-synthetic classification is what is the same with regard to scheme change as outlined above and what is particular to this kind of classification?

For the enumerative scheme it seems that we have an unwritten assumption about the relationship between the old edition and the new edition of the scheme. If a library adopts a new edition of the scheme it can decide to re-class books based on the new coherent scheme. The fact that purely enumerative schemes allow you to re-class more simply means this is sometimes and option. It is more complicated for analytico-synthetic schemes however. While it is true in this latter case we can conceptualize a new editions as coherent, we are constructing classes, not simply assigning them to documents. Parts of the class number in an analytico-synthetic scheme will be revised and some will not. Some will look the same as those already on the shelf, but will have drifted in meaning because of the change in semantics over time. We thus have a kaleidoscope view of semantics because of the fragmented structure of the evolving analytico-synthetic classification and its semantic echoes found in the collection already classed. The semantics of facets and isolates are also considered in relation to each other in the scheme for classification. They have an *ecological* relationship.

This kaleidoscopic view and ecology perspective of change in analytico-synthetic classification lays bare the differences between enumerative scheme change and analytico-synthetic scheme change. We can see this with examples from the Colon Classification.

When we examine facets and isolates in the various editions of the Colon Classification we can see the effects of both ecological change and word-use change. Starting from the third edition [2] when postulates and principles were mature in Ranganathan's thought, we followed GENETICS, ALTERNATION OF GENERATION, and ONTOGENY. We can see the lexical change reflected in the headings that go with the isolate numbers. With Genetics we see an erasure of a refined meaning because the editors drop Phylogeny as a qualifying term. *See* Table 1.

Table 1: Biology Isolate Numbers in a Sample of Editions of the Colon Classification

Date and Edition Number	Isolate Number	Isolate Heading
1950 3rd Edition [1]	6	Genetics, phylogeny
1952 4th Edition [2]	6	Genetic, phylogeny
1960 (1969) 6th Edition [3]	6	Genetics (phylogeny)
1987 (1989) 7th Edition [5]	6	Genetics

We can infer that phylogeny is not, according to the editors, the only way to conceptualization and describe genetics by 1987. And this tracks the change in the science. So we see how the line breaks here. This is word-use change.

Table 2 shows the ecological change in the same area of the Colon schedules.

Table 2: Sample Isolate Notation in Four Editions of Colon Classification

Notation	1950 3rd Edition	1952 4th Edition	1960 (1969) 6th Ed.	1987 (1989) 7th Ed.
7	Ontogeny	Ontogeny	Development (ontogeny)	Development (Ontogenesis)
71	Fertilisation	Fertilisation		
715	Artificial fertilisation	Artificial fertilisation		
7192	Twins	Twin		
72	Germination	Germination		
73	Embryology	Embryology		

Notation	1950 3rd Edition	1952 4th Edition	1960 (1969) 6th Ed.	1987 (1989) 7th Ed.
75	Growth after birth	Growth after birth		
751	New born	New born		
752	Toddler	Toddler		
755	Infant	Infant		
76	Pre-adolescent	Pre-adolescent		
77	Adolescent	Adolescent		
78	Old age	Old age		
791	Death	Death		

The 7th Edition has this note: “Divisions as for "7 Development" in the Schedule of (1MP1) isolates for "L Medicine" in Chap EL. Schedule of (1MMt1) Substance isolates. Divisions as in the schedule of (1P1) isolates "E1 General Chemistry" Chap EE. Schedule (1E) Action isolates (For use also in (1E) of GT, GV, I, and K” [5]. This directs the classifier to another part of the schedule.

Table 2 is a clear example of ecological change. We removed isolate numbers from this subject, removing the expressivity. From this we can see how the line is broken from one edition to another.

The final example from this part of the Colon Classification ALTERNATION OF GENERATION, has a single change in the 7th Edition. We add a synonym. It then reads, ALTERNATION OF GENERATION (METAGENSIS). It is not clear what effect this has on the semantics. It could be either a lexical or ecological change if METAGENSIS was defined or used elsewhere.

3 FACETS AND ISOLATES AND THE KALEIDOSCOPE PERSPECTIVE

Typical to his holistic style of thinking, Ranganathan considered facets as part of an ecology of tools useful to dynamic classification. Inspired by toy sets that had combinable pieces, Ranganathan, used that metaphor to describe subjects and parts of subjects. This is a fine starting point for accommodating a wide range of new subjects made of parts of extant subjects or new parts. However, this is only one view of time and meaning. It is a distinctly *rationalist*.

I have argued elsewhere that Ranganathan was a *postulational rationalist* [6]. Whereas rationalism posits eternal and fixed concepts that transcend time and space, I suggest that Ranganathan's fundamental categories of Property, Matter, Energy, Space, and Time were postulated and are available for revision should the scheme need it. However, I have a harder time seeing that perspective in this ecology of structure and semantics. From this investigation it seems that even with quite a bit of word-use change in the Colon Classification there is an assumption that words and meanings are fixed.

The only amelioration here is to resituate classification in its context of joint exhaustivity – where all that needs to be said about subjects is provided in the scheme for classification. For us to guarantee this means that designers would need a method for defining each facet and isolate in relation to the interrelationships in the scheme, with the literary warrant, and with the text collection described by the scheme. Further we would have to say that any change in this context would trigger a reevaluation of the whole context, or a turning of the cylinder of the kaleidoscope to see a new configuration of facets and relationships. We must document the current classification and context to manage changes to them both.

4 CONCLUSION

We are able to show at this point that there are three levels of analysis of change in an analytico-synthetic scheme for classification. We must (1) document change of facets in relation to each other and (2) change in potential subjects constructed from combining facets. Finally, (3) we must document change in the explicit relationship structure over time in the Colon Classification, our example.

In the case of our biological examples above we can see deletion of facets and pointing to other areas in the schedule for classification. This is the first level of analysis. The change in the potential subjects that can be represented seems straightforward. By 1960 we cannot use G7192 for twin ontogeny. We have to start with G7 (ontogeny/development), and then add a connecting digit without direction. In 1987 we have guidance on this. So there are at least three potential notations for the ontogeny of twins in the life of the Colon Classification. This is the second level of analysis. The third level requires us to link these three notations. This third level is ongoing research and will be reported elsewhere.

Change in an analytico-synthetic scheme for classification is much more a web of connections, and the complexity of mapping these changes is quite large. However, there is value in the exploration of this complexity for our understanding of both improving systems, and revisiting our theory of meaning in knowledge organization. We are forced to consider which contexts matter and which do not in our pragmatic sysetms design mentality.

S.R. Ranganathan worked tirelessly to improve this theory of dynamic classification; I hope that thinking about change in this way allows us more insight into his contributions and the remaining research questions in this space. He was the father of library science in India, and his work still resonates and makes curious the rest of the world.

REFERENCES

1 Ranganathan, S. R. (1950) Colon Classification. Ed. 3, Asia Publishing House.

2 Ranganathan, S. R. (1952) Colon Classification. Ed. 4, Madras Library Association.

3 Ranganathan, S. R. (1960) Colon Classification. Ed. 6, Asia Publishing House.

4 Ranganathan, S. R. (1967) Prolegomena to Library Classification. 3rd Edition. Asia Publishing House.

5 Ranganathan, S. R. (1989) Colon Classification. Ed. 7. Gopinath, M.A. (ed), Sarada Ranganathan Endowment for Library Science.

6 Tennis, J. T. (2008) Epistemology, Theory, and Methodology in Knowledge Organization: Toward a Classification, Metatheory, and Research Framework. **In** *Knowledge Organization*. 35(2/3): 102-112.

7 Tennis, J. T. (2012) Facets and Fugit Tempus: Considering Time in Faceted Classification Schemes. **In** *Proceedings of the 12th International Conference for Knowledge Organization.* (Mysore, India). Advances in Knowledge Organization vol. 13. Ergon: Würzburg: 58-62.

8 Tennis, J. T.; Thornton, K. and Filer, A. (2012) Some Temporal Aspects of Indexing and Classification: Toward a Metrics for Measuring Scheme Change. **In** *Proceedings of the 2012 Conference*.

8

The Lexicalization of Syntagmatic Relationships

Rebecca Green and ***Carol A. Bean***

A language expresses meaning primarily in its vocabulary (lexical units) and through the grammatical structures in which the units are combined (syntax). Relationships between the words in a language can exist based on their inherent meanings (paradigmatic relationships) or based on their occurrences, roles, and combination in larger contexts such as sentences (syntagmatic relationships). Lexicalization is often used to realize syntagmatic relationships that might otherwise be expressed in these larger linguistic contexts. Semantic frames are a useful way to characterize the interplay among words/phrases in natural language, syntactic structures, and the expression of syntagmatic relationships.

Keywords: Semantic relations, Syntagmatic relations, Semantic frames, Lexicalization

1 INTRODUCTION

Alas! The title of our paper—"The Lexicalization of Syntagmatic Relationships"—turns out to be ironic, although altogether unintentionally so. We had set out to discuss how words can communicate the relationships that might more typically be expressed in extended phrases or sentences, and here we begin by using terms like *lexicalization* and *syntagmatic relationships*, which are unknown to all but a few. We would say, "shame on us," except that the words we have selected best reflect the meanings we wish to discuss. The fault may lie not so much with the unfamiliarity of the words as with the unfamiliarity of the concepts they express. With that in mind, let's start by finding out a bit about lexicalization and about syntagmatic relationships.

1.1 Lexicalization

Lexicalization is defined as "the realization of a meaning in a single word or morpheme rather than in a grammatical construction" (http://www.merriam-webster.com/dictionary/lexicalization). Lexicalization is both the general process by which a language (or sublanguage or dialect) acquires its vocabulary and also the individual results of that process.

We find what may be the earliest documentation of lexicalization in the Biblical account of creation. In Genesis 2.20, before even the creation of Eve, all the living creatures are brought to Adam so he can name them, that is, so he can create words to represent certain classes of beings. As we see, the process of lexicalization goes back a long way.

Although the relationship between what a word sounds like and the concept or meaning it lexicalizes seems largely arbitrary, which concepts get lexicalized is anything but. Lexicalization is based on warrant: We create words for the concepts we experience the need or desire to communicate about; we don't lexicalize concepts just in case the need might arise. But the sorts of meanings that end up being lexicalized exhibit variety: They can be concrete objects, abstract qualities, ideas, states, locations, actions, events, relationships, and so forth.

As an integral part of the process of communication, lexicalization relies on social contract. The whimsical humor of Humpty Dumpty's assertion, "When I use a word, it means just what I choose it to mean—neither more, nor less" [1], lies precisely in the realization that if we use words to mean just what we individually choose for them to mean and not what we collectively agree for them to mean, communication will be thwarted rather than facilitated. Lexicalization is the linguistic equivalent of a computer programming macro, gathering into a single term what we otherwise would need an extended sequence of words to communicate. But surely we would not always produce the same sequence of words in place of the single term, so lexicalization also helps make what we communicate more uniform. Lexicalization thus supports both efficiency and effectiveness in communication.

1.2 Syntagmatic Relationships

With that understanding of lexicalization in hand, we turn to gain a preliminary understanding of the other major concept in our title, syntagmatic relationships. Naturally, given that we are considering the lexicalization of these relationships, syntagmatic relationships involve relationships between words. The reader might think, "Oh, yes, I know: You mean the relationships, say, between *dog* and *canine*, *sports* and *cricket*; or maybe between *depart* and *arrive*, *hot* and *cold*; or between *month* and *January*. But do you mean all of these, or just some of them?" Ah, gentle reader, none of them. Those relationships are what we call paradigmatic relationships—relationships that exist between the words based on their meanings, relationships we characterize as *a priori* because they do not depend on context. The types of relationships we are interested in are those that arise from the use of words in combination in some particular context, for example, among the words in a sentence, as in *The woman hit the car with an umbrella* or in *The man flew Air India from London to Mumbai*. Then what is the relationship between *umbrella* and the remaining words in the sentence in '*The woman hit the car with an umbrella*'? Answer: The umbrella is the instrument of the hitting event. And what is the relationship between *London* and the remaining words in the sentence in '*The man flew Air India from London to Mumbai*'? Answer: London is the departure location of the flying event. Thus, we see that syntagmatic relationships of words in sentences concern the semantic role played by that which they refer to (their "referent") in the event or state communicated by the sentence. (Because of our larger context in the areas of knowledge organization and information retrieval, we will focus our interest in syntagmatic relationships on those involving noun phrases. Elsewhere [6] we have referred to these relationships as "conceptual syntagmatic relationships.")

1.3 Syntagmatic Relationships Lexicalized

What does the lexicalization of a syntagmatic relationship then mean? If syntagmatic relationships depend on contextual occurrence, how can they be lexicalized? We will see two ways in which the syntagmatic relationships of interest to us are lexicalized. The first way involves the lexicalization of the event or state in which the syntagmatic relationship occurs. The second way involves the lexicalization of the specific role played by a participant in that event or state. For example, in our first example sentence, *The woman hit the car with an umbrella*, it is the verb *hit* that lexicalizes the event being talked about and it is the preposition '*with*' that signals that its object (*the umbrella*) is the instrument of hitting. We see the same pattern repeated in our second example sentence, *The man flew Air India from London to Mumbai*: It is the verb *flew* that lexicalizes the event of flying and it is the preposition '*from*' that signals that its object (*London*) is the departure location of the flying. As we explore our subject further, we will find that the lexicalization of syntagmatic relationships is more complex than this initial characterization, but the basic picture will hold: The event or state in which the syntagmatic relationship occurs can be lexicalized (indeed, typically will be lexicalized) and the specific role played by participants in that event or state may be lexicalized.

1.4 Application to Information Retrieval

One of the reasons we care about the lexicalization of syntagmatic relationships is that, on the one hand, syntagmatic relationships are important to information retrieval, and, on the other hand, we rely heavily on words for such retrieval. Syntagmatic relationships are important to information retrieval in at least two ways. First, the control of syntagmatic relationships facilitates precision of retrieval, since we often want to retrieve works in which a subject plays a specific role in a specific event or state (which is just another way of saying works in which the subject is in a specific syntagmatic relationship). Second, we may want to retrieve works because they address some overall syntagmatic relationship. Our reliance on words for information retrieval means that we are limited in the effectiveness of information retrieval by the degree to which we understand the semantic structure of language. It stands to reason then that an understanding of how words express syntagmatic relationships will be an aid in more effective information retrieval [1].

2 A SYNTACTIC PERSPECTIVE ON SYNTAGMATIC RELATIONSHIPS

2.1 Lessons from Phonological Syntagmatic Relationships

We have characterized syntagmatic relationships in terms of the relationships between words occurring in combination, but we could just as well have used a broader characterization, since syntagmatic relationships exist between other kinds of linguistic elements occurring in combination, not just words. For example, we also have phonological syntagmatic relationships between the sounds that go into the pronunciation of a word, say, between the three sounds (/k/, /æ/, and /t/) that go into the pronunciation of *cat*. It may be easier to see some of the properties of syntagmatic relationships in this phonological context. For one thing, it is not the case that any sequence of sounds can be put together; assuming the standard pronunciations associated with each letter, we know that "zxcvb" is not a word because the corresponding sounds do not combine without intervening vowels. For another thing, we can see in the phonology of English how sounds in

---

[1] *See* Green, 1989 [4] on the development of an index language focused on the expression of syntagmatic relationships; *see* Green, 1995a [5] and Green, 1995b [6] for issues and misunderstandings surrounding the expression of syntagmatic relationship in index languages; *see* Green and Bean, 1995 [7] for the relationship of syntagmatic relationships tc relevance

combination assimilate to one another. Our first example of this requires that the reader undertake a short experiment by observing differences in the placement of the tongue when forming an /l/ sound before different vowels. Without actually pronouncing the vowels, note the tongue placement and the slight differences in pronunciation of /l/ in preparing to say *lay, Lee, low, loo,* and *law*; the differences will be most noticeable when alternating between /l/ before a front vowel (*lay, Lee*) and a back vowel (*low, loo, law*). How we pronounce /l/ assimilates to the sound that follows it. Our second example involves the sound combination represented by "in-" (meaning not), which varies depending on the sound that follows; consider the sound combinations in ***inc**omprehensible* , ***ind**ecent,* ***inf**allible,* ***inj**ury,* ***inn**ate,* ***ins**ulin,* ***int**ent,* ***inv**alid,* vs. ***imb**ecile,* ***imb**ibe,* ***imb**ued,* ***imm**ature,* ***imm**obile,* ***imm**utable,* ***imp**ossible,* ***imp**enetrable,* ***imp**atient* vs. ***ill**egible,* ***ill**iterate,* ***ill**ogical,* vs. ***irr**egular,* ***irr**ational,* ***irr**eversible.* The use of "in-" is the default, but we see that when the sound that follows is /b/, /m/, or /p/, "im-" is used instead; we see also that "il-" is used before /l/ and "ir-" is used before /r/. What wants explanation is why "im-" appears before /b/ and /p/. The answer lies in the fact that /b/, /m/, and /p/ are all bilabial consonants—that is, consonants formed using both lips. The specific variant of "in-" used is the one that is most like the sound that follows.

Similarly, when dealing with syntagmatic relationships between words, it is also the case that only certain combinations of words are valid combinations. We note that the first part of the word "syntagmatic" bears a resemblance to "syntax." It is not surprising, then, that allowable combinations of words are governed by syntactic rules. Ultimately, we will see that the syntagmatic relationships of interest to us go beyond valid syntactic structures and are also meaningful conceptual or semantic structures. That is, valid combinations of words "fit" both syntactically and semantically.

2.2 Predicate-Argument Structure

For starters we will look at the lexicalization of syntagmatic relationships from a predominantly syntactic perspective. Given our specific interest in syntagmatic relationships involving noun phrases, we can look to predicate-argument structure for a model to explain the syntactic basis of syntagmatic relationships. The overall model is this: The predicate (typically a verb) acts as a function over one or more arguments (typically nouns or noun phrases). The predicate's arguments can be characterized as participants in the action, situation, etc., conveyed by the predicate. Alternatively, arguments may be said to complete the meaning of the predicate [2].

In our first example sentence, *The woman hit the car with an umbrella, hit* is the predicate, while *the woman, the car,* and *an umbrella* serve as arguments. The verb *hit* is a transitive verb, meaning that it takes a direct object, in this case, *the car.* Indeed, each of the arguments can be characterized in terms of both its syntactic role in the sentence and the thematic role it plays relative to the predicate. When *hit* appears in active voice, its subject (here *the woman*) typically is the participant who does the hitting (the hitter) and its direct object (here *the car*) is the participant receiving the action of the hitting (the "hittee," the thing that was hit). In this particular instance, the woman does the hitting through an instrument, expressed as the object of a prepositional phrase governed by the preposition *with*. (Note that the instrument could even be a part of the woman's body—*The woman hit the car with her fist.*) When *hit* appears in passive voice, the "hittee" becomes the subject, the hitter occurs as the object of a prepositional phrase governed by *by,* and the instrument occurs still as the object of a prepositional phrase governed by *with—The car was hit by the woman with an umbrella.* Knowledge of a verb predicate involves knowing the syntactic patterns in which it may occur, and for each such pattern, the mapping between syntactic roles and thematic roles. (For background on predicate-argument structure and thematic roles, *see* [11],[2]).

2.3 Lexicalization and Thematic Roles

These thematic roles—hitter, "hittee," and instrument—are nothing less than syntagmatic relationships specific to hitting. Where does lexicalization enter the picture? First, almost too obvious to deserve mention, the event in which these syntagmatic relationships occur is lexicalized in the predicate *hit.* Second, we have seen that some of the thematic roles of this predicate are signaled (or 'marked') by prepositions: The instrument is introduced by the word *with*, while the hitter is introduced by the word *by* when the verb is in passive voice (that is, if the hitter is

---

[2] In linguistics, a distinction is drawn between arguments and adjuncts, depending on whether the role played is specific to the given predicate [as is the case with arguments] or the role applies to events or states generally [as is the case with adjuncts]. Roles pertaining to time (e.g., *on Wednesday*] and place [e.g., *in San Francisco*], for example, are typically designated as adjuncts. The distinction is not critical for our purposes—indeed, it is not always clear cut—and so we will not observe it, using the term "argument" for both arguments and adjuncts

expressed in that context; actually, if the hitter is not expressed in that context, but the instrument is expressed, the instrument gets "promoted" to being introduced by the word *by—The car was hit by the umbrella*). Note, however, that the thing hit, in this case the car, never appears as part of a prepositional phrase. We may say that it is 'unmarked,' which reflects the fact that we cannot have an instance of hitting without including an argument corresponding to the thing hit, even if we have to use a generic word like *something*. Thus we can say, *The woman hit the car, The car was hit, The woman hit something,* but *The woman hit* and *The woman hit with the umbrella* are not complete utterances.

Our explanation so far is limited to one set of related sentences in English. The restriction to English affects the phenomenon of lexicalization inasmuch as English uses prepositions to mark some thematic roles where other languages might rely on cases [6]. (Since cases typically are expressed as affixes appearing in conjunction with word roots—that is, they are not themselves words—we do not consider them to be lexicalizations.) Languages using cases can also use a freer word order, another tool in the language arsenal for expressing thematic roles. English exhibits a strong preference for the subject to appear before the verb and for any objects of the verb to appear directly after it. It is word order patterns that permit core arguments of predicates to go unmarked. It is likewise word order patterns that allow speakers of English to distinguish between the thematic roles played by two objects appearing directly after the verb. For example, in *The man gave his son a book*, the first object, *his son*, is mapped to the beneficiary role, while the second object, *a book*, is mapped to the gift role. Thus, our topic, the lexicalization of syntagmatic relationships, allows for more to be said with regard to English than with regard to languages that retain case systems.

2.4 Lexicalization and Semantic Types

At the same time, there is more to be said about the lexicalization of syntagmatic relationships in English than we have touched on so far. A key aspect that we have bypassed thus far is the relationship between thematic roles and semantic types. For example, the thematic roles of the verb *hit*, the hitter, the thing hit, and the instrument of the hitting, cannot be filled by just any noun phrase. Consider the absurdity of *The piano hit sincerity with a planet,* in which, ostensibly, *the piano* is the hitter, *sincerity* is the thing hit, and *a planet* is the instrument of the hitting. A piano can't be the hitter because a hitter has agency--it intends to hit and takes action to make the hitting happen—but a piano, as an inanimate object, cannot be an agent. Sincerity can't be the "hittee," because the thing hit must be concrete, while sincerity is an abstract concept. And if a piano could be the agent of hitting, a planet is so massive that a piano could have no control over it in order to use it as an instrument. Conversely, a woman can be an agent of hitting by intending to and taking action to do so; a car, as a concrete object, can be the object of hitting; and an umbrella is not only a concrete object, but is of a size and weight that a person can exercise control over it and use it as an instrument.

As just seen, semantic types (e.g., agent, concrete [object]) can be very general, so that while they rule out some number of potential noun phrases, they also permit a large number of noun phrases. But in some cases, semantic types can be fairly restrictive. For example, in our second example sentence, *The man flew Air India from London to Mumbai*, we have an air travel event, as signaled by the word *flew*. The thematic roles expressed in the sentence include a traveler (*the man*), a vehicle (*Air India,* i.e., an Air India plane[3]), a departure location (*London*), and a destination location (*Mumbai*). Let's examine a little more carefully the situation with the departure location (marked by the word *from*) and the destination location (marked by the word *to*). Location is clearly a more specific thematic role than agent or concrete object. But it's not sufficient that *London* and *Mumbai* are both locations. *The man flew Air India from the Taj Mahal to the Pacific Ocean* doesn't work, even though the Taj Mahal and the Pacific Ocean are also both locations. Neither is the right kind of location for the departure or destination location of a flying event; neither mausoleums nor oceans provide the appropriate context for an airport. The reader may object that this distinction relies on real world knowledge, not on the meanings of words. We respond that this is not a question where only one or the other can apply. Yes, we are relying on real world knowledge to rule out the Taj Mahal and the Pacific Ocean as appropriate locations for airports. But isn't real world knowledge built into our understanding of the meaning of many, perhaps all, words? On a practical level, if we hope that natural language processing will ever be able to distinguish between the felicity of *The man flew Air India from London to Mumbai* and the infelicity of *The man flew Air India from the Taj Mahal to the Pacific Ocean*, the requisite real world knowledge will have to be built into the meanings of the word *fly*, as well as *London, Mumbai, Taj Mahal*, and *Pacific Ocean*. And if that real world knowledge is built into the meaning of those words, it has been lexicalized.

---

[3] In this sentence, *Air India* seems to be doing double duty, as it metonymically supplies the vehicle in which travel takes place and explicitly supplies the service provider. The latter role might more naturally be expressed as the object of a prepositional phrase governed by *on*: *The man flew on Air India from London to Mumbai.* The verb *fly* so strongly implies the vehicle type that no direct object is required

3 A MORE SEMANTIC PERSPECTIVE ON SYNTAGMATIC RELATIONSHIPS

Up to this point, we have discussed in some detail two specific sentences. In each of the sentences the verb serves as a predicate, while noun phrases in the sentence serve as arguments of that predicate. We have seen that the arguments can be characterized both in terms of syntactic roles (e.g., subject, direct object, object of prepositional phrase) and semantic/thematic roles, which may be given generally (e.g., agent) or more specifically (e.g., hitter, traveler, destination location).

What are the more specific semantic roles specific to? It might seem that the best answer is the predicate, but that possibility turns out to be too specific. Consider other verbs that are used to communicate events akin to hitting (e.g., *jab, slap, smack, strike*) or vehicular travel (e.g., *drive, hitchhike, ride, sail*). It is not uncommon for verbs that can be used to talk about similar situations to share syntactic behavior to a large degree, although that is by no means necessary. Differences in syntactic behavior may reflect slight differences in the set of thematic roles that can be expressed, but if the verbs don't share a core set of thematic roles, they aren't used to communicate about basically the same situation. Indeed, the capability of making similar assertions about the same thematic roles may be used as a criterion for identifying which predicates are akin to one other.

3.1 Semantic Frames: The Overall Idea

Following the lead of Fillmore [3], we will use "semantic frame" to reference what the semantic roles are specific to. A semantic frame is "a script-like conceptual structure that describes a particular type of situation, object, or event along with its participants and props. For example, the Apply heat frame describes a common situation involving a Cook, some Food, and a Heating Instrument, and is evoked by words such *as bake, blanch, boil, broil, brown, simmer, steam,* etc. We call these roles frame elements (FEs) and the frame-evoking words are [lexical units (LUs)] in the Apply heat frame" ([10], p5).

For example, in FrameNet (https://framenet2.icsi.berkeley.edu/), an online database of semantic frames, our vehicular transportation situation is called the Ride_vehicle frame, which is characterized in this manner: "In this frame a Theme is moved by a Vehicle which is not directly under their power. The Source, Path, Goal, or Area of the motion may be indicated. The Distance traveled or the Speed of motion may also be indicated. A Route or Road may be present and the Manner in which the Theme moves may be given."

We see that a semantic frame has associated with it a set of frame elements / semantic roles, which interact with each other in a well-defined way. FrameNet's description of this frame distinguishes between core frame elements and non-core frame elements, as shown in Figure 1. We should note that core elements are not quite the same as mandatory elements. For example, in the set of frame elements above, the expression of Area is incompatible with the expression of Path/Source/ Goal. Typically some indication will be given of where the travel takes place, either as a general area or as a path.

Type of frame element	Frame element	Meaning of frame element
Core	Area	The location where the motion takes place
	Goal	The endpoint of the trajectory of motion (our destination location)
	Path	The trajectory of the motion
	Source	A starting-point of the motion (our departure location)
	Theme	The entity which moves by means of the Vehicle (our traveler)
	Vehicle	The means of conveyance of the Theme
Non-core	Cotheme	A theme that rides in the same Vehicle as the main Theme
	Depictive	The state of the Theme or Vehicle during the motion
	Distance	The extent of the motion
	Duration	The amount of time the motion takes
	Manner	A property of the motion not related to its trajectory
	Purpose	The Purpose for which the Theme rides a vehicle.
	Road	The thoroughfare on which the Vehicle travels
	Route	The usual path that the Vehicle travels
	Speed	The rate at which the motion occurs
	Time	When the riding takes place

Fig. 1: Frame elements of Ride_vehicle frame in FrameNet

3.2 Evoking a Semantic Frame

Also associated with each frame is a set of words, phrases, or lexical units that are said to "evoke" the frame. What this means is that the lexical unit introduces into the conversation the entire frame with which it is associated. As predicates, verbs typically evoke frames. Nouns whose meaning corresponds closely to a frame element also evoke frames. Any time a lexical unit evokes a frame, that word or phrase lexicalizes a syntagmatic relationship. The word *passenger*, for instance, evokes the Ride_vehicle frame. Anyone who understands the word will know upon encountering it that we are talking about a situation in which a person is riding in—but not driving—some type of vehicle, which is moving along a path from a source location to a goal location. Not only does the frame-evoking word introduce the frame, but in this case it can also be said to profile [8, I: p183-189], or focus on, a specific part of the frame, the Theme frame element. Similarly, *patient* evokes FrameNet's Medical_interaction_scenario frame and profiles the person whose health status is of concern and who receives care from medical professionals to maintain or restore their health. *Batter* evokes a baseball frame (a frame that FrameNet has not yet analyzed) and profiles a specific participant in the frame—the person standing at the plate with bat in hand, who by following the rules of baseball attempts to reach base by hitting a thrown ball, and eventually to score.

The reader may now be objecting, "How can you say that *patient* evokes a Medical_interaction_scenario frame and not a Rashness frame, or that *batter* evokes a baseball frame and not a Food-related frame? Well, of course, we don't mean that the word *patient* always evokes a Medical_interaction_scenario frame, or that the word *batter* always evokes a baseball frame. Frame semantics can't make polysemy disappear. We mean that the relevant senses of those words evoke the indicated frames.

3.3 The Interplay of Frame Elements and Syntax

We should contrast the case of polysemy, where the various senses of an orthographic form evoke completely different frames, with the case of various uses of a single word, which may evoke different, but related, frames. Let us, consider, for example, several uses of *hit* and the frames they evoke as shown in Figure 2, or several uses of *fly* and the frames they evoke as shown in Figure 3.

Frame	Characterization of frame	Example sentence
Impact	An Impactor makes sudden, forcible contact with the Impactee.	The rock hit the sand with a thump.
Cause_impact	An Agent causes an Impactor to make sudden, forcible contact with an Impactee.	The juggler hit the ceiling with every other ball.
Experience_ bodily_harm	An Experiencer is involved in a bodily injury to a Body_part.	She fell and hit her head.
Cause_harm	An Agent or a Cause injures a Victim.	The robber hit the woman on the head with a stick.

Figure 2: Closely-related FrameNet frames evoked by *hit*

Frame	Characterization of frame	Example sentence
Motion	Some entity (Theme) starts out in one place (Source) and ends up in some other place (Goal), having covered some space between the two (Path).	The ball flew over the fence.
Self_motion	The Self_mover, a living being, moves under its own direction along a Path.	The bird flew above the coastline.
Ride_vehicle	A Theme is moved by a Vehicle which is not directly under their power.	The man flew from London to Mumbai.
Operate_vehicle	A Driver controls the motion of a Vehicle.	The Navy pilot flew twenty combat missions.

Figure 3: Closely-related FrameNet frames evoked by *fly*

One way to explore the differences among these frames is by considering the role of Body part in the frames evoked by *hit* and the role of Vehicle in the frames evoked by *fly*. Body part is not a frame element in the Impact or Cause_impact frames: As soon as Body part is introduced into the Impact or Cause_impact mix, we shift to the Experience_ bodily_harm, where Body part or Cause_harm frames; in the Experience_bodily_harm frame, Body part is expressed as a direct object, but in the Cause_harm frame, Body part is expressed as the object of a prepositional phrase governed by *on*. The case with Vehicle and *fly* is similar, but even more complex. Vehicle is not a frame element of the Motion and Self_motion frames; its addition to the participant mix brings the Ride_vehicle and Operate_vehicle frames into play. With a verb like *fly*, which implies the mode of transportation, the Vehicle frame element can be expressed metonymically through the company that owns the (fleet of) Vehicle(s). Hence, as we have seen, we can talk about *flying Air India* or *flying on Air India* in the Ride_vehicle frame, but would talk about *flying for Air India* in the Operate_vehicle frame. This pattern holds for other verbs that imply mode of transportation, e.g., *sail Carnival Cruise Lines* or *sail on Carnival Cruise Lines* in the Ride_vehicle frame and *sail for Carnival Cruise Lines* in the Operate_vehicle frame. But if we use verbs that do not imply mode of transportation (e.g., *go* or *travel)*, the Vehicle or Vehicle owner frame element is expressed as the object of a prepositional phrase governed by *by* in the Ride_vehicle frame (e.g., *went by car* or *travel by bus*).

What are we to make of these subtle differences in how frame elements are expressed across related frames, if they are indeed allowed to be expressed at all? The differences reflect the strong syntactic basis of FrameNet's frames; that is, syntax and semantics work together in the expression of syntagmatic relationships. By the same token, this syntactic specificity sometimes allows us to differentiate between frames, simply on the basis of the syntactic role of a frame element or on the basis of the preposition that introduces it.

3.4 Prepositional Marking of Frame Elements Extended

We have seen evidence indicating that if a preposition is used to introduce a frame element with one predicate evoking a semantic frame, it tends to be used to introduce that frame element for other predicates evoking that frame. Not only is this true for a specific frame, but it can be true also for frames that are hierarchically, compositionally, or metaphorically related. For example, the paired use of *from* to mark a departure location / source and to mark a destination location / goal occurs in many contexts beyond literal motion- and transportation-related frames, as seen in Figure 4. (Note that in some cases, the source occurs as the subject of the verb and therefore lacks prepositional marking.)

Scenario	Example sentence	Source	Goal
Vehicular travel	He flew Air India from London to Mumbai	London	Mumbai
Self-locomotion	He walked from home to his place of work.	home	his place of work
Movement	She turned her head from right to left.	right	left
Education	The teacher imparted her knowledge of Sanskrit to her new student.	teacher	her new student
Commercial transaction	The merchant sold the desk to his #1 customer.	merchant	his #1 customer
Alphabetical range	Those with last names from A to M are asked to bring desserts.	A	M
Numerical range	The little boy can count from 1 to 100.	1	100
Temporal range	The monsoon season lasts from July to September.	July	September

Figure 4: Various scenarios using *from* and *to* for source and goal

3.5 Lexicalization and Semantic Frames

We have asserted that when a lexical unit evokes a frame, it lexicalizes a syntagmatic relationship. This is practically a tautology, because semantic frames express syntagmatic relationships of the sort we are interested in. We have seen this pattern of lexicalizing syntagmatic relationships in three distinct ways: (1) specific senses of verbs typically evoke specific frames; (2) some nouns evoke frames while at the same time profiling frame elements; and (3) prepositions can mark frame elements, sometimes in the context of a highly specific frame, but also sometimes in the context of a set of frames.

4 CONCLUSION

Readers will be wondering if the syntagmatic relationships of interest to us aren't really just the same thing as facets. Yes, of course—that's why we chose this subject! As we have seen, these syntagmatic relationships are closely associated with thematic roles and with frame elements in semantic frames. Semantic roles have become an increasingly important resource in computational linguistics [9]. That is, many different disciplines and schools of thought have felt the need to work with the relationships that bind the participants of a clause/assertion/ premise.

What we hope to have added to the conversation via our cognitive linguistics perspective is some sense of the interplay among words and phrases (i.e., lexical items) that occur in natural language, syntactic structure, and the expression of syntagmatic relationships. We have seen in semantic frames a particularly useful resource for characterizing this interplay. We believe the application of semantic frames to the knowledge organization context has great potential.

REFERENCES

1 Carroll, Lewis. (1872) Through the looking-glass, and what Alice found there: By Lewis Carroll. With fifty illustrations by John Tenniel. London.

2 Croft, William. (1991) Syntactic categories and grammatical relations: the cognitive organization of information. Chicago: University of Chicago Press.

3 Fillmore, Charles J. (2003) Form and meaning in language: Volume I, Papers on semantic roles. Stanford, Calif: CSLI Publ., Center for the Study of Language and Information.

4 Green, Rebecca. (1989) The expression of syntagmatic relationships in frame-based indexing. Thesis (Ph. D.)--University of Maryland, College Park, 1989.

5 Green, Rebecca. (1995a) Syntagmatic Relationships in Index Languages: A Reassessment. *The Library Quarterly*. 65(4): 365-385.

6 Green, Rebecca. (1995b) The Expression of Conceptual Syntagmatic Relationships: A Comparative Survey. *Journal of Documentation*. 51(4): 315-38.

7 Green, Rebecca and Carol A. Bean. (1995) Topical Relevance Relationships. II. An Exploratory Study and Preliminary Typology. *Journal of the American Society for Information Science*. 46(9): 654-62.

8 Langacker, Ronald W. (1987). Foundations of cognitive grammar. Stanford, Calif: Stanford University Press.

9 Palmer, Martha Stone; Daniel Gildea and Nianwen Xue. (2010) Semantic role labeling. [San Rafael, Calif.]: Morgan & Claypool Publishers.

10 Ruppenhofer, Josef; Ellsworth, Michael; Petruck, Miriam R. L.; Johnson, Christopher R. and Scheffczyk, Jan. (2006) FrameNet II: Extended Theory and Practice. Berkeley, California: International Computer Science Institute. Available: https://framenet2.icsi.berkeley.edu/docs/r1.5/book.pdf.

11 Somers, H.L. (1987) Valency and case in computational linguistics. Edinburgh: Edinburgh University Press.

9

Challenges of Knowledge Organization and ISKO

H. Peter Ohly

Traditionally 'Knowledge Organization' is the ordering of documents on a bookshelf and the indexing of these in a more or less one-dimensional catalog. Now with the Web, its many and hyperlinked, distributed and heterogeneous sources the plain terminological approaches are no longer sufficient. Given this, ISKO has to rethink its mission. The *new* Knowledge Organization, which aims at the Semantic Web 3.0 tries to combine different Knowledge Organization systems by shared metadata and formalized ontologies. While the semantic approaches have quite an opposite approach to the user driven systems the future might lay in a combination of logical descriptions, specialized evaluation, and self-organizing principles, what could be named "Self Organizing Knowledge Organization Systems". There are open questions which need to be solved in future by ISKO and similar organizations.

Keywords: Knowledge organization; ISKO; International Society for Knowledge Organization; Semantic web;

1 WHAT IS KNOWLEDGE ORGANIZATION?

Dahlberg [8] defines Knowledge Organization as "... the science of structuring and systematically arranging knowledge units (concepts) according to their inherent knowledge elements (characteristics) and the application of concepts and classes of concepts ordered by this way for the assignment of the worthwhile contents of referents (objects/subjects) of all kinds". More precisely, Dahlberg [7] defines knowledge organization as:

> A subject area encompassing the organizing of a) units of knowledge concepts and b) all types of objects (minerals, plants, animals, documents, pictures, museum objects, etc.), related to particular terms or categories, so as to capture what is known about the world in some orderly form allowing it to be further shared with others.

Knowledge organization encompasses the following:

1. the epistemological, mathematical, system-theoretical, cognitive scientific and scientific theoretical premises of order of concepts as well as their historical background,
2. the knowledge of elements and structures of systems of concepts,
3. the methodology of construction, conservation, revision and evaluation of this system;
4. the methodology of intellectual and machine applications of this system via classification and indexing,
5. special taxonomies and classification systems including documentation language (thesauri),
6. questions arising from related areas such as linguistics (~ linguistics mathematics) and terminology; including the retrieval problems, especially in online access,
7. the entire periphery of knowledge organization in the workplace, individual centers, societies, countries and in international areas, as well as the question of education, the economy, the user, etc.

With respect to e.g. social tagging, the systematic approach and the presumption of inherence of the knowledge elements are not obvious. Traditionally 'Knowledge Organization' was understood as the ordering of documents on a bookshelf and the indexing of these in a more or less one-dimensional catalog. At least with more specialized documents (e.g. journal articles), the growth of databases and the availability of sophisticated retrieval techniques, these approaches were not satisfactory and term based organization became increasingly important. Now with the Web, its many and hyperlinked, distributed and heterogeneous sources the plain terminological approaches are no longer sufficient. Zeng [32] sees an increase of dimensionality and functions with the development from term lists, via metadata-like models and classifications, to relationship models (*see* Fig. 1). In principle this reflects a shift from more subjective views of knowledge and its order to more objective ones. Hence it is important to examine how far e.g. ISKO (International Society for Knowledge Organization) has to change its mission.

There are many disciplines which are applied in Knowledge Organization, e.g. Linguistics, Cognitive Science, and Philosophy. Some emerging frontiers include

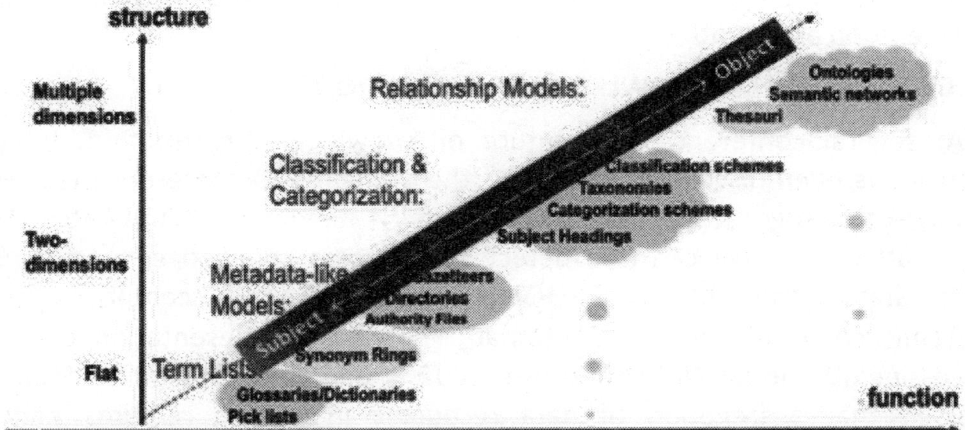

Major functions						
eliminating ambiguity	xxx		xxx	xx	xxxx	xx
controlling synonyms		xxxx	xxx	xx	xxxx	xx
establishing relationships: hierarchical			x	xxxx	xxx	xxx
establishing relationships: associative					xxxx	xxxxx
presenting properties						xxxxx

Fig. 1: KOS types (amended from Zeng 2008, p.161 [32])

Knowledge Management and Knowledge Engineering (cf. Fig. 2). In Knowledge Management the main focus is to make profit out of the knowledge within an enterprise and its business. The codification and retrieval of knowledge for management processes are part of it. Knowledge Engineering tries to mechanize knowledge storage, its maintenance, and its integration. Human models of understanding the universe of knowledge are part of it. Whereas Knowledge Management and Knowledge Engineering are appropriate to shape the primary

Discipine		Area	Methods	Applications
Knowledge Organization	(KO)	Library	Metadata	KOS
Knowledge Management	(KM)	Enterprise	Profit	BI
Knowledge Engeneering	(KE)	Informatics	Maschine Logic	AI KBS
KO+KM+KI ?		interdisciplinary	Semantic Web ?	eScience ? eCommerce ? eGovernment ? eDecision??

Fig. 2: Characteristics of Knowledge Disciplines (Ohly 2011a) [24]

scope of Knowledge Organization, these are also related disciplines worthy of consideration as essential collaboration fields.

2 CHALLENGES FOR KNOWLEDGE ORGANIZATION

At several conferences the future of Knowledge Organization, Information Science has been discussed. In 2006 at the Vienna ISKO conference [22] Winfried Schmitz-Esser suggested that a world model is needed that integrates means of organization and that can also detect and process knowledge in texts. Gerhard Budin stated that Knowledge Organization nowadays comprises cognitive, epistemic, communicative, and automatic knowledge representation, creation, and processing. At the IKONE[1] conference 2007 in Bangalore Maxmilian Stempfhuber stressed that aggregation of data resources in portals requires handling of heterogeneity with respect to user demands. One of the most demanding statements given at this conference was by Prasad Bharat Ram: "Give me what I want, not what I ask for" [23]. Means for that might be procedures that deal with misspellings, spam ranking, user models. A conference on 'Scientific Communication of the Future' in Jülich [1]) yielded in diversification of knowledge and types of knowledge communication distinguishing between mainstream knowledge and ingenious knowledge creation. These discussions indicate that users as well as indexers have a fluid notion of knowledge and document contents. These users are very different with respect to their individual or public tasks and their observing or constructing role, especially with the "Social" Web 2.0 [31; *see* Fig. 3]. Whereas in the pre-digital world the experts were dictating the values to the users, in the digital word the public and skilled users are setting the norms [cf. 26]. There is need to support the possibility of adopting information sources from yesterday to questions of tomorrow (*see* Fig. 4). A prerequisite - though not sufficient - is the trust in the information and its creating institutions. The retrieval should apply sophisticated and robust processing techniques that are able to mine important information from many and heterogeneous databases. Hence the demanding question will be: How can old information be transformed and reused for future problems. Nevertheless unobvious user expectations can hardly be matched by a mechanical information system. More recent conferences (ISKO France 2009, Lyon and 2011, Lille; ISKO Germany 2009, Bonn; UDC Seminar 2011, Den Haag; DGI 2012, Düsseldorf) had similar discussion rounds but focused more on the issues of Web

[1] International Conference on Future of Knowledge Organization in the Networked Environment, 2007, DRTC, Bangalore [30]

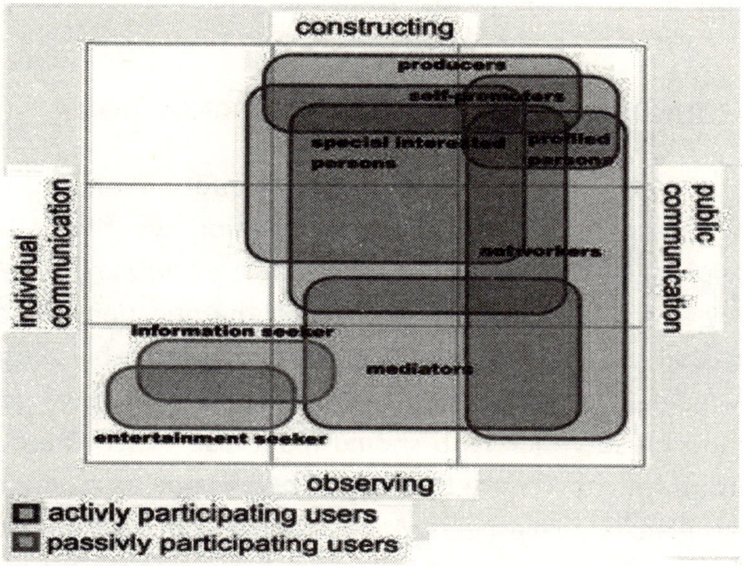

Fig. 3: Web 2.0 Users Typology (translated from Trump 2007)

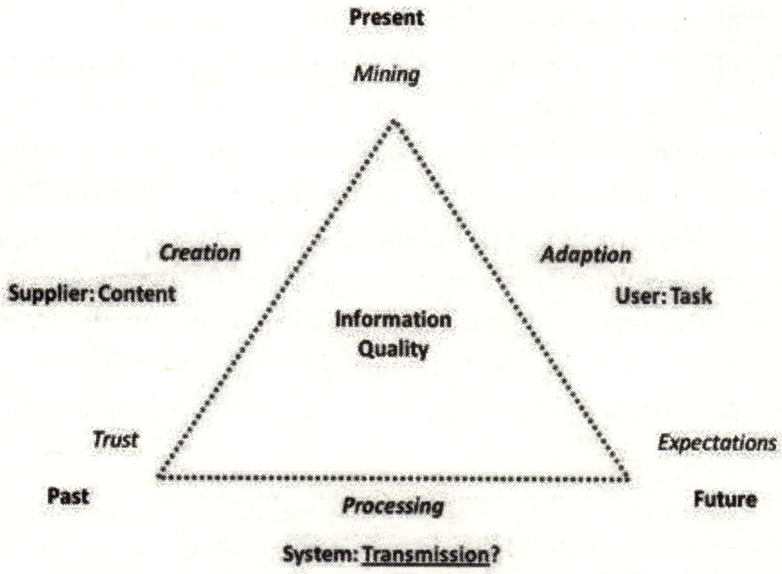

Fig. 4: Past-Present–Future of Information [25]

semantics, the conflict with new social media and the computer science dominance[2].

3 THEORETICAL FOUNDATIONS OF KNOWLEDGE ORGANIZATION

One key question is the theoretical foundation of information and knowledge organization work. Going back to Dahlberg's definition we find questions of application and periphery of Knowledge Organization. The founders of classification systems, like Dewey and Otlet [27] went far beyond the question of locating and ordering books on shelves. Focus on usability is accompanied by questions like: What kind of knowledge is worth being collected? Where should we get it from? How can we use and preserve it? Who should make use of it? There are many theories offered from Activity Theory to Design Theory, not to mention theories that include ecological and global aspects. A look only at Complexity Theory (Morin [20])[3] shows the wide range of theories nested with it under different aspects (*see* Fig. 5): Systems Theory (Bertalanffy) and Cybernetics (Wiener) up to Global Network Society (Castells)[4]. Thus Knowledge Organization must be aware of different theoretical positions that enforce certain tasks and visions and must be able to lay its emphasis and principles on those theories that are appropriate in its special application area and for its user clientele. Certain positions determine the kind of information as well as expectations of the users. Not at least psychological theories, how we are attracted to use information (Berlyne: Activation Theory) and which design of information will be fashionable (Bürdeck: Design Theory), as well as sociological theories, how information gets diffused (Rogers: Diffusion Theory) and psycho-social dynamics of opinion leadership (Lewin: Group Dynamics) have to be considered[5]. Hjørland [12; *see*: Fig. 6] distinguishes between Empiricism (induction from data), Rationalism (logical modeling), Historicism (historical background), and

---

2 <http://pro.ovh.net/~iskofran/?q=node/13> and <http://liste.cilea.it/pipermail/isko/2010-January/000259.html>; <http://conferences.isko-france.asso.fr/en/programme.htm>; <http://www.mail-archive.com/wiss-org@gesis.org/msg00051.html>; <http://seminar.udcc.org/2011/programme.htm>; <http://dgiinfo.informationsassistent.de/index.php?option=com_content&view=article&id=288&Itemid=122>

3 *See also*: Montuori 2004 [19]

4 Bertalanffy 1957 [3]; Wiener 1948 [33]; Castells 2005 [5]

5 Berlyne 1967 [2] (*see also*: Scott 1966) [29]; Bürdek 2005 [4]; Rogers 1962 [28]; Lewin 1935 [16]

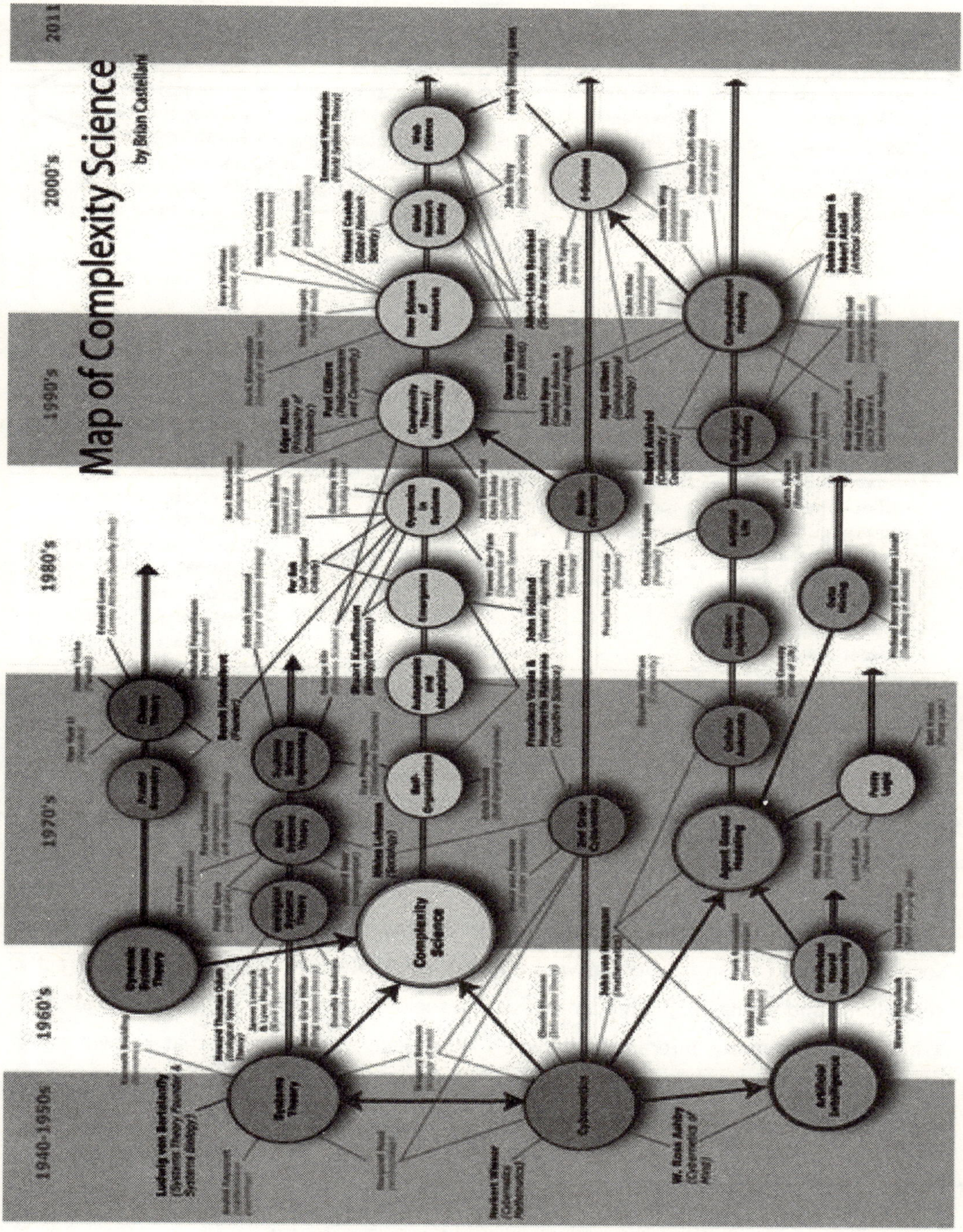

Fig. 5: Complexity Map (from Castellani 2009 [6])

Empiricism	*Rationalism*	*Historicism*	*Pragmatism*
Relevant: Observations, sense-data. Induction from collections of observational data. Intersubjectively controlled data.	Relevant: Pure thinking, logic, mathematical models, computer modeling, systems of axioms, definitions and theorems.	Relevant: Background knowledge about pre-understanding, theories, conceptions, contexts, historical developments and evolutionary perspectives.	Relevant: Information about goals and values and consequences both involving the researcher and the object of research (subject and object).
Non-relevant: Speculations, knowledge transmitted from authorities. "Book knowledge" ("reading nature, not books"). Data about the observers' assumptions and pre-understanding.	Low priority is given to empirical data because such data must be organized in accordance with principles which cannot come from experience.	Low priority is given to decontextualized data of which the meanings cannot be interpreted. Intersubjectively controlled data are often seen as trivia.	Low priority (or outright suspicion) is given to claimed value-free or neutral information. For example, feminist epistemology is suspicious about the neutrality of information produced in a male dominated society.

Fig. 6: Epistemological Schools (amended from Hjoerland 2002 [12])

Pragmatism (goals and values of information and users). Hjørland [11][6] explains the "Pragmatic Theory of Knowledge"[7] as follows:

> "Since living and acting constitutes the a priori of knowledge, knowledge is constructed in such a way that an application of well constructed knowledge will directly or indirectly serve living and acting" […][8] "in a bio-physical, a socio-cultural and a subjective world". […] "There is a continuous interaction between knowledge and action so that knowledge is created in and through action and so that experiences that the actor acquires through action influences subsequent action".

6 Extract from Hjørland [11]: <http://www.iva.dk/jni/lifeboat_old/Positions/Pragmatism.htm>

7 Under which he subsumes his information concept of Activity Theory [17]

8 Order changed by the author

He himself (with reference to (Andersen, 2005)) is a defender of Activity Theory as theoretical basis for information work: "The most important issues in the criticism of empiricism, rationalism and "positivism" probably are the neglecting of knowledge as a social and historical product made to serve certain purposes and interests and by implication the need reconsider knowledge claims in the light of new purposes, conditions and interests" [13]. For practical classification work he is rather critical about user-based/cognitive views, facet-analytic approaches, empirical (numerical) and as well as social (citations) classifications, but proposes a domain-analytic view, where only the cooperation with subject specialists will result in applicable and acceptable knowledge organization systems. As he says: "The difference between a good and a bad classification is that the good classification reveals deep insight concerning the possible choices and dilemmas and is well argued" [13].

4 NEW KNOWLEDGE ORGANIZATION

The *new* Knowledge Organization, which aims at the "Semantic" Web 3.0 tries to combine different Knowledge Organization systems in the Internet by shared metadata and formalized ontologies. Examples for these are the NKOS group with recommendations for thesauri description schemes [21] and SKOS which applies machine-readable resource description languages to knowledge organization systems such as thesauri, classification schemes, and other concept schemes [18]. The SKOS data model provides basic sets of documentation properties, semantic relation properties, lexical labeling, label relations, concept collections, and concept mapping. These sets provide a framework that can be adapted to more specific needs.

Whereas the semantic approaches have quite an opposite approach to the user driven "social" systems[9] the future might exist in a combination of logical expert based descriptions and self-organizing principles, what could be labeled "Self Organizing Knowledge Organization System" (SOKOS). A first attempt in harmonizing Knowledge Organization systems with a machine-readable world is given by the ISO norm 25964 Information and Documentation, part 1 and 2 [15][10],

[9] *See* e.g. Flickr < http://www.flickr.com/>

[10] *See also*: Dextre Clarke 2011 [9] and 2011/2012 [10]

that revises the existing international standards for retrieval thesauri and is also intended for their interoperability with other vocabularies in a Semantic Web context.

Knowledge Organization has to turn back to formal, semantic approaches, such as facetted concept systems. But it also has to be logically more precise and adequate with the aim of enabling specialized reasoning over multiple sources in the Web environment. Also approaches such as social indexing and its quantitative exploitation can be neglected no longer.

5 CONCLUSIONS FOR ISKO

ISKO as a specialized society in this field has to help its clientele to get orientation in an unclear offer of competing approaches and specific realizations. Means for this are international and interdisciplinary congresses, articles in its specialized journal (Knowledge Organization), access to classical texts, text books, repositories, and exchange relations with other societies (cf. [14], Art. 4). The theoretical background of information, resp. knowledge, and its coding and exchange must be re-furbished, especially it has to include the social dimension. A step forward in this direction are repositories with classical readings and old Knowledge Organization journal issues, as well as a specialized bibliography open to the community and the encouraging of norms and evaluations concerning the field of Knowledge Organization. Knowledge Organization textbooks have to include the question of ontologies, machine processing, and Web environment. Exchange with other disciplines or even special groups requires more active contacts with other scientific societies in the field as well as clear exchange rules with these. Nevertheless ISKO has to define its boundaries to other sciences.

But there are still open questions that might be solved in future by ISKO and neighbor societies:

1. What are the indicators for a "good" Knowledge Organization System?
2. How can Knowledge Organization Systems based on different principles (faceted, numerically clustered, social, etc.) be combined?

3. How can local heterogeneity be combined with the aim of a global e-science?
4. What is the profile of a Knowledge Organization profession?
5. Will Knowledge Organization only become a mere application of Knowledge Engineering in the field of information brokering?

6 OUTLOOK

Knowledge Organization is an everlasting demand for efficient storage, retrieval, and processing of information codified in text and other human artifacts. Similar to Information Science it is so common that it is sometimes not seen as an independent discipline with the prerequisite of getting standardized, established, mediated, and updated. With the development of more and more complex information and communication technologies it became increasingly dependent on these and is sometimes understood as sub-discipline of these. Without any intention to subordinate one to the other it must be clearly seen that engineering means and the semantic cultural logic are different aspects of one more or less application problem. The problem is to provide knowledge of a special kind for a special purpose (cf. knowledge management in enterprises). These situations should be defined by Knowledge Organization and then knowledge engineering techniques can be applied in cooperation. On the other hand Knowledge Engineering is demanded for the development of adequate techniques for Knowledge Organization in whatever context if the intention is clearly enough specified. Currently we have the offering of available techniques without knowing how appropriate they are for application problems. E.g. the combination between open and closed techniques is a question for knowledge workers according to its social functionality and desirability. It is up to Knowledge Organization to provide a transfer from one to the other. Information technology (now computer based) is a prerequisite for every information designer but not the only one and not the main focus. To find its role it is necessary to explore the philosophical background for current knowledge intermediation.

REFERENCES[11]

1 Ball, Raffael. (2007) WissKom 2007: Wissenskommunikation der Zukunft. Juelich: Forschungszentrum Juelich. <juwel.fz-juelich.de:8080/dspace/bitstream/2128/2893/1/Ball_2007.Wisskom.pdf>

2 Berlyne Daniel, E. (1967) Arousal and reinforcement. **In**: Levine, David: *Nebraska symposium on motivation*, 1967. Lincoln, Nebraska: University of Nebraska Press, p. 1-116.

3 Bertalanffy, Ludwig von. (1957) Allgemeine Systemtheorie. Wege zu einer Mathesis universalis. **In:** *Deutsche Universitätszeitung*, 5/6: 8-12.

4 Bürdek, B.E. (2005) Design: History, theory, and practice of product design. Boston, MA: Birkhauser-Publishers for Architecture.

5 Castells, Manuel. (2005) The network society: From knowledge to policy. **In**: Castells, Manuel; Cardoso, Gustavo: *The network society: From knowledge to policy*. Washington, DC: Johns Hopkins Center for Transatlantic Relations, p.3-21. <www.umass.edu/digitalcenter/research/pdfs/JF_NetworkSociety.pdf>

6 Castellani, Brian. (2009) Map of complexity science. <http://www.art-sciencefactory.com/complexity-map_feb09.html> (with link to Lucas, Chris 2008: Self-Organizing Systems (SOS) FAQ <http://www.calresco.org/sos/sosfaq.htm>

7 Dahlberg, Ingetraut. (1998). Wissensorganisation. **In**: Schneider, H..J., *Lexikon: Informatik und Datenverarbeitung. Version 4.0*, München: Oldenbourg Verlag.

8 Dahlberg, Ingetraut (2006) Definitionen aus dem Begriffsfeld Wissensorganisation. <http://www.isko-de.org/index.php?id=dahlbergdefinitionen>.

9 Dextre Clarke and Stella, G. (2011) ISO 25964: A standard in support of KOS interoperability. <http://www.iskouk.org/conf2011/mp3/ISKO-UK-2011_StellaDextreClarke.mp3>

10 Dextre, Clarke and Stella, G (2011/2012). ISO 25964: A standard in support of KOS interoperability. Gilchrist, Alan; Vernau, Judi: *Facets of Knowledge Organization*; 2011 Jul 4-2011 Jul 5; London. London: Emerald; 2012. <http://www.iskouk.org/conf2011/papers/dextreclarke.pdf>

11 Hjørland, Birger (1997) Information seeking and subject representation. *An activity-theoretical approach to information science*. Westport & London: Greenwood Press.

12 Hjørland, Birger (2002) Principia informatica. Foundational theory of information and principles of information services. **In**: Bruce, Harry; Fidel, Raya; Ingwersen, Peter; Vakkari, Pertti: *Emerging frameworks and methods. Proceedings of the fourth international conference on conceptions of library and information science (CoLIS4)*. In. Greenwood Village, Colorado, USA: Libraries Unlimited,p. 109-121. <http://www.iva.dk/bh/Core%20Concepts%20in%20LIS/articles%20a-z/principia_informatica.htm>

13 Hjørland, Birger (2013) Theories of knowledge organization — theories of knowledge. *Keynote given at the 13th Meeting of the German ISKO (International Society for Knowledge Organization)*, Potsdam, 19th to 20th March 2013 (will be published in: Knowledge Organization 2013).

11 All Internet links visited April 28th 2012

14 ISKO (1989) International society for knowledge organization (ISKO). Charter and preamble. **In**: *International classification 16-3,* p. 165-167. <http://www.isko.org/charter.pdf>

15 ISO norm 25964 Information and documentation, part 1 and 2 (2011/2013) <http://www.iso.org/iso/home/store/catalogue_tc/catalogue_detail.htm?csnumber=53657 and http://www.iso.org/iso/catalogue_detail.htm?csnumber=53658>

16 Lewin, Kurt. (1935) A dynamic theory of personality. New York: McGraw-Hill.

17 Leontev, Aleksei N. (1978) Activity, consciousness, and personality. Englewood Cliffs, NJ: Prentice-Hall. <http://lchc.ucsd.edu/MCA/Paper/leontev>

18 Miles, Alistair and Bechhofer, Sean. (2008) Simple knowledge organization system: Reference:W3C Working Draft 25 January. <http://www.w3.org/TR/2008/WD-skos-reference-20080125>

19 Montuori, Alfonso. (2004) Edgar Morin: A partial introduction. **In**: *World futures 60,* 5, p.349-355 http://www.ciis.edu/Documents/Academic%20Departments/TID/morin_a_partial_introduction.pdf

20 Morin, Edgar. (2007) Restricted complexity, general complexity. **In**: Gershenson, Carlos; Aerts, Diederik; Edmonds, Bruce: *Worldviews, Science and Us: Philosophy and Complexity. World Scientific* Publishing Co., p. 5-29. <http://cogprints.org/5217/>

21 NKOS (1998) Networked knowledge organization systems (NKOS) Registry. *Reference document for data elements.* <http://nkos.slis.kent.edu/registry3.htm>

22 Ohly, H. Peter. (2008a) Knowledge organization pro and retrospective. **In**: Clement Arsenault and Joseph T. Tennis. *Culture and identity in knowledge organization. Advances in knowledge organization* 11, p. 210-215.

23 Ohly, H. Peter (2008b) The future of knowledge organization in the networked environment. A brief report. *IFLA SET Bulletin*, 9(1): 33-35.

24 Ohly, H. Peter. (2011a) Organization, management and engineering of knowledge. Paper presented at: *Concepts et outils pour le management de la conaissance. 1er colloque international ISKO-Maghreb 2011.* http://www.isko-maghreb.org/index-quick.php?dims_op=doc_file_download&docfile_md5id=0e5b168e52682b12611795598fa2c3db

25 Ohly, H. Peter. (2011b) Information: A Question of Quality? **In**: Haton, Jean-Paul; Sidhom, Sahbi; Ghenima, Malek; Benzakour, Khalid: *Information systems and economic intelligence. Proceedings 4th SIIE'2011*, Marrakech, p. 255-259. (*see also*: **In**: *Scire – Representatión y organización del conocimiento* 17-1, p. 17-21)

26 Quoniam, Luc; Lucien, Arnaud. (2009) Du Web 2.0 à l'Intelligence compétitive 2.0. **In**: Hassoun, Mohamed; El Hachani, Mabrouka: *Intelligence collective et organisation des connaissances*, p. 15-23. <http://www.isko-france.asso.fr/pdf/isko2009/QUONIAM_ARNAUD.pdf>

27 Rayward, W. Boyd. (2010) Organizing and disseminating knowledge: theoretical and instrumental innovations of Paul Otlet. **In**: Gnoli, Claudio; Mazzocci, Fulvio: *Paradigms and conceptual systems in knowledge organization. Advances in knowledge organization 12*. Würzburg: Ergon. p. 14.

28 Rogers, Everett M. (1962) Diffusion of innovations. New York: Free Press.

29 Scott, William E. (1966) Activation theory and task design. **In**: *Organizational behavior and human performance,* 1, p. 3-30.

30 Stempfhuber, Maxmilian. (2007). Heterogeneity and information fusion driven by user. **In** Raghavan, K. S. Ed. *Future of Knowledge Organization in the networked environment*. Indian Statistical Institute Platinum Jubilee Conference Series, p.153-170

31 Trump, Thilo; Klingler, Walter; Gerhards, Maria. (2009) Web 2.0. Begriffsdefinition und eine Analyse der Auswirkungen auf das allgemeine Mediennutzungsverhalten. Köln: Result. <http://www.result.de/wp-content/uploads/2009/10/web-2.0-studie_result_swr_februar_2007.pdf >

32 Wiener, Norbert. (1948) Cybernetics or control and communication in the animal and the machine, Paris: Hermann & Cie Editeurs; New York: John Wiley & Sons, Inc.

33 Zeng, Marcia Lei. (2008) Knowledge organization systems (KOS). **In**: *Knowledge organization*, 35(2/3): 160-182.

10

What does Knowledge Organization mean in a Big Data Environment?

Michael Shepherd** and **Carolyn Watters

Big Data changes the context and functional requirements of knowledge organization. It is necessary to view knowledge organization through the lens of Big Data, in particular, through the dimensions of Volume, Velocity, Variety and Veracity, as well as through the Functional Goals of the user. In this paper, we explore the challenges of knowledge organization in the Big Data Environment and suggest that knowledge organization must evolve to support the integration of structured, semi-structured, and unstructured data (Variety), support real time use of streaming data (Velocity), and provide confidence and support metrics (Veracity), all in the support of the functional goals of the user..

Keywords: Knowledge organization; Big Data; Web Environment; Digital Environment

1 INTRODUCTION

"Big data is a term applied to data sets whose size is beyond the ability of commonly used software tools to capture, manage, and process the data within a tolerable elapsed time." [17] Consequently, Big Data is relative to the capabilities of our tools to manage and process that data. Data sets that we may have considered "big" ten years ago, may no longer be considered "big" as our hardware and software tools to manage and process that data have advanced tremendously in the past ten years.

When we speak of Big Data today, we are typically referring to datasets that are terabytes (10^{12}), petabytes (10^{15}), and larger. We recognize that the amount of data generated is growing exponentially. By some estimates, 90% of all the data in the world has been generated over the last two years [11] and it is estimated that in 2011 alone, 1.8 zettabytes (10^{21}) of data were generated. For instance, Google processes about 24 petabytes of data per day and 100 billion queries per month, high-energy particle accelerators can generate 15 petabytes per year, climate data are measured in petabytes as are ocean studies and health data. The sensors on a jet produce 10 terabytes of data for every 30 minutes of flight [3]. Wal-Mart handles more than one million customer transactions every hour, feeding databases estimated at more than 2.5 petabytes—the equivalent of 167 times the books in America's Library of Congress. Facebook, a social-networking website, is home to 40 billion photos [12].

At the same time the number of both sources of data and access points to data have also grown exponentially as more devices produce data and more people use information in both the work environment and the home environment. As illustrated in Figure 1 [15] the growth in unstructured data is far outstripping the growth in structured data. This growth in unstructured and semi-structured data has implications for Knowledge Organization (KO) as most KO systems have been designed to deal with semi-structured (text) but will have to accommodate unstructured data as from sensors.

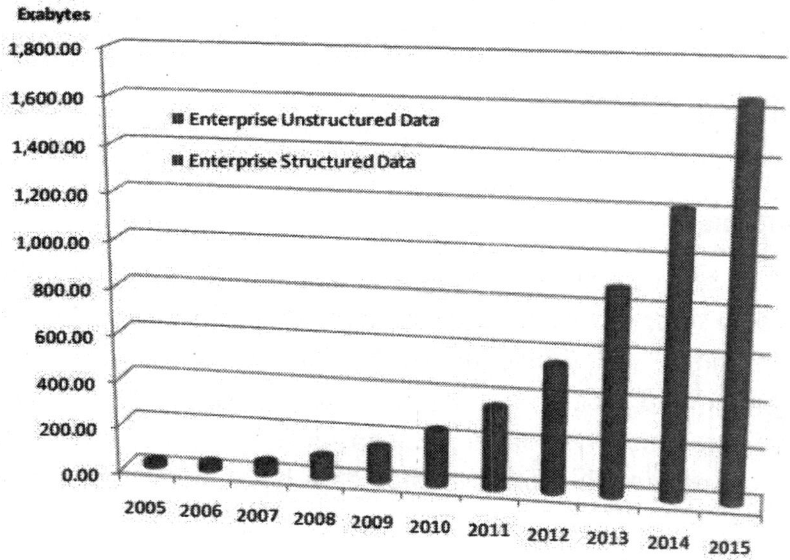

Fig. 1: Total Enterprise Data Growth 2005-2015 [Walker, 2013]

The recognition of the potential impact of Big Data is gaining momentum and is now of major importance in addressing economic, scientific and social problems.

Big Data has real value only when properly analyzed, because it can then yield actionable information and identify patterns that lead to new knowledge and better decision-making. Patterns can be found that would not be readily apparent in smaller datasets. In business, this leads to competitive advantages. In science, this leads to new discoveries. For example, in astronomy, modern space telescopes are producing hundreds of gigabytes of science data every day. Satellite-based remote sensing generates significant amounts of data for monitoring the effects of climate change on vegetation, ice-cover and on tagged animals. Ocean tracking networks monitor the movement of fish stocks and other marine animals. In health, this leads to the acceleration of medical discoveries and better health outcomes. Data-based understanding of the human genome has led to an understanding of rare genetic diseases, and is now engaged in the search to fuel a revolution in personalized medicine. Research in genetics, biology, and computational neuroscience has been making steady progress in understanding brain function. Social media data has changed the landscape for individuals and for large systems to provide business-relevant insights, to detect epidemics early, and to monitor and anticipate social and political change.

The problem we are now faced with is how to manage, organize and interact with this data so that we can harness its potential. What is knowledge organization in a Big Data environment? How can humans and systems exploit the knowledge contained in these huge data sets? Can we extrapolate from our current paradigms or are we on the cusp of a shift in the way we conceptualize and manage KO in this context?

This paper first discusses the characteristics of Big Data in order to frame a discussion of the characteristics of a new generation of knowledge organization fit forthe Big Data environment. We then examine current approaches through the lens of those Big Data characteristics to identify the gaps. Finally we propose criteria to provide guidelines in the development of KO for the world of Big Data.

2 DIMENSIONS OF BIG DATA

Big Data is not just volume or the number of bytes in a dataset. Four dimensions are used to describe these datasets, often referred to as the four Vs. The four "V" dimensions of Big Data are Volume, Velocity, Variety and Veracity [8].

- Volume is the matter of scale, i.e., these data sets are larger than can currently be processed using conventional database systems.
- Velocity is the rate at which data streams arrive for processing. This may be so fast that there is not enough time to capture and manipulate the data in order to make near real-time decisions based on the data stream. Indeed, the data may be getting generated faster than it can be manipulated for real

time or near real time evaluation. Applications in which Velocity is a factor include identifying network attacks, credit card fraud, detection of pathogens in air, health sensors, etc.

- Variety is the reality that data sets are seldom well structured and contain a variety of data types including structured data, such as text and numeric data, and unstructured data such as sensor data, audio, video, and click streams.
- Veracity is the requirement of trust in the data. That is the need to quantify and track uncertainty associated with data that is used to form actionable results. Failure to account for veracity may have serious repercussions. For example, during the recent financial crisis, banks and rating agencies had been relying on models that, although they required a vast amount of information to be fed in, failed to reflect financial risk in the real world [12].

To this list we add the dimension of Functional Goal.Functional Goal is the need to be fit for purpose. That means that the characteristics of a Big Data system must reflect the many uses of that data, either known or as yet unanticipated. Table 1 provides an extracted overview of the range of functional goals associated with Big Data [2].

Table 1: Examples of analytical applications and associated functional goals (IBM)

Functional Goals	Sample Analytical Applications
Prediction	Revenue prediction, Disease spread prediction
Reporting	Financial reporting, Social network analysis
Pattern Matching	Topic/Sentiment analysis. Search, Document management
Recommendation	Customer retention, Music/Video recommendation
Alerting	Fraud detection, Web-traffic analysis, Intrusion detection

Simply put, the problems with Big Data are that it is big and it is complex. It is difficult to capture, store, manage, analyze, and ultimately represent the results of this analysis for human decision-making. Data Analytics is an emerging field of study that brings together tools and techniques to address these data problems in support of evidence-based decision making.

Tools are not enough to leverage the value in these supersized and complex data sets. Knowledge organization structures that accommodate the parameters of the data and the parameters of the functional goals of the users within the domain of application are required.

3 KNOWLEDGE ORGANIZATION

Knowledge Organization (KO) is both theory and practice [16]. While there are many different approaches to the subject, there are two general paradigms: top down and bottom up. The top down approach is based on the *a priori* knowledge of the area of interest. The bottom up approach is based on an acceptance that knowledge and knowledge organization may be extracted and identified *post hoc* from the data itself. Of course, these are not strictly oppositional views and many examples can be seen where the two approaches are complementary. To date most KO systems have adopted pragmatic approaches to organize knowledge in order to make it possible to satisfy defined information needs.

Traditional KO systems are often based on the use of *a priori* lists including free text and/or term lists such as authority lists, glossaries and dictionaries; classifications and categories such as subject headings and classification schemes; and relationship lists such thesauri, semantic networks and ontologies [7]. Even using these basic text based organization tools, there are many different approaches to knowledge organization including prescribed classification schemes, facet-analytical processes, and unstructured information retrieval [6]. Less traditional KO systems use techniques such as data mining and regression analysis, to "discover" rules and relationships *post hoc* as they exist in the data to uncover the structure of the knowledge.

The question being considered in this paper is, "What is Knowledge Organization in a Big Data Environment?" Knowledge Organization and the development of a new generation of Knowledge Organization Systems are critically important in a Big Data environment and will need to combine the best of traditional and less traditional approaches. To explore this question we first review the KO through the dimensions of Big Data introduced earlier.

4 KNOWLEDGE ORGANIZATION AND THE DIMENSIONS OF BIG DATA

By way of examining the issues of knowledge organization in this context, we explore the impact of the four dimensions of Big Data plus the Functional Goal dimension that differentiate the requirements of KO in these environments to get at the complexity of applying current KO structures in the Big Data context.

- *Volume.* One of the purposes of knowledge organization is to organize large volumes of data so that the information needs of the user can be easily satisfied. In Big Data this is an issue of scale of processing, managing, and analysis and is largely a question of software and hardware capability.

- *Velocity*. A differentiating factor for Big Data is the increasing demand for real time and near real time analysis.
- *Variety*. The growth of unstructured and unmanaged data ranging from text to sensors now available for use in decision making also differentiates Big Data.
- *Veracity* is an issue that knowledge organization always dealt with and is accentuated by the increasing difficulty of verifying much of the data available.
- *Functional Goals* and unanticipated use of large data sets made more widely available differentiate the requirements of KO from more traditional uses.

We examine herefour of theapproaches to knowledge organization as suggested by Hjørland [6] in the context of Big Data.

*Traditional approaches.*Classification systems have evolved from those used in libraries (DDC, LCC, etc.) for hundreds of years. The most effective of these have fixed vocabularies and are applied manually. These approaches work well in libraries, including digital libraries, but do not scale well to the very high volumes we are now encountering. To put things in perspective, Wal-Mart databases are 167 times the size of the Library of Congress collection [12].

In terms of volume and velocity, real time and highly dynamic data sets are currently beyond the scope of these techniques to perform within acceptable degrees of precision. Again, to put things in perspective, "the text in all the books in the Library of Congress would fit on a stack of DVDs the height of a single-story house" [3], while "Last year, the world created enough digital data to fill a stack of DVDs that would stretch from Earth to the moon and back" [5].

Classification systems have been developed to reflect the order of knowledge as it is currently recognized rather than as it might be suggested by the incoming data. Yet, the variety of data types in more and more of these data sets are not restricted to structured homogeneous data and do not readily lend themselves to these types of classification systems. Furthermore, more and more data sets contain vast amounts of non-textual data integrated withother types of unstructured data from sensors and weather data to video and social media data. Big Data sets often do have structure, but seldom do they have or use predefined classification structures into which data items can be vetted and fit. Rather the expectations are that the structures emerge and are uncovered through *post hoc* applications of analytics techniques. The veracity of large data sets and the results of the analysis of that data is often unknown and may be, in some case, unknowable. That is, some of the data and knowledge extracted from that data or assignment to KO markers may be totally reliable and totally accurate but this is not a certainty. The functional goals for which traditional approaches have been most successful are search, pattern matching, and recommending.

*The facet-analytical approach.*The faceted approach has been used successfully for library collections and also in non-traditional environments. This approach differs from the traditional classification approach in that it establishes rules for encoding relationships rather than prescriptive categories. This approach has been used in a range of domains for KO including in the design of web-pages [9] and the exchange of web page metadata [4], and in the development of libraries of software for reuse [10]. Perhaps the most relevant feature of the facet-analytical approach in this discussion is its ability to accommodate new knowledge through the combination of existing elements.

Faceted schemes involve a relatively fine-grained analysis of the text that may be problematic at scale and at high rates of data streams. Entity extraction has been used in text analytics applications such as topic and sentiment analysis. This usually involves Natural Language Processing to extract implied relationships from textual data to build facets and instances of schema. To date, little has been done with data other than text although one can certainly imagine combinations of techniques that would include faceted analysis from complementary data sources of different types of data. Faceted techniques support a variety of functional goals including search, pattern matching, prediction, and alerting.

The information retrieval (IR) approach. Information retrieval is the most widely adopted KO for datasets of the size of the current Internet. IR approaches are normally defined by a common goal of selecting documents that the system has deemed to match the expressed need of the user. Internet search engines, such as Google, are the best examples of this approach for big text datasets. The traditional approach to retrieval from a large text corpus is to assign index terms to each item. These index terms may be assigned manually or extracted automatically from the texts. Querying of these text data sets is usually via a query language and the query is executed against the lists of assigned index terms.

Information retrieval is, of course, a core of Big Data analytics, but given such large data sets, expectations have grown and now we expect to be able to uncover structures and patterns in the data that would not normally be found using traditional information retrieval techniques. Such techniques include clustering, discovering networks through hyperlinks and statistical co-occurrence, and the discovery of relationships using association rule mining [1].

Sophisticated indexing techniques have been used to handle the volume of very large textual data sets, such as we find on the web today. The KO structure is largely simply based on the indexing of terms within the text and is relatively light weight. Given expectations on cloud storage capacity this has not, to date, put a practical limit on the size of these datasets.The unstructured and unpredictable nature of the data, the domain independence, and speed of creation and changes in these datasets, however, impose a limit on the practicality of any in-depth analysis of these datasets of the sort that is needed to move beyond simple retrieval of chunks of text into the useful extraction of chunks of knowledge for the user. More problematic is the dramatic shift of the creation of the types of data from predominantly text or numeric to data from sensors, video capture, audio files, and noise data. IR techniques especially at scale have had little success outside of textual datasets. The reliability and credibility of data returned in response to a user query rests on the ability of the user to have trust in the data source. As we move from document or web site retrieval to responses that are more than simple extraction identifying credibility becomes problematic. The functional goals of IR systems remain largely search, reporting, and recommending.

User-oriented view approach. While the overall goal of knowledge organization is to satisfy the user's information need, current approaches largely exclude the user, especially for very large very complex datasets. However, there have been approaches that leverage the KO of the user with the knowledge organization system of the data. These approaches include user feedback for re-ranking of results and for query modification, incorporating user profiles into the process itself and, more recently the development of folksonomies that are user developed classification systems based on user assigned tags.

Visual Analytics is a user-oriented view approach that connects the human with the data [14] by providing tools and techniques that support people in synthesizing information and deriving insight from "massive, dynamic, ambiguous, and often conflicting data; detect the expected and discover the unexpected; provide timely, defensible and understandable assessments, and communicate assessment effectively for action" [13]. The key to this approach is that the user is seen as a vital part of the system. The human capacity for finding patterns and insight from presentations of data and organizational representations of data is leveraged to optimize the impact of the algorithmic underpinnings of these systems. This approach uses the knowledge of the user to examine and explore the data and relationships visually, often allowing the user to manipulate the visualization by changing parameters in real time.

User-oriented visualization provides *post hoc* analysis of large data sets. The goal of these systems is to reduce the complexity of the dataset. This allows maximal flexibility in the organization and presentation to the user. Thus, very large datasets can be managed by the users. By including the capabilities of the user in the KO through interaction and manipulation of the data presentation, patterns and structures can be detected real time.Visualization also allows the presentation of parallel views of different types of data, much like multimedia streaming does for video and music editing. By incorporating the knowledge of the user and the ability of users to derive insight from patterns in data, these approaches expand the functional capabilities of KO systems into areas of prescription, prediction, and quantitative analysis.

Figure 2[1] is an example of a user-oriented visualization. In this instance, the user has been able to overlay sea surface temperature data with leatherback turtle migration data and manipulated the data dynamically through to discover the relationships over time.

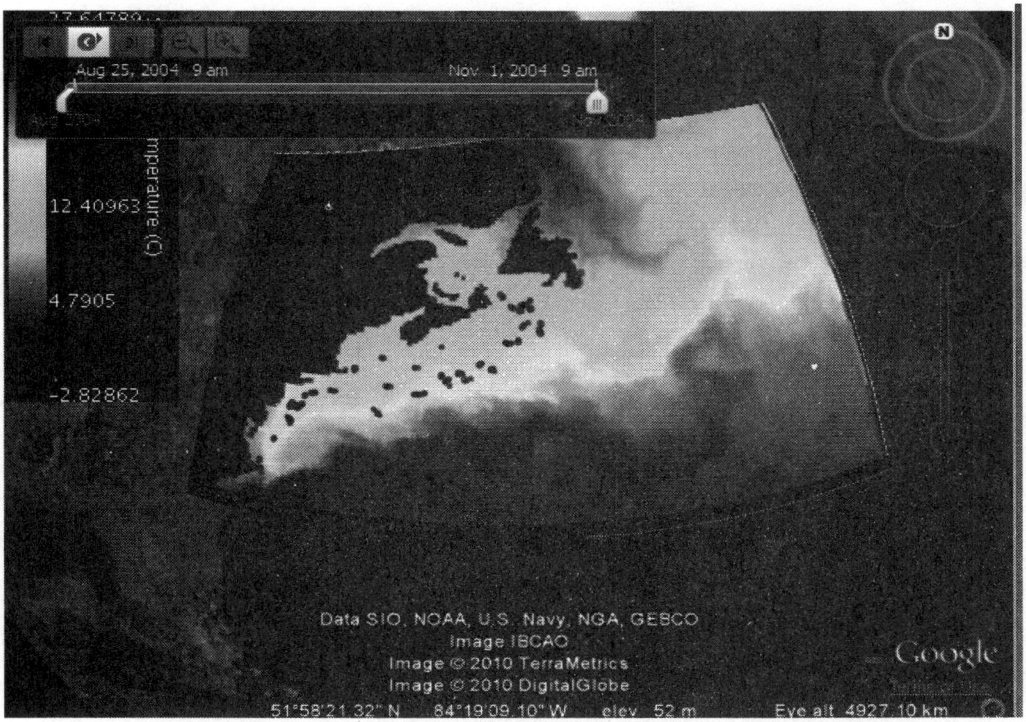

Fig 2: Leatherback Turtle Migration and Sea Surface Temperature

[1] Courtesy of S.S.R. Abidi. Platform for Ocean Knowledge Management. Dalhousie University

The goal of knowledge organization is to facilitate the information need of the user. This simple statement is, as we know, quite complex. Table 2 maps the functional goals to knowledge organization in the context of big data.

Table 2: Functional Goals and Knowledge Organization

Functional Goal	Example Application	Knowledge Organization
Prediction	Epidemics	Classification, visualization
Reporting	Social Networks	Entity Extraction, facets
Pattern Matching	Document retrieval	Classification, faceted, IR
	Topic/Sentiment Analysis	Entity extraction
Recommendation	Customer Retention	User profiles, association mining
	Product Recommendation	User profiles, association mining
Alert	Intrusion Detection	Classification
	Fraud detection	User profiles, classification
	Web-traffic analysis	Classification

5 EVOLUTION OF KNOWLEDGE ORGANIZATION IN A WORLD OF BIG DATA

Just as the model of KO has evolved from the organization of sets of books to the organization of documents on the Web to extraction of found knowledge by data mining, the requirements of KO systems to cope with the dimensions of big data indicate that a new generation of KO systems is needed. Perhaps, rather than trying to manipulate existing knowledge organization models and approaches for the new reality of huge unstructured and heterogeneous real time data sets and unknown user needs, we should redefine knowledge organization for the exploding context of data analytics for Big Data. The goal, to satisfy the information need of the user, is not changed rather the characteristics of the data and knowledge organization are changing.

We can begin to take a broader view of what we mean by functional goals. Just as we have moved from mass production of goods to mass customization of the production of goods, so have we moved from the one size fits all retrieval engine to the extraction of information that is highly dependent on the user and the user's task. These tasks are addressed by the functional goals of the analytical applications of Table 2.

We have looked at knowledge organization for Big Data through the lens of the four V's and these functional goals. In particular, we focussed on variety, velocity and functional goals, largely because volume is a given and veracity is a very hard dimension to tackle as a general proposition.

Traditional Knowledge Organization systems, which function well for repository data, do not operate well in the case of streaming text data. For instance, information retrieval on unindexed streaming text is less effective at scale than is the same query processed against an indexed data store. This is largely because in the case of streaming data, the data is processed against the query while in traditional retrieval the query is processed against the stored data. If the streaming paradigm becomes complicated, such as looking for network attacks or fraudulent transactions, then it becomes a different type of pattern recognition problem, usually implemented through a machine learning approach. In this instance, the knowledge organization system must "learn" what legal patterns look like and then identify patterns that cannot be classified as legal. Similarly when datasets have multiple types of data components, the KO system must incorporate multiple extraction techniques and learn to recognize new knowledge structures.

Sensor data is even more difficult to deal with as it is streaming at us virtually non-stop. Whether it is sensor data from satellites monitoring space, ocean tracking sensors, or sensors tracking air quality, it is streaming fast and we have to be able to make decisions. We have to be able to categorize it on the fly, and this usually means a machine learning-based application.

Veracity is a difficult dimension for KO systems. Perhaps techniques can be borrowed from approaches such as association rule mining. In this approach, given a set of terms, the analysis searches for other terms that do not appear in the original set of terms but do appear frequently with subsets of the original terms. An "association" between the original terms and the discovered terms and the confidence and support for this association may be calculated statistically [1].

In summary, characteristics can be identified that differentiate KO for Big Data contexts from the current state of KO. We propose the following guidelines for the development of a framework for Next Generation Knowledge Organization for this environment. We propose that Knowledge Organization should:

- Support the integration of structured, semi-structured, and unstructured data (Variety);
- Support real time use of streaming data (Velocity); and
- Provide confidence and support metrics (Veracity).

all in the context of the functional goals of the user. Big Data is relative. It is only "Big" when it is beyond our current capabilities to manage the data. Nonetheless, it raises challenges for Knowledge Organization now and in the future.

REFERENCES

1 Agrawal, R.; Imielinski, T. and Swami, A. (1993) Mining Associations between Sets of Items in Massive Databases, Proc. of the ACM-SIGMOD 1993, *Int'l Conference on Management of Data*, Washington D.C.

2 Bordawekar, Rajesh; Blainey, Bob and Apte, Chidanand. (2012) Analyzing analytics. *IBM Research Report*. RC25317 (WAT1209-067) 22.

3 Connor, Marcia. (2012) Data on big Data. http://marciaconner.com/blog/data-on-big-data/. 18.

4 Dijck, Peter Van. (2003) Introduction to XFML.http://www.xml.com/pub/a/2003/01/22/xfml.html.

5 Golub, Ben. (2011) Storage in a Big Data World. http://blogs.computerworld.com/18351/a_stack_of_dvds_to_the_moon_and_back.

6 Hjørland, Birger. (2008) What is Knowledge Organization (KO)? Knowledge Organization. *International Journal devoted to Concept Theory, Classification, Indexing and Knowledge Representation,* 35(2/3): 86-101.

7 Hodge, Gail. (2000) Systems of Knowledge Organization for Digital Libraries: Beyond Traditional Authority Files. *The Digital Library Federation*.

8 IBM. (2013) http://www.ibmbigdatahub.com/infographic/four-vs-big-data. Accessed 29, September, 2013.

9 La Barre, Kathryn. (2006) The use of faceted analytico-synthetic theory as revealed in the practice of website construction and design. Ph.D.-dissertation submitted at the school of LIS at Indiana University.June.

10 Prieto-Diaz, R. (1990) Implementing faceted classification for software reuse. 12th International Conference on Software Engineering.

11 Science Dailey. (2013) Big Data, for Better or Worse: 90% of World's Data Generated over Last Two Years. http://www.sciencedaily.com/releases/2013/05/130522085217.htm.

12 The Economist. (2010) Data, Data, Everywhere.http://www.economist.com/node/15557443. 25, February, 2010.

13 Thomas, J James and Cook, A Kristin. (2006) A Visual Analytics Agenda. *IEEE Computer Graphics and Applications*, 26(1): 10-13.

14 Thomas, J.J. and Cook, K.A. eds., (2005) Illuminating the Path: The Research and Development Agenda for Visual Analytics, IEEE CS Press.

15 Walker, Michael. (2013) Structured vs. Unstructured Data: The Rise of Data Anarchy. [http://www.datasciencecentral.com/profiles/blogs/structured-vs-unstructured-data-the-rise-of-data-anarchy]. Accessed 29, September 2013.

16 White, Hollie. (2011) Theories of Knowledge Organization Literature Review Chapter. [http://sites.duke.edu/holliewhite/files/2011/10/Theory-of-Knowledge-Organization-lit-review-Mar-2010.pdf] 2011

17 Wikipedia. (2013) [http://en.wikipedia.org/wiki/Cloud_computing] Accessed 29, September 2013.

11

Supporting Multiple Points of View in Knowledge Organization

Kavi Mahesh and ***Pallavi Karanth***

Knowledge organization schemes typically assume a single point of view and a consequent single scheme of classification and a single set of categories with "standard" definitions and conceptual relationships. The real world, on the other hand, is full of multiple points of view that result in different conceptualizations and categories which are incompatible with each other. This article attempts to formulate the present lack of support for multiple points of view as a formal problem in ontological modeling and proposes a solution that enables multiple, incompatible views of the world to co-exist in a single KO scheme. Although a particular view in such a KO scheme is likely to be inconsistent with other views within the same scheme, the solution guarantees that each view presents a consistent conceptualization of the world or domain being organized. The proposed solution is expected to be of significant practical value in supporting multiple conceptualizations resulting from cultural, historical, philosophical, linguistic and political differences. This article also examines the gaps in current standards such as OWL and proposes an extension to OWL to enable multiple points of view.

Keywords: Knowledge organization; Ontology; OWL; Multiple conceptualization

1 WHY SUPPORT MULTIPLE POINTS OF VIEW

Knowledge organization schemes – including classification schemes, standards, tools and technologies – typically assume that the community of members or, mankind in general, has a single point of view. As a consequence, they support a single scheme of classification and a single set of categories with "standard" definitions and conceptual relationships. The real world, on the other hand, is full of multiple points of view that result in different conceptualizations and categories which are incompatible with each other. The current state of the art either prevents the community of users from developing an ontology, thesaurus, taxonomy or other scheme of knowledge organization that is acceptable to all members, or forces some of the members to accept the points of view of others.

Multiple points of view (POV) can arise from cultural, historical, philosophical, linguistic and political differences. Moreover, new categories may be introduced over time or even existing instances may change their membership in categories. For example, *Pluto,* which was considered a *planet* till recently is no longer a member of that category. Rather, it is considered a *dwarf planet.* In other cases, the subcategories of a category may vary in different points of view. For example, while the term *agriculture* includes *animal husbandry* and even *fisheries* in the Western view of the world (which is "standardized" in Wikipedia, for instance), it refers only to the growing of plants in India and many other parts of the world. This is evidenced not only from common usage of the term but also from how the term is translated in Indian languages and, more importantly, the governance structure of both state and central governments of India where *animal husbandry* and *fisheries* departments are not under the department of *agriculture* [5,13].

Multiple points of view and the current lack of support for representing and managing them can also have business implications. For example, the concept of *vegetarianism* has several points of view which could result in significant confusion and customer dissatisfaction in handling requests for special meals in the airline industry, apart from conflicts in cultural practices and religious beliefs in the society at large. Airlines nowadays offer long menus of special meals and passengers often have to learn unfamiliar terminology such as *OvoLacto* to decide which meal to get.

This article attempts to formulate the present lack of support for multiple points of view as a formal problem in ontological modeling and proposes a more democratic solution that enables multiple, incompatible views of the world to co-exist in a single knowledge organization (KO) scheme. Although a particular view in such a KO scheme is likely to be inconsistent with other views within the same scheme, the solution guarantees that each view can present a consistent conceptualization of the world or domain being organized. The article also examines the gaps in current standards such as OWL [14,2,9] and proposes an extension to OWL to enable multiple points of view. The proposed solution is expected to be of significant practical value in supporting multiple conceptualizations in KO schemes with minimal changes to existing practices, standards, tools and technologies.

2 MULTIPLE POINTS OF VIEW: CONFIGURATIONS

In order to analyze what is possible in current KO schemes and technologies, let us consider several different configurations in classification schemes in which multiple points of view can occur. The simplest configuration is one where the same instance is a member of different categories in different views. For example, gravitational objects in the solar system are classified as *star, planet, dwarf planet* and *satellite.* Here, *Pluto* has been classified as both a *planet* and a *dwarf planet* in different periods of scientific observation. From 1854 to 1930 and 2006 to the present, *Pluto* is not classified as a *planet.* Only between 1930 and 2006, *Pluto* was considered a *planet.* From 2006 onwards, *Pluto* has been classified as a *dwarf planet.* Nevertheless, multiple points of view of this kind can be handled by having separate versions of the KO scheme for different periods of time. In any case the terminology (T-Box [9]) is common to all the points of view since *Pluto* is an instance (or individual) and its membership in a category (i.e., rdf:type) such as *planet* or *dwarf planet* is an assertion (A-Box). The only representation that is not acceptable is the one where *Pluto* is simultaneously an instance of both *planet* and *dwarf planet* since those two categories are mutually disjoint. Figure 1 shows the two different points of view on what *Pluto* is.

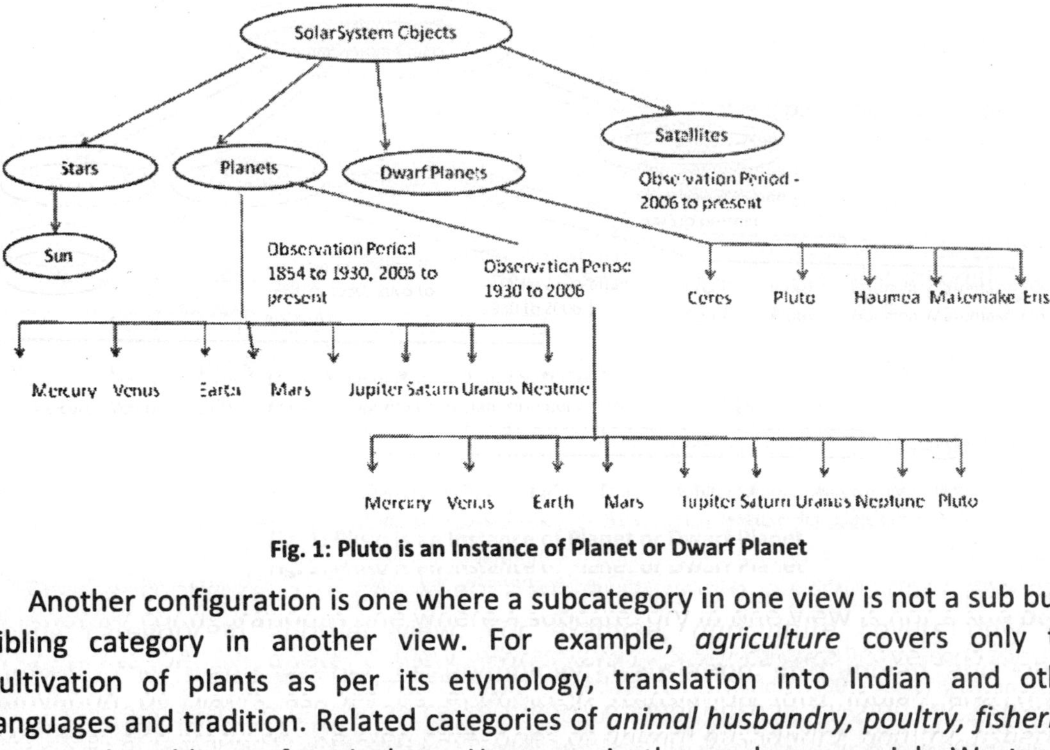

Fig. 1: Pluto is an Instance of Planet or Dwarf Planet

Another configuration is one where a subcategory in one view is not a sub but a sibling category in another view. For example, *agriculture* covers only the cultivation of plants as per its etymology, translation into Indian and other languages and tradition. Related categories of *animal husbandry, poultry, fisheries,* etc. can be siblings of *agriculture.* However, in the modern – mainly Western – point of view, *animal husbandry* and *fisheries* are included as sub-categories of *agriculture.* It is important to support both points of view not only to accommodate the social, cultural and religious implications of each configuration, but also for more practical reasons such as the structure of governance of corresponding departments in a state or nation. For example, in both Union Government of India and the state of Karnataka, the Departments of *Animal Husbandry* and *Fisheries* are not under the Department of *Agriculture* [5,13]. Figure 2 shows the two different configurations of *agriculture* and related categories. Similar configurations may arise where the alternative positions of the categories in different views may appear to be farther apart (i.e., as "cousins" or "nephews") but the situation is not really more complex.

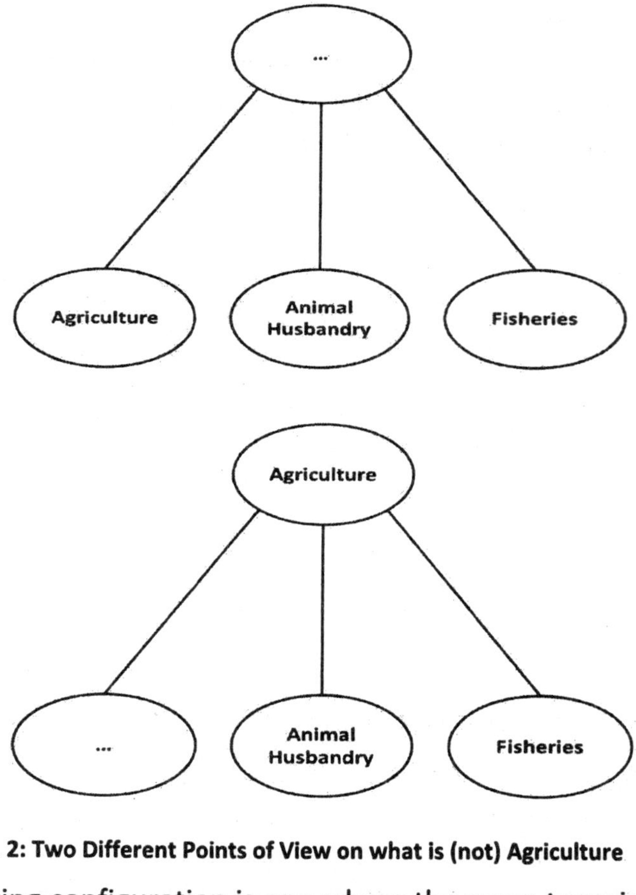

Fig. 2: Two Different Points of View on what is (not) Agriculture

A more challenging configuration is one where the same term is conceptualized in different ways in different points of view. For example, consider representing different conceptualizations of the concept of *vegetarianism*. Figure 3 shows a diagram where six different conceptualizations of *vegetarianism* are shown as subcategories of a broad category labeled *vegetarian.* There are several problems with this solution:

- the parent *vegetarian* concept is a dummy; no individual wants to be its member;
- believers of any one kind of *vegetarianism* will not accept some of the other kinds as *vegetarians;* and
- members do not like the technical-sounding long names for their own categories; they all want their conceptualization to be called *vegetarian.*

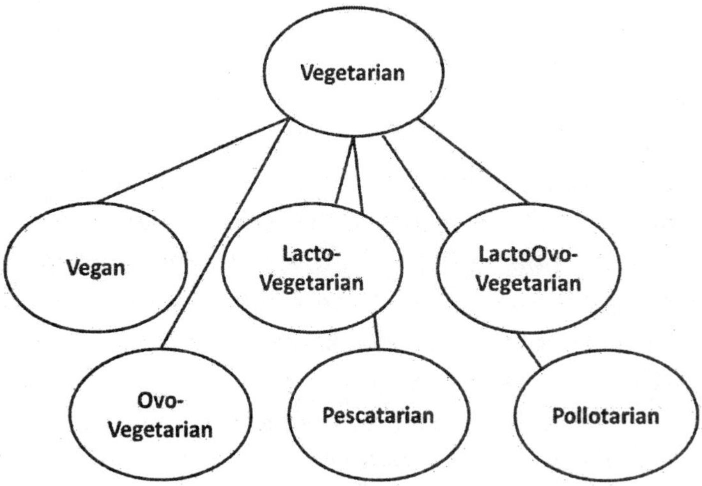

Fig. 3: Multiple Points of View of the Concept of Vegetarian

In order to analyze how the semantics of the six types of *vegetarianism* differ from each other, let us examine their representation in the Web Ontology Language – OWL – a recommendation of the World Wide Web Consortium [14,2,9]. Any knowledge representation mechanism would require precise semantics in order to be manipulated by a machine. OWL ontologies provide for exploiting precise semantics and delegating inferences to programs known as reasoners [9]. Knowledge Representation languages such as OWL are expressive enough to represent various KO scenarios in a variety of domains.

Each of the six subcategories of *vegetarian* are defined in OWL using an *objectProperty* called *eats* which has *person* as its domain and *food* as its range. The following snippet shows how the *Vegan* class is defined as a subclass of *vegetarian* and also of the class of entities that *eat* only *plant products:*

```
<Class rdf:about="#Vegan">
  <rdfs:subClassOf rdf:resource="#vegetarian"/>
  <rdfs:subClassOf>
    <Restriction> <onProperty rdf:resource="#eats"/>
      <allValuesFrom rdf:resource="#plantProducts"/>
    </Restriction>
  </rdfs:subClassOf>
</Class>
```

Before concluding that the present form of the OWL language does not allow us to represent together multiple incompatible conceptualizations of *vegetarianism* that is acceptable to members of each kind, let us explore alternative constructs in the OWL standard to see if they meet the requirements of the present example. Can each kind of *vegetarianism* be represented in a separate version of the OWL ontology? Although OWL clearly supports multiple versions of ontology files, such a solution does not allow us to represent multiple points of view together in a single ontology. It is adequate only where different points of view are held by completely disjoint communities with no useful interaction among them. Nor is it adequate to simply have an undefined term such as *vegetarian* with no semantics; such a solution does not support even the most basic requirement of automatically classifying individuals into one of the categories arising from a particular point of view.

Multiple inheritance is also not a solution, even if it is used with non-monotonic inheritance [1]. Such a scheme is suitable only where multiple points of view are in fact compatible, at least partially. For example, *platypus* is classified as a *mammal* due to its body fur and its ability to feed young ones with its milk, as a *reptile* because of its looks and its venom, and as a *bird* as it lays eggs and has duck like feet. Since it is all these at all times, multiple inheritance is the right solution. If some of the properties of *reptiles, mammals* or *birds* are not applicable to *platypus,* they can be blocked or overridden through non-monotonic inheritance. Figure 4 depicts *platypus* and its multiple inheritance.

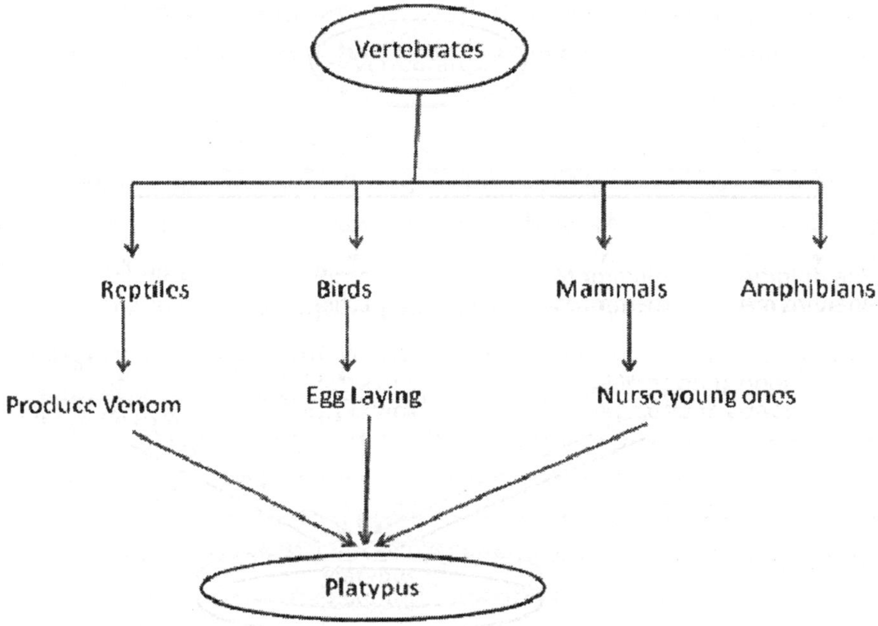

Fig. 4: Multiple Inheritance but a Single Point of View for Platypus

3 RELATED APPROACHES

The field of Ontological Engineering provides a technique known as Ontological Design Patterns (ODP) [3] which enables efficient solutions to certain problems that arise when building ontologies. There are several types of Ontological Design Patterns grouped into various families [6]. However, the varieties of design pattern types that have been developed were found to be inadequate for the present purpose of representing multiple incompatible points of view. Notable among ODPs is Context Slices which provides a solution for encoding of binary relations which hold only in a certain context. Here, it provides an alternative approach to reifying the relations holding in some context, thereby retaining the expressivity of the language in representing transitivity of a binary relation. Context Slices refers mainly to binary relations in a context and does not apply to our requirement of also reifying "is-a" relations.

Another Ontology Design Pattern known as Normalization pattern is applicable where there are a number of super classes resulting in a poly hierarchy which can be untangled by defining each subsumption relation as a restriction rather than a class-subclass hierarchy. Normalization is applicable to cases of multiple inheritance where an entity clearly belongs to multiple parent classes at the same time (or in the same point of view, as in the platypus example above) without any disagreement or incompatibility.

View Inheritance pattern is an Ontological Design Pattern which also deals with multiple inheritance cases where the classes involved in inheritance can be subclasses of either the same or different abstraction criteria. However, in such a configuration, there is no ambiguity when it comes to the type of an entity as the classes involved in inheritance are not mutually disjoint.

Ontology Views is a project undertaken at Structural Informatics Group of University of Washington [7], where queries are executed over reference ontologies to generate application specific ontologies. Ontology Views are very much similar to relational database views where queries are executed over the database tables to extract a portion of database instances to generate a conceptual table. A complementary way of defining views on ontology has been suggested in a paper where a central concept is chosen from which relationships are traversed to include other concepts in the view which is known as a Traversal View [4]. Ontology Views differ from our problem scenario in that views are defined to extract portions of the ontology specific to particular needs of applications where the reference ontology is completely consistent without any disagreement or ambiguity on the type of any entity.

Inconsistency in ontologies is fairly common in cases where an ontology is built by merging from different sources created by different authors. A framework for reasoning with inconsistent ontologies has been presented in another paper [15]. An inconsistency reasoner chooses a selection function in order to reason with an inconsistent ontology. The selection function determines which consistent subsets of the inconsistent ontology are to be considered for the purpose of reasoning. Selection functions can be based either on syntactic relevance or semantic relevance and are specific to individual queries.

It must also be noted here that Resource Description Framework (RDF) [11] provides a framework to assert anything about the world. Although it provides a very simple way to model information, it does not prevent anyone from making assertions which may be inconsistent with other assertions. RDF provides a construct rdf:Alt which allows alternative values for property assertion. However, RDF operates at a more primitive level where precise semantics cannot be expressed to serve the purposes of supporting multiple points of view about various semantic categories. We need the more expressive constructs in OWL to address our concern of supporting different conceptualizations of the world to exist in a single KO scheme.

Similarly, the Simple Knowledge Organization System (SKOS) [12] as an application of RDF allows us to model thesauri, taxonomies and terminologies. It is not expressive enough to capture richness and subtleties of the commonalities and distinctions between different points of view about a concept such as vegetarianism. We can only model broader, narrower and related term relations in SKOS. One feature of SKOS that deserves a mention is Concept Schemes which allow us to represent concepts belonging to various (sub)domains as multiple vocabularies within a single KO scheme. However, this too is inadequate to address the current problem of representing multiple views for concepts in a single KO scheme.

4 EXTENDING OWL TO SUPPORT MULTIPLE POV

We propose to extend the current Web Ontology Language (OWL or OWL-2) to support multiple points of view. It must be emphasized here that an extension is necessary since none of the available constructs support the representation of multiple points of view. Further, there cannot be multiple OWL classes (i.e., concepts or categories) in a single ontology all of which have the same name.

We first present the extended syntax and then the semantics of the new construct. This extension becomes usable when the straightforward changes suggested below are implemented in any of the tools and technologies used for editing, managing with reasoning with the OWL ontologies.

4.1 Additional Syntax

A new XML attribute called POV is proposed for all constructs of the OWL language except those that declare a class or property. In addition, a built-in class called POV (which is a subclass of the universal class *owl:Thing*) is introduced. The value of the POV attribute can be any individual of the POV class. For short hand, multiple comma-separated values can be specified if the particular construct applies to more than one point of view. The POV class is a mere placeholder and is not expected to be extended or specialized in nontrivial ways.

For example, six instances of the POV class are created to represent the six different conceptualizations of *vegetarian* shown in Fig. 3: *VeganPOV, LactoPOV, LactOvoPOV, OvoPOV, PescatarianPOV* and *PollotarianPOV.* These are now used to constrain the *eats* property of each point of view of *vegetarian* as shown in the following sample snippet:

```
<Class rdf:about="#vegetarian">
  <rdfs:subClassOf rdf:resource="#person"/>
  <rdfs:subClassOf POV="#LactoPOV">
    <Restriction> <onProperty rdf:resource="#eats"/>
      <allValuesFrom>
        <Class> <unionOf rdf:parseType="Collection">
            <rdf:Description rdf:about="#dairyProducts"/>
            <rdf:Description rdf:about="#plantProducts"/>
          </unionOf>
        </Class> </allValuesFrom> </Restriction>
  </rdfs:subClassOf>
  <rdfs:subClassOf POV="#VeganPOV">
    <Restriction> <onProperty rdf:resource="#eats"/>
      <allValuesFrom rdf:resource="#plantProducts"/>
    </Restriction>
  </rdfs:subClassOf>
</Class>
```

In this OWL representation, the class *vegetarian* is defined as a subclass of *person* irrespective of any point of view since no POV attribute is mentioned. In the *LactoPOV* point of view which is indicated for the next *subclassOf* relation, *lacto-vegetarians* are defined as those who *eat* only *plant* or *dairy products.* Within the same *vegetarian* class, another point of view *VeganPOV* is defined by qualifying the next conjunctive *subclassOf* relation with a *POV="#VeganPOV"* attribute wherein *vegetarians* can only *eat plant products.*

A POV attribute mentioned in an element applies to all descendant elements. For example, there is no need to mention the POV attribute in the embedded elements such as *Restriction, onProperty* or *allValuesFrom.*

The POV attribute can be applied to all constructs of OWL including:

- *objectProperty* range constraints used to define classes using *subClassOf* or *EquivalentClass* expressions that use *someValuesFrom, allValuesFrom* or *hasValue;*
- *datatypeProperty* range constraints used to define classes (e.g., in POV *"low calorie"* may mean calories less than 800 and in another POV 600);
- cardinality constraints on property values using *minCardinality, maxCardinality* and exact *cardinality;*
- axioms of equivalence, disjointness, etc.;
- property domain definitions;
- property range definitions; and
- *rdf:type* or other equivalent constructs for declaring the class to which an individual belongs.

However, the POV attribute cannot occur in class and property declarations (although they can occur within them in other constructs as seen in the vegetarian example above).

4.2 Semantics

The ontology as shown above with the POV attribute will lead to undesirable results if used under the current semantics of the OWL language. For example, the entire *vegetarian* concept with its multiple POV-specific *subclassOf* constraints is reduced to just the *vegan* concept since that has the strongest restriction on what can be eaten. Further, present day tools such as the Protégé ontology editor [10] ignore and in fact erase all the POV attributes when the ontology is saved in a file.

We propose a simple pre-processor mechanism for a multiple-POV OWL ontology that works as follows. Given a POV and an ontology, it filters all parts of the ontology that have a mismatched POV attribute value. That is, any element without a POV attribute is retained and all elements with a matching POV attribute value are also retained. All other elements of the ontology are filtered out. The semantics of the filtered OWL ontology is the same as the standard semantics of

OWL or OWL-2. Thus, POV extension can also be applied to all the dialects of OWL – Lite, DL and Full – as well as all profiles of OWL-2 such as the EL, QL and RL [8].

No change is needed for reasoners or any other tools in this simple extension to OWL as long as the preprocessor is first applied to the ontology. However, if reasoning with multiple POVs is desired, the reasoner must be extended to maintain multiple concurrent definitions of the affected classes. This can be accomplished by hyphenating class names with the value of the POV attribute. The reasoner must take care to append an appropriate POV name whenever a class is referred without any specific POV. For example, there is no longer a class called *vegetarian;* there are instead six different definitions of it which can be maintained internally by the reasoner with names such as *vegetarian-VeganPOV, vegetarian-LactoPOV,* and so on. As far as the users of the KO scheme are concerned, they all see each of the points of view simply as *vegetarian.*

5 CONCLUSION AND FURTHER WORK

In this article, we have presented a simple extension to the OWL language that enables multiple incompatible points of view to be represented and managed in ontologies and other knowledge organization schemes. The proposed solution is expected to go a long way in bringing greater democracy into the way in which categories are defined and used in a variety of systems across the globe. Diverse view points and opinions held by various communities can now be accommodated in a single knowledge organization scheme without imposing any one's view on others, while still allowing deep and precise representation of the semantics of each category in each point of view (as opposed to just terminological labels). This new capability is expected to be a key enabler in supporting globalization in general and global e-commerce and e-governance in particular by including all communities of users and their various points of view.

In our future work, we plan to first develop the formal semantics of the proposed extension using the approach of model-theoretic semantics [9] applied to the family of description logic languages. This is important to figure out the various implications of the proposed extension. For instance, it is not possible to declare that two points of view are the same using *owl:sameAs* or *owl:equivalentClass,* although a reasoner should be able to infer the equivalence of two or more points of view.

We also plan to develop plug-ins and extension to popular open-source editing and browsing tools for ontologies, reasoners and application programming interfaces to encourage widespread use of multiple points of view in representing and managing knowledge organization schemes. We also plan to use the POV extension to implement the capability of personalizing a KO scheme with one's own idiosyncratic points of view without affecting the overall function of the scheme. This may eventually support the idea of "each user, his own categories."

6 ACKNOWLEDGEMENTS

This work is supported in part by the World Bank/Government of India research grant under the TEQIP programme (subcomponent 1.2.1) to the Centre for Knowledge Analytics and Ontological Engineering (KAnOE) at PES Institute of Technology, Bangalore, India.

REFERENCES

1 David, S.; Touretzky, John F. and Horty, Richmond H. Thomason. (1987) A Clash of Instuitions: The Current State of Nonmonotonic Multiple Inheritance Systems. **In** *Proceedings of International Joint Conferences on Artificial Intelligence*, 1: 476.

2 Dean Allemang and James Hendler. (2011) Semantic Web for the Working Ontologist, 2nd edition, Morgan Kaufmann.

3 Mikel Egana Aranguren. (2009) Role and Application of Ontology Design Patterns in Bio-Ontologies, Thesis submitted to Manchester University.

4 Natalya, F. Noy and Mark, A. Musen. (2004) Specifying Ontology Views by Traversal, **In** *Proceedings of International Semantic Web Conference - 2004*, LNCS 3298, p. 713-725, 2004.

5 Official Website of Government of Karnataka – List of Departments, http://www.karunadu.gov.in/pages/departments.aspx

6 Ontology Design Patterns. http://www.ontologydesignpatterns.org

7 Ontology Views Project. Structural Informatics Group, University of Washington, http://sig.biostr.washington.edu/projects/ontviews/

8 OWL2 Web Ontology Language Profiles. W3C Recommendation, www.w3.org/TR/owl2-profiles/

9 Pascal Hitzler; Markus Krotzsch and Sebastian Rudolph. (2010) Foundations of Semantic Web Technologies, CRC Press.

10 Protégé, Open Source Ontology Editor and Knowledge-Base Framework, Stanford University, http://protege.stanford.edu/

11 Resource Description Framework. W3C Recommendation, www.w3.org/RDF/

12 Simple Knowledge Organization System Primer. http://www.w3.org/TR/2009/ NOTE-skos-primer-20090818/

13 Union Government Departments, Government of India, http://goidirectory.gov.in/ union_organisation.php?ct=E003

14 Web Ontology Language. W3C Recommendation, www.w3.org/2004/OWL/

15 Zhisheng, Huang; Frank, van Harmelen and Annette, ten Teije. (2006) Reasoning With Inconsistent Ontologies: Framework, Prototype and Experiment, *Chapter 5, Semantic Web Technologies: Trends and Research in Ontology-based Systems*, John Wiley and Sons, 2006.

12

Discovery and Access Systems: Discussion of Value added dimensions using Twitter

Hemalata Iyer and ***Amber J. D'Ambrosio***

The use of hashtags in Twitter closely resembles the use of controlled vocabulary in online library catalogs. This natural link between this micro-blogging tool and library catalogs offers an opportunity to consider how Twitter and its accompanying hashtags can contribute to innovations in the 21st century library catalog. One of the most important aspects of libraries as physical places is their role as social spaces, a role they have yet to successfully fulfill in their online presence. Incorporating social media tools such as Twitter into library catalogs offers a venue for conversation and interaction to simulate the experience of users present in physical library spaces. Twitter's hashtags offer a means of aggregating conversations and information on topics from the catalog, librarians and users and facilitating the growth of online communities. The benefits of integrating Twitter into the online library catalog can be viewed from the framework of the Eisenberg-Dirk modification of Taylor's value-added model, which acknowledges the developing interactivity of information systems. Additional insight is possible by using the Chang Iyer morphological box of Twitter application, which is based on Ames and Newman's taxonomy of tagging motivations, to analyze possible value-added attributes of each interface feature].

Keywords: Online catalogues; OPAC; Next generation Catalogues; Twitter

As libraries face the challenge of remaining relevant in a world dominated by Google and the Internet, one of the richest resources of the library, the catalog, faces the greatest struggle. Many library catalogs still display records in a way that resembles the now largely defunct card catalog and require significant navigation to find relevant information about a resource. For millions of users now familiar with the instant gratification of keyword searching online, library catalogs seem slow, unwieldy, contain unfamiliar terminology and little interactivity. However, the design of online catalogs has been shifting over the last few years. Both the proprietary and the open source fields provide libraries with the opportunity to overlay Web 2.0-rich interfaces onto their online public access catalogs, allowing users to interact with the catalog and making it more dynamic as a result. Web 2.0 extends libraries' reach to the users and creates new channels to connect with the user and community. People turn to each other for help with information needs and libraries need to figure out how to become part of those conversations [12]. Web 2.0 offers the best opportunity for libraries to know that those conversations are taking place and contribute positively to them.

The reason for incorporating Web 2.0 technology goes beyond it being the latest and greatest in a long line of technological innovations. The strength of Web 2.0 is its ability to simulate, and stimulate, social interactions online. LibraryThing stands as a kind of popular online catalog because it is almost purely interactive and dynamic, allowing users to catalog their own personal libraries and identify overlaps with their friends among the many other features. The library world has made a move toward this type of next generation catalog, though by their very nature library catalogs will never be as fluid as the primarily user-created content of LibraryThing. Even without reaching that level of user-centered dynamism, Web 2.0 features add many attractive facets to library catalogs. WorldCat.org has incorporated many interactive social features into its worldwide union catalog. WorldCat now has features like personal profiles where users can create identities that include interests, library affiliations and links to other accounts, etc.; lists to which users can add items cataloged in WorldCat, group items owned by their local library, and share lists with friends; ratings and reviews; social tagging; and RSS feeds/notifications that continuously push or pull defined sets of information out of WorldCat [11]. Innovative Interfaces offers a proprietary interface known as Encore that offers many similar features as does the open source interface known as VuFind. Even if some online public access catalogs have come this far with Web 2.0 features, many libraries have been unconvinced of their merits or unable to afford their implementation. However, these features do make strides toward creating an online library environment that is as close to the social spaces of libraries as an online environment can be.

Usability studies on the open source catalog overlay VuFind demonstrate that users do find Web 2.0 features in the library catalog more engaging than the traditional online library catalog [5]. The steps that have been taken in this direction can go still further. It has been pointed out that "Library catalogs are traditionally not where people share their interests. People take catalog references to library assets and share them where other enthusiasts gather" [10]. If library catalogs provide a means for users to share the information from the catalog with their friends, colleagues or fellow enthusiasts, libraries will be tapping into the inherently social nature of sharing information. For example, allowing users to share catalog records readily with friends on Facebook will provide users with an ability of which they frequently take advantage with websites and online articles. However, another very important trend in social media and Web 2.0 in recent years that has yet to make an appearance in library catalogs is Twitter, the first in a possible series of micro-blogging platforms. Twitter is already in use in libraries [1] and has been suggested for mining information to use in collection development decisions [6]. However, until recently its primary use in libraries has been as a means of announcing events rather than actively engaging with users or encouraging interactivity outside of some casual use for reference services [9]. The similarity between Twitter hashtags and controlled vocabularies provides a window for viewing the possibilities for melding micro-blogging to the online public access catalog. WorldCat.org has already made inroads into utilizing the hashtag function of Twitter with their union catalog. They provide a new Twitter-based service that returns a WorldCat search when a user sends a tweet with the tag #Ask4Stuff. The user will get a tweet back with results that can be localized by including the local library name as another hashtag. A search can be shared with a user's social network and marked with other hashtags or it can be saved in the user's Tweet stream [8].

Several cataloging sites, both professional and social, have adopted Twitter. The following table presents the adoption of Twitter and the use of Hashtags by the leading library and social cataloging sites during the period, September 1st 2011 to November 17th 2011. It presents the Twitter profile and the tweeted hashtags by OCLC, Worldcat, LibraryThing, the Library of Congress and Goodreads, during that period (*see* Table 1).

Acknowledging the similarity between controlled vocabularies and the use of hashtags to indicate a topic in Twitter opens up the possibilities for exploring the use of Twitter and its accompanying hashtags in library catalogs, which currently rely almost solely on controlled vocabularies. The one exception to this has been the integration of social tagging in the OPAC overlays mentioned above. These tools allow social tagging to be enabled and then users can create tags to describe resources in the catalog, which operates in a similar way to Twitter hashtags assigned by users to indicate topics. Users in general tend to prefer the flexibility involved in expressing through their own vocabularies to convey their ideas for personalized information organization [2]. With tagging already a feature of Web

2.0 catalog overlays, it is worth considering whether or not Twitter and its accompanying hashtags can bring anything innovative and worthwhile to the catalog. The primary advantage of Twitter is its potential to create an interactive experience for the user, thus furthering the goal of making an online library website and catalog a social space for users. Hashtags can contribute to this venture, but they will by no means be the only variable. Hashtags alone cannot offer the full benefits of Twitter, or rather micro-blogging, as an entire platform and therefore, to take complete advantage of the social possibilities Twitter itself needs to be integrated into the online library catalog.

Table1: Twitter Adoption and Hashtag Use of Leading Library and Social Cataloguing Sites [4]

Twitter account	@OCLC	@Worldcat	@library congress	@Library Thing	@Goodreads
Description of the Twitter account	"OCLC is about connecting people to knowledge through library cooperation."	"WorldCat is the world's largest library catalogue and is a great place online to find materials in libraries, worldwide."	"We are the largest library in the world, with millions of books, recordings, photographs, maps and manuscripts in our collections."	"Watch this space for feature announcements, site news, and more from the team at Library Thing.com"	"The largest site for readers and book recommendations. Find new books, recommend books, track your reading, join book clubs, win advanced copies, and much more!"
Twitter profile	Following: 162 Followers: 5605 Tweets: 2016 Favorites: 0 Joined on April 8, 2009	Following: 258 Followers: 2293 Tweets: 594 Favorites: 1 Joined on April 8, 2009	Following: 6 Followers: 302,385 Tweets: 1579 Favorites: 0 Joined on June 29, 2007	Following: 3022 Followers: 4398 Tweets: 1303 Favorites: 3 Joined on January 20, 2011	Following: 10,160 Followers: 223,784 Tweets: 1963 Favorites: 1 Joined on August 19, 2008
Recent two-month tweeted hashtags	#oclcr (4)	#WorldCat	#natbookfest (15)	#LibraryThingReads (10)	#quoteoftheday(9)
	#orrapcap	#Spotify	#thankyousteve	#fridayreads (9)	#NBA 2011
	#wms4aca	#declaration		#bookhaiku (4)	#Goodreads Choice (10)
	#orss (2)	#wanttohelp		#AllHallowsRead	#neardalert
	#orarchivegrid	#birthdays #oclc #ala11		#ows	#weekendgoodreads
	#wcid	#playlearn		#NatBookFestival	
	#DDC11	#librariannerdhumor			

Note: The number within parentheses indicates the frequency of tweeted hashtags from September 1, 2011, to November 17, 2011.

The most ideal possibility would be to incorporate a Twitter "box" into the catalog. Rather than just appearing on the library's main webpage or just on the main page of the catalog, the box would ideally appear at every stage of a user's search process. As when Facebook is integrated into websites like the *New York Times*, this box could allow the user to sign in to their Twitter account or simply show the library catalog's Twitter feed. The box would be there every step of the way as the user performs searches and explores the catalog. Any questions users have about resources, search strategies or results could be posed instantaneously in the Twitter box and addressed by a librarian or another user. To facilitate the use of Twitter in the catalog, users could have the option of attaching hashtags to catalog records that could then be used to pull together lists of records with the same hashtags, much in the way tagging works in catalogs that have enabled it to date. These hashtags could also be utilized in the Twitter box when discussing resources with other users or librarians. Librarians would also provide predetermined hashtags to assist with searching and discussing issues. Hashtags would provide a more natural language solution to describing and indexing items in the catalog, particularly with regard to confusing terminology used by catalogers to describe carriers/formats, treatments of a topic, etc. Searches for particular hashtags can be saved on the library's or catalog's Twitter account so that all tweets that mention a particular hashtag can be seen at log on. This would enable librarians to easily follow the use of a hashtag in the catalog, see trends and respond. There are also social media aggregators like TweetDeck and HootSuite that allow users to follow various social media presences at once and hashtags can be added to columns in such programs to bring it all together. However, the key to all of this is making it engaging for the user, making them want to interact via Twitter with the librarians and other users. One way to accomplish this might be by having librarians adopt a "persona" for the catalog itself, making it more than a static information system. The users would seem to communicate with the catalog rather than a librarian. This might require someone with a ready and clever knack for language to provide appeal for users. Another way is for librarians to offer unsolicited suggestions, such as new resources with links to their records in the catalog and links to reviews of those resources. Twitter is a social media tool meant for in-the-moment interaction and socialization, and the use of hashtags is not much different from any other form of folksonomy without the possibilities for interaction that Twitter provides. The goal is to encourage users to engage and interact, to have a social experience in the catalog or with the catalog. The next step is to consider the value of incorporating Twitter and hashtags into the catalog.

The most well-established structure for such an assessment derives from the work of Robert Taylor and his value-added model for assessing information systems.

Robert Taylor is known for his work emphasizing user perspective in the context of reference interviews. His question negotiation model recognizes four layers of needs: the visceral need in which the user has a vague and inexpressible need; conscious need where the user understands in his or her mind but is unable to define or describe it; formalized need expression that is rational and results in a formal statement of the need; and compromised need when the question is tailored to the expectations of the information system. The third layer in the process involves the actual question negotiation wherein the reference librarian engages the user in a conversation to understand his or her real information need underneath the stated need. The fourth layer requires the translation of this into the language, vocabulary and search strategies permitted by the information system [14]. Taylor later developed his value-added model in which he once again recognizes meeting the users' information needs as central to the information system [13]. Its processes and algorithms exist to meet the needs of the user, and they are intended to add value in meeting their needs. This model offers a framework for evaluating the processes in terms of their value to the users. It addresses six user criteria and for each of these user criteria he specifies the Interface (values added) and the System (value added processes). In 2008 Eisenberg and Dirks modified Taylor's model and developed the Eisenberg-Dirks value-added model that considers the new trend in interactive information systems as its basis [7].

Chang and Iyer have created a morphological box of Twitter hashtag application based on a table created by Ames and Newman [4]. Ames and Newman's table considers the taxonomy of tagging motivations in Twitter and how it fulfills both self and social purposes in terms of its functions for organization and communication [3]. The significant aspect of the resulting table consists of functional characteristics (interface features) and functional attributes (value-added examples) for each user requirement: *communication* and *organization* as seen in the Table 2.

In this paper the morphological box for Twitter hashtag applications proposed by Chang and Iyer has been chosen as a framework for discussing the use of Twitter and Twitter hashtags in library catalogs because it best addresses the needs of 21st Century users who expect interactivity from information systems.

Table 2: Morphological box of Twitter hashtag applications

User Requirements	Communication		Organization		
Function Characteristics (Interfaces)	Memory	Social Signaling	Search	Directory	Archive
Function Attributes (Value-Added examples)	self-publishing	Retweet	Tweets	Interest	Compile
	scheduling to send tweets	Mention	Time	Subject	Save
	archiving	sharing photos/ videos	#hashtag	Industry	Analytics
	saved searches	sharing organized tweets URL	Keyword	recent searches	Visualizations
			Language	Location	recent 500-1500 tweets
			from @name	real-time trends	making it public or private
			mentioning @name	user-contributed definitions of real-time trends	

The Chang and Iyer Twitter application box has used *communication* and *organization* from Ames and Newman's taxonomy to analyze possible value-added attributes of each interface feature. The value-added examples specifically address function attributes of Twitter. From here this paper will consider interface features of Twitter as iterated in the Chang and Iyer box, then do the same with the modified Taylor value-added model as developed by Dirks and Eisenberg and discuss the added value of integrating Twitter into a library catalog. The advantage of using the morphological box is that modifications can be made depending on the goal of the analysis. In this case study, the focus is on Twitter as a social platform that can make the virtual library a community space as a modified version of a physical library as place. Ames and Newman discovered that the primary motivation behind tagging is a social function to share organized information and while Chang and Iyer touch briefly on this function of Twitter, it is not explored to the depth that Ames and Newman's results suggest it can be. Chang and Iyer also observed that social cataloging sites do more to create this social space and engage with the user community than professional cataloging organizations do.

The first user requirement in the morphological box of Twitter hashtag application is *communication*. The two function characteristics associated with communication are *memory* and *social signaling*. Two of the function attributes of *memory* in relation to Twitter in a library catalog would be archiving and saved searches as listed in the Chang and Iyer box. While the Ames and Newman table considers the *memory* attribute of Twitter as *self-communication*, that is, in essence the user motivation to tag is to provide a personal context and also provide memory cues for one's self., it can also be thought of in terms of collective memory and social-communication both in the broad world of the Internet and in the context of a library catalog. Thus a hashtag applied to a specific search or question that then aggregates all responses inside a library catalog could be seen and utilized by other users to recall search results or responses to questions. This is a direct result of the next interface function, *social signaling*, and how Twitter creates a social space in a virtual context. Retweeting, mentioning, sharing of photos and videos, and sharing a URL for organized tweets are all listed in the Chang and Iyer box as value-added examples of this. The community memory created by hashtags spreads through these methods. A dialogue forms, fulfilling the user requirement for social communication, and it can be used to advantage by libraries if they engage in the way their users do with each other.

The second user requirement is *organization*, which is more in line with the traditional way that librarians want to think about information and their role in its accessibility. The three function characteristics drawn from the Ames and Newman table are *search*, *directory*, and *archive*. Following the Chang and Iyer morphological box vertically down from *search*, the important function attributes for integrating Twitter into a library catalog would be #hashtag, keyword, language, from @name, and mentioning @name. All of these methods would assist users as well as librarians in managing tweets relevant to the library catalog that could comprise the virtual social fabric proposed above. They allow users to aggregate information from Twitter. A book title, author, subject, etc. could be searched by these methods and shared among users of the catalog.

The *directory* characteristic of the interface would provide a pre-determined pool of information similar to what is gained by searching. These are often found on sites other than Twitter but pull the information from Twitter so that users can have simplified access to it. Tracing the Chang and Iyer box down provides a glimpse of the kinds of directories that might benefit a catalog using Twitter: interest, subject, industry, recent searches, location, real-time trends, user-contributed definitions of real-time trends. Any one of these and perhaps many others could prove useful in a library catalog and to its users.

The final function characteristic of *organization* is *archive*. This might have more appeal for librarians than for users, but it provides the ability to compile and save as well as analytics, visualizations, and the ability to make the information public or private. From this point the paper will continue to explore the use of Twitter in the catalog in a similar fashion but now drawing from the Taylor model that Dirks and Eisenberg modified.

The Dirks-Eisenberg model first looks at *Ease of use* from four function characteristics: *browsing, formatting, mediation*, and *orientation*. *Browsing* refers to how an information system collocates information for a user in such a way that there it is probable the users will serendipitously find information of value to them. Catalogs allow searching by subject, author, title, etc. and that allows a user to browse results gathered by those criteria. The current run of next generation catalogs take this to the next step by incorporating faceted browsing, which allows users to do a broad keyword search as they might in a search engine and then narrow down to what they specifically want to browse. Incorporating Twitter and its hashtags into this process would not only allow users to aggregate catalog results by user-assigned hashtags but also provide a means of pulling together information on help topics. Questions asked to librarians by previous users that have been identified by a specified hashtag will be easily pooled for the user to browse and seek information on how to resolve their problems. Other applications could be to develop trend clouds and real time trends, referring the users to new trends or the ones that are promoted and often used.

The next element, *Mediation*, refers to intervention to promote understanding and reconciliation between the system and the user. Twitter is intended to be interactive and serves as a tool for communication between the librarian and the user at point of need. Similarly, Twitter can be utilized to support the *Orientation* aspect of the model by helping the user gain familiarity with using the catalog. The librarian can provide links to documents containing catalog use instructions and also provide immediate assistance. *Formatting* is about presenting information in ways that facilitates easy scanning and selecting. In the case of library catalogs the record can be presented in a user-friendly way with natural language captions such as "title", "author", "publisher", etc. that is easy for the user to understand. Next generation catalogs have made great strides in presenting users with the most relevant information to them, such as availability and location, when browsing results. This saves them time and effort and a great deal of confusion. An incorporated Twitter box would allow users to aggregate information in the format of tweets, which might offer them familiarity and quick browsing.

The second user criterion that the model addresses is *Quality* which includes the elements: *accuracy, comprehensiveness, currency, reliability, validity* and *authority. Accuracy* refers to error free information and conformity to the original piece of information. In a catalog, which is designed using accepted bibliographic standards, even if some discrepancies exist, the user is usually unable to detect them as they are not conversant with the standards. However, such discrepancies may impact the user negatively when searching. A constantly present Twitter feed would allow the librarian to immediately address search-related problems and attempt to restore accuracy to a user's search with supplemental information. Librarians would also be able to monitor and respond to inappropriate content should it appear in the catalog's Twitter feed. *Comprehensiveness* encompasses complete or, at least, broad coverage of the subject sought by the user. Catalogs allow this through subject searches and the use of lists of subject headings that facilitate grouping of records under a particular heading. Twitter hashtags created for frequently searched topics and the analysis of tweets about topics can help librarians develop topical hashtags that will support comprehensiveness. Users can also create and attach hashtags to records, allowing for multiple perspectives on the subject of a resource and adding another layer. *Currency* involves representing the current modes of thinking on the subject sought by the user. Catalogs are dynamic and add newer records that reflect the current modes of thinking and also use subject headings that are dynamic and reflect the current terminology and usage. Librarians can leverage Twitter to provide links to new materials added to the collection, possibly with additional resources like reviews. Twitter also in and of itself represents currency as it is intended as an *in-the-now* means of communication. Searching by hashtags will enable librarians and users to see current trends in information seeking and current research interests of other users.

Reliability,validity and authority also support quality in an information system. *Reliability* reflects the trust that a user develops in the system because of the consistency of its quality of performance and *Validity* refers to the soundness of information provided by the system. Through Twitter the user can seek other users' opinions on items discovered in the catalog. This together with the librarian's assessment and views on the item could help users make decisions about which resources to choose. Over a period of time it is likely that users will grow to trust the sources and information contained in the catalog records. This also suggests a certain degree of dependability and suitability of the catalog as a resource-finding tool. In addition, providing trend comparisons, editor's reviews, and analytics will enhance credibility. Top ten trend analysis and review of how a user interacts with Twitter in the library's catalog on a weekly or monthly basis will add value.

Adaptability is the third user criteria in the model and addresses: *contextuality, flexibility, simplicity, transaction, trust, feedback, community, individualization, localization* and *privacy. Transaction* is about meeting the specific needs of individuals through human intervention. This involves having knowledge of their personal bias, level of sophistication, learning style, etc. Interacting with users via tweets will help librarians to understand the personal context of users and tailor responses and assistance to individual needs and idiosyncrasies. This is also the definition of *individualization*, something that would prove much easier if a user could instantly communicate with librarians. Using Twitter within the catalog also lends *flexibility* of enabling the system to offer multiple approaches with a dynamic adjustment to the changing information needs during transaction. The use of hashtags adds an element of flexibility for the user to aggregate or find information, and a librarian's intervention could provide a dynamic adjustment to the user with regard to changing search strategies and needs. Also, over a period of time the information gathered from tweets may help when making changes to the catalog, especially in how the information is delivered to the user. For example, a hashtag like #yoursuggestions would collect feedback to the librarians. Although librarians have been conducting user surveys, employing Twitter for gathering feedback while users are in the process of using the catalog adds a different dimension. It can provide a new user perspective on the issue because it is instantaneous and relevant to the user's immediate situation. *Simplicity* refers to the lucid clear and uncomplicated way in which information is presented while the system adjusts and adapts to the users changing needs. The help offered by librarians via Twitter must be written in a clear manner. As tweets allow for only 140 characters, there should be a conscious effort towards clarity and brevity.

Trust in this model is the willingness of the user to see the system as trustworthy and responsive to cumulative reviews, certificates, etc. This connects to the elements of *Quality* discussed above as quality establishes a foundation for trust. Catalogs are in themselves a trustworthy source as they are institutional resources. The selection and processing of materials is carried out by professional librarians and that lends credibility and authority. Twitter adds another dimension to this through interaction with librarians to personalize the search process and can enhance the trust that the user already has. It makes the tool more dependable for finding relevant material because of the instant help that the user can receive from authoritative sources. *Feedback* in the model refers specifically to users utilizing and assessing information or an information system. Twitter offers an immediate and effective means for users to do more than simply provide feedback; they can actively engage in a conversation about their opinions and needs.

The most relevant element of the model with a social media tool such as Twitter is *community*, which deals specifically with building a community.While users might build online communities around the types of resources found in libraries, they do not do so in the library's online space. Community building is one of the greatest advantages of incorporating social media. Twitter will not only encourage conversations and social interaction in the library's online space, the use of hashtags for topics of interest, such as #sports, #Shakespeare or #presidential election, would allow users to share common interests and communicate with each other and librarians about the resources the library offers to support their interests. This would enable the library to become as much of a virtual community space as it is a physical community space. *Privacy* is another element but engaging in Twitter in the library's catalog, in the community created in that space, means that the tweets are open to all and there is no question of privacy. However, searching the catalog would remain private unless the user chose to discuss their search on Twitter with the librarian.

Performance is omitted as this study does not address an existing system with actual performance specifications and so the final aspect of the user criteria given by this model is *Pleasing*. This somewhat unusual term covers *aesthetics, entertainment, engagement, stimulation, satisfaction*. All of these aspects revolve around how much users enjoy interacting with an information system. Next generation catalogs have taken steps in this direction by incorporating Web 2.0 features into the overlays. Physical libraries are social spaces but online libraries are not. If librarians choose to provide the catalog with a "persona" for Twitter, then when users tweet while in the catalog they will seem to receive responses from the catalog itself. If the catalog's persona is entertaining and intelligent, it will encourage users to engage in a conversation with the "catalog." Incorporating Twitter into the catalog encourages users to engage with the catalog, librarians, and with each other. Users will have an outlet for voicing thoughts, ideas and concerns and having conversations about their searches or needs. The catalog has the potential to become a stimulating space for users rather than a static list of results generated by a system. The use of hashtags for current topics or interests will allow the users to engage with a familiar method of classifying the subject of their search or their needs while in the catalog and it will allow a thread to develop on a specific topic that can be browsed by users or librarians. Users might develop a kind of "affection" for the catalog if it engages them on a social and interactive level that heretofore has not been the case with library systems. Thus sophisticated functionalities can be achieved by proper utilization of Twitter, resulting in the enhancement of library systems, especially the catalog.

Embedding Twitter on the catalog main page and result pages can serve as a social space for users to interact with the community and librarians. It will also allow the librarian to intervene and help users with searches and other concerns at the moment they need assistance. This is likely to impact the user's perception of the library and the catalog and encourage them to visit and revisit the catalog and use the library collection. The use of Web 2.0 in next generation catalogs takes a step in the direction of making libraries' online environment social and community spaces. However, in order for libraries to simulate an online space as close to the physical community space as possible, they need to go further toward actual interaction with their users and enabling users to interact with each other in the online library environment. A micro-blogging tool like Twitter, with its own system of semi-controlled vocabulary, offers librarians an opportunity to do what they have always done in the physical library space in the broadening virtual world that their users now frequently inhabit. As technology and social media move inevitably forward, more and better opportunities for creating interactive online library spaces will arise, but tools already exist for beginning that journey into the future of libraries and their catalogs.

REFERENCES

1 Aharony, Noa. (2010) Twitter use in libraries: An exploratory analysis, *Journal of Web Librarianship.* 4(4): 333-350; Forrestal, Valerie. Making Twitter work: a guide for the uninitiated, the skeptical, and the pragmatic, *The Reference Librarian*, 52(½): 146-151; Stuart, David. What are libraries doing on Twitter? *Online*, 34(1): 45-47.

2 American Library Association. (2005) Current issues and developments related to metadata: Thoughts and opinions, Library Technology Reports, Nov/Dec 2005, 41(6): 45-57; Iyer, Hemalata and Lucy Bungo. (2011). An examination of semantic relationships between professionally assigned metadata and user generated tags for popular literature in

complementary and alternative medicine. *Information Research*, 16(3) paper 482. Available at http://InformationR.net/ir/16-3/paper482.html

3 Ames, M. and Naaman, M. (2007). Why we tag: Motivations for annotation in mobile and online media, **In** *Proceedings of the SIGCHI Conference on Human Factors in Computing Systems*: 971-980.

4 Chang, Hsia-Ching and Hemalata Iyer. (2012) Trends in Twitter hashtag applications: design features for value-added dimensions t future library catalogues. *Library Trends*, 61(1): 248-258.

5 Denton, William and Sarah J. (2011) Coysh. Usability testing for VuFind at an academic library. *Library Hi Tech*, 29(2): 301-319.

6 Dominguez, Daisy V. and Steven Ovadia. (2011) What's next for collection management and managers, *Collection Management*, 36(3): 145-153; Petit, Joan. Twitter and Facebook for user collection requests, *Collection Management*, 36(4): 253-258.

7 Eisenberg, Michael B. and Lee Dirk. (2008). Taylor's Value-Added Model: Still relevantafter all these years, Paper presented at *the iConference, iFutures: Systems, Selves, Society, February 2008*, Los Angeles, CA. http://www.ischools.org/conference08/pc/PA3-4_iconf08.pdf (accessed November 18, 2011); Scholl, Hans J.; Michael B. Eisenberg; Lee Dirks, and Timothy S. Carlson. The TEDS framework for assessing information systems from a human actors' perspective: Extending and repurposing, *Journal of American Society for Information Science and Technology*, 62(4)(2011): 789-804.

8 Havena, Andy. (2008) Three new ways to experience WorldCat.org, *NextSearch*, 16: 14-15,20.

9 Mathews, Brian S. (2010) Twitter and the library: Thoughts on the syndicated lifestyle, *Journal of Web Librarianship*, 2(4): 589-593.

10 Smith-Yoshimura, Karen. (2010) Social metadata, *NextSearch*, 15: 14-15.

11 Storey, Tom. (2007) A WorldCat community, *NextSearch*, 7: 16-17.

12 Storey, Tom. (2009) The ripple effect: Pt.1 Extending the library reach, *NextSearch*, 13: 4-9.

13 Taylor, R.S. (1982) Value-added processes in the information life cycle, *Journal of the American Society of Information Science*, 33(5): 341–346; Taylor, R. S. *Value-added processes in information systems*. Norwood, NJ: Ablex, 1986.

14 Taylor, Robert S. (1968) Question-negotiation and information seeking, *College and Research Libraries*, 29(3): 178-194.

13

Ranganathan's Contributions to Knowledge Organization and Presentation

K.S. Raghavan and ***A. Neelameghan***

Knowledge Organization tools can be used for a variety of purposes including arranging information objects, representation of their *'aboutness'*, displaying semantic relations between concepts and even for presentation of ideas in texts. The paper highlights some of the major contributions of Ranganathan to the theory and practice of knowledge organization.

Keywords: Knowledge organization, Ranganathan, S.R.; Colon Classification; Fundamental categories

1 INTRODUCTION

Knowledge Organization (KO) is a sub-discipline at the core of Information Studies. Although Bliss titled one of his works as *Organization of Knowledge in Libraries*, the term *knowledge organization* is of comparatively recent origin. The sub-discipline has its origins in philosophy, as early classificationists were philosophers. The history of modern KO begins in the mid 19th Century and even more clearly in the last quarter of the 19th Century with the works of Melville Dewey and Charles Cutter. In the initial decades, however, *Classification* and *Cataloguing* were treated as two related but distinct sub-disciplines. Even that branch of *Cataloguing*, viz., *Subject Cataloguing* was being treated independently of developments in *Classification*. This dichotomy was more due to the limited understanding that *Classification* is a means for assigning notation to documents to facilitate their arrangement on library shelves and *subject cataloguing* as concerned with assigning subject headings to documents for use in card catalogues. The term *subject indexing* was also brought into vogue. However, over time, it was realized that all these activities have identical purpose, viz., representation subjects of discourses in a precise and unambiguous manner to support storage and retrieval of information. Since then *Classification* and *Indexing* are being treated more or less as synonyms. More recently Svenonius adopted an even broader approach to *information organization* (as she prefers to refer to the sub-discipline) and looks at a unified theory of KO inclusive of bibliographic systems of all kinds – schemes of classification, codes of cataloguing, controlled vocabularies, etc [15]. Souza [et al] have gone a step further and have developed a typology of KO systems [14]. Knowledge organization systems are used in information systems for a variety of purposes that include:

- Arranging information objects (artifacts such as documents and / or their metadata records) in a helpful and logical sequence to support browsing;
- Representing information objects and their '*aboutness*' to support search and retrieval of information;
- Displaying relationships between information objects and concepts to support navigation and enhancement of information retrieval.

S.R. Ranganathan's contributions to knowledge organization have not only been substantial, but have also influenced much of subsequent work and thinking in the area of knowledge organization. In this paper an attempt is made to briefly examine Ranganathan's contributions to the broad area of knowledge organization and their impact.

2 THEORETICAL BASE

Knowledge Organization Systems as understood by the LIS community today and even the facet analytical approach did exist before Ranganathan. The *Universal Decimal Classification*, the development of which was initiated during the last decade of the 19th Century (and, to a limited extent, even the *Dewey Decimal Classification* had synthetic features, e.g. in the form of *General Auxiliaries*. The approach was carried further in Kaiser's *Systematic Indexing*. However, what characterized Ranganathan's approach was his search for a theoretical base for every tool and technique that he developed. Ranganathan published his *Five Laws of Library Science* in the 1920s and these *Five Laws* are the most explicit statements of the goals and objectives of libraries (and of all kinds of information systems).

- *Books are for use*
- *Every reader his or her book*
- *Every book its reader*
- *Save the time of the reader*
- *Library is a growing organism*

All his practices, tools and techniques were designed and evaluated against these *Five Laws*. The *Five Laws* have been adapted and re-formulated for the Web environment, and continue to be relevant in spite of the very many changes that the digital and web environments have brought about in terms of the ways in which information is generated, packaged, communicated and accessed. In other words the *Five Laws* continue to serve as the broad parameters against which all tools, techniques and practices aimed at improving and enhancing access to and discovery of information could be assessed and evaluated. It is from these *Five Laws* that Ranganathan derived more specific *Canons* and *Principles* to guide the development of tools and techniques for specific areas of library science and service such as the Canons and Principles of Classification and Cataloguing. In the following sections we briefly examine Ranganathan's approach to knowledge organization [1].

3 RANGANATHAN'S APPROACH TO KNOWLEDGE ORGANIZATION

While there is hardly any aspect of library science or service that Ranganathan has not touched, it is his contributions to Classification and Cataloguing that are the subject of interest here. There was not much by way of theory of classification when Ranganathan came on the scene, although it is important to note the contributions of Bliss and Sayers. It must be remembered that Ranganathan was in-charge of organizing a large library collection. His approach to designing a knowledge organization system should be seen within this broad mandate of organizing a collection of documents (primarily books) in the physical environment of a library. His *Colon Classification* (CC) and the *Classified Catalogue Code* (CCC) need to be seen in this context. However, what came out eventually in the form of a *General Theory of Classification* contained in his *Prolegomena to Library Classification* and later writings by himself and his associates had significant applications outside the conventional library. His *Theory of Library Catalogue* (first published in 1938) is another important contribution to knowledge organization. The Canons and Principles that Ranganathan enunciated in this book formed the basis for his *Heading and Canons*, which is probably the first comprehensive comparative study of codes of cataloguing [10]. We shall return to this later in this paper. To begin with let us examine Ranganathan's approach to classification.

---

[1] Ranganathan did not employ the term *'knowledge organization'* in his works. Although two of the principal works of Bliss carried the phrase *'organization of knowledge'*, the term has largely been brought into wide usage among the LIS community by Dahlberg

3.1 Planes of Work and Fundamental Categories

Ranganathan explicitly defined and identified the three planes of work in designing knowledge organization systems, viz., the Idea Plane (the plane of logic and intellection), the Verbal Plane (the plane of terminology) and the Notational Plane (the plane of symbols):

- *Idea Plane*: The work of identifying concepts that collectively constitute a domain (universe of interest), categorization of these concepts, identifying and defining the relationships (hierarchical and non-hierarchical lateral relationships) between the concepts, arranging the concepts in a logical helpful sequence;
- *Verbal Plane*: The work of labeling the concepts using terms in a natural language; and
- *Notational Plane*: The work of assigning notation to denote the concepts.

The work in the Verbal and Notational planes is primarily *'Representation'* of concepts identified in the Idea Plane. The facet-analytic approach constitutes the core of Ranganathan's contribution to the work in the Idea Plane. It is important to clearly differentiate between the facet-analytic approach as a methodology for identifying and categorizing concepts and Ranganathan's own schema of categories that formed the basis for his *Colon Classification*. There is no doubt that the facet-analytic approach is now generally accepted as the basis for design of knowledge organization systems. That *categories* are the basic building elements of a knowledge organization system is now generally conceded. There is a considerable volume of literature documenting the use of faceted classification and interestingly enough, this is by no means limited to the LIS environment and extends to, e.g., E-commerce websites. In a paper in this volume Vanda Broughton mentions that, since 2010, over 450 papers have appeared on facet-analytic approach clearly indicating the interest in and recognition of the usefulness of the approach in knowledge organization pioneered by Ranganathan. In the initial years after the development of the facet-analytic approach, the only other group outside India that did substantial work by way of application of the technique for designing systems of knowledge organization was the British Classification Research group. While the members of this group did differ from one another with regard to the nature and number of categories, the single most obvious difference between this group and Ranganathan (and his associates) relates to *Fundamental Categories*. It is in this context that we need to examine another important component of

Ranganathan's theory of classification, viz., the *postulational approach*. In adopting the postulational approach, the principal questions that Ranganathan considered relate obviously to adequacy and helpfulness of the postulate in a given context. Obviously Ranganathan found that the five *Fundamental Categories* were both adequate and helpful in categorizing concepts going with the various *'Basic Subjects'*. He argued that even *'Basic Subjects'* are to be postulated depending on such factors as literary warrant, etc. Postulating *Basic Subjects* was a necessity for Ranganathan as he was, like Dewey, building a library classification. One finds that in Derek Austin's PRECIS, designed to build alphabetical indexes and not a library classification, the notion of *Basic subjects* does not exist. Coming back to the notion of *Fundamental Categories*, some alternatives have been suggested; the most widely suggested schema of universal categories is the one proposed by B. C. Vickery. G. Bhattacharyya's schema of *Elementary Categories* (*Discipline*, *Entity*, *Property*, and *Action*) is also suggested as a universal schema applicable across domains. Clearly, therefore, there are two broad schools of thought in applying facet-analytic approach to knowledge organization: One school of thought that advocates a schema of universal categories (Ranganathan, Vickery, Austin, Bhattacharyya, etc) and the other that suggests that the number and nature of categories are domain-dependent. Clearly the second approach dominated the initial years of developmental work by members of the CRG and, in more recent time, it dominates the application of facet analysis for design of E-commerce websites. The first approach has been widely used in design of knowledge organization systems such as Macrothesauri, classauri and the like. The question of adequacy of the five *Fundamental Categories* in categorizing concepts across domains still remains. However, the question applies equally to other schemas of categories. It is doubtful if there is an appropriate alternative to Ranganathan's method of postulates.

A major criticism of Ranganathan's *Fundamental Categories* relates to "lack of clear definition" of the categories. One can recall Norman Robert's paper criticizing Ranganathan's treatment of *'Personality'* category [13]. It is true that Ranganathan suggested the use of the 'Principle of Residues' in his writings to identify the facets belonging to *'Personality'* in a subject. However, subsequently the five *Fundamental Categories* have been adequately defined and their connotation clearly indicated [2,8]. Knowledge organization systems are concerned with conceptual categories and unless we use the labels employed by domain specialists to name categories in a domain, it is difficult to provide precise definitions of categories in a schema. But this is not feasible in any schema of universal categories.

Whether or not one agrees with Ranganathan's five *Fundamental Categories*, there is no question that his facet-analytic approach and his schema of categories have been the basis for all schemas that have emerged since then. Ranganathan's *Basic Subject, PMEST* model clearly reflects systems thinking and it is not difficult to see the commonality between his schema and those that emerged later. The *Thesaurofacet* of Jean Aitchison, the *Classaurus* of G. Bhattacharyya apart, even conventional subject terminology schemas such as LCSH have realized the importance of the facet-analytic approach. The FAST (Faceted Application of Subject Terminology) derived from the Library of Congress Subject Headings (LCSH) which is a family of eight modular, complementary vocabularies designed to support faceted retrieval is a case in point.

3.2 Sequence of Ideas

Ranganathan also devoted considerable attention to the issue of formulating principles for the sequencing of facets / ideas in a logical sequence. His 'Wall-Picture Principle' referred to by Hutchins as the 'Principle of Dependence'. Stated simply the Wall-Picture principle suggests that a concept follows the concept to which it is subordinate either in a classificatory or grammatical sense. His principles of facet sequence (Whole-organ Principle, Actand-Action-Actor-Tool Principle Commodity-Raw material Principle, etc) and the Principle of Context-Dependence in PRECIS could all be derived the Wall-Picture principle. Ranganathan stressed the need for search for a natural syntax of facets – the syntax of facets most helpful to most people – i.e. the *'absolute syntax'* of facets [11].

3.3 Semantic Relations

Ranganathan recognized a few broad categories of semantic relations, viz. *Array* relations, *Chain* relations and *Phase* relations. These correspond to non-hierarchical associative relations (RTs) and hierarchical relations (BT & NT). These were subsequently labeled by G. Bhattacharyya as COSSCO (Coordinate, Super-ordinate, Subordinate and Collateral) relations. Neelameghan and Maitra [3], based on an analysis of facet relations occurring between concepts in a wide range of subjects, identified different types of non-hierarchical associative relations (RTs). These have been expanded in more recent papers by Neelemeghan and Raghavan [5,6].

3.4 Ranganathan's Contributions to Cataloguing

Reference has already been made to *Heading and Canons*, a comparative study of five catalogue codes. Ranganathan placed a great deal of emphasis on developing a theory to guide practice and this is evident from the Canons and Principles of cataloguing that he formulated as reference points to guide cataloguing work. Apart from preparing the first complete code in the English language for a classified catalogue, his other most important contribution is Chain Indexing. Interestingly enough Chain Indexing had its major large scale application outside the Madras University Library in the *British National Bibliography* which used the indexing system to generate the alphabetical index to the classified part of the bibliography for 20 years since its inception in 1950 till 1970. Mills in his introduction to U.D.C. recommended Chain indexing as ideal for indexing a classification scheme. John Phillip Immroth tested the system's applicability to LC classification. The system in form continues to be widely used in many bibliographies and indexing services; its greatest advantage when applied to any classification scheme is its ability to group together related subjects that are scattered by the scheme; a feature referred to as '*symbiosis*' by Ranganathan and '*collocation of distributed relatives*' by Jack Mills. This is achieved by the simple process of inverting the classificatory hierarchy while generating the index entries, a feature Dewey had introduced in his *Relativ Index*. Ranganathan's Chain Index is the basis for all string indexes (to borrow a term used by Timothy Craven) – PRECIS, POPSI, etc. in the sense that it was Chain Index which first introduced the idea of ordering terms in an index entry in a logical sequence (reverse order of the classificatory hierarchy) [1]. This coupled with Ranganathan's paper in the *Journal of Documentation* in 1964 could be seen as triggering the search for new systems of indexing that eventually resulted in PRECIS and POPSI. This paper is significant because it signaled a shift in emphasis from Notational Plane to the Verbal Plane for effective information retrieval. That the facet structure suggested by Ranganathan in his General Theory of Classification (especially the *'Title in Standard Terms'*) could be used as the basis for subject heading structuring has been demonstrated in several later publications [2,8,9].

4 S.R. RANGANATHAN AND PRESENTATION OF INFORMATION

According to Ranganathan, classification and categorization are neural necessities; Human beings make categories of concepts and of entities or find and use relevant existing categorization [12]. This is largely guided by the purpose on hand. In a text, in a classified bibliographic file or on the shelves of a library, the ideas / items are presented in a linear sequence. This amounts to reducing the multi-dimensional universe into a uni-dimensional sequence. The ability to sort and present items / ideas by every possible characteristic (facet), which is possible in today's digital world / Cyberspace, was not available at the time of Ranganathan and one could only think of physical organization of items in a linear fashion. This is why he came up with such ideas as *'APUPA'* pattern and *'helpful sequence'* – a sequence helpful to a majority of end users. End users search patterns and sorting (of information objects) requirements are many and varied and there is no single method of physical organization of information objects that can meet all the different approaches. The utility and value of facet-analytic techniques in organizing and presenting information objects in Cyberspace in a desired order dictated by the purpose on hand has been brought out in an article by David Weinberger [16]. Ranganathan also came up with the idea of *'seminal mnemonics'* - concepts that are equivalent at the seminal level. The similarity in the presentation of ideas in text in some of the works of some of the greatest thinkers of the 20th Century and that dictated by the application of *seminal mnemonics* has been shown in a paper by Prataplingam [7]. In a recent paper Neelameghan and Raghavan have examined the impact of culture on knowledge organization and, with examples from the domain of Carnatic music, have shown how different kinds of presentation of information could be made to meet different requirements [4]. What is important is that such organization and presentation of information / information objects in different ways to meet different requirements is possible only via the application of facet analytic techniques.

5 CONCLUSION

It is appropriate to conclude this paper by quoting from David Weinberger. "The architecture of Ranganathan's system is perfectly designed for computer manipulation: Create a set of fields, or facets, and keep track of the values plugged into those fields. Then let people browse the fields in any order they want, creating their own trees: Browse first by consultant location, then by cost, then by skill set, or whatever combination a particular query dictates. This is how browsing is organized at Apple Computer's iTunes page, Monster.com, and sites run by Eddie Bauer, the National Aeronautics and Space Administration, and many others. It's as if Ranganathan designed colon classification in 1933 specifically for the kind of instant reshuffling that computers made feasible decades later". "Facets are all about manipulating multidimensional space", says Steve Papas, co-founder of Endeca, which uses Ranganathan's system in its software. "You can't do that in the physical world. But Ranganathan was ahead of his time. The constraints of the physical world didn't inhibit his imagination".

6 ACKNOWLEDGEMENT

One of the authors, Dr. K. S. Raghavan, would like to place on record his deep sense of gratitude to the support provided under the TEQIP programme (subcomponent 1.2.1) of the World Bank / Government of India research grant to the Centre for Knowledge Analytics and Ontological Engineering (KAnOE) at PES Institute of Technology, Bangalore, India.

REFERENCES

1 Bhattacharyya, G. and Neelameghan, A. (1969) Postulate based subject heading for a dictionary catalogue system. *Annual Seminar (DRTC); 7; 1969, Paper CA.*

2 Neelameghan, A. and Gopinath, M.A. (1975) Postulate-based permuted subject indexing. *Lib. Sc.*, 12, Paper H.

3 Neelameghan, A. and Maitra, Ranjita. (1978) Non-hierarchical associative relations among concepts: identification and typology /. FID/CR Report No. 18, Part A.-- Bangalore: FID/CR Secretariat, Documentation Research and Training Centre.

4 Neelameghan, A. and K.S. Raghavan. (2012.) Frames of Knowledge: A perspective of Vedic Hinduism and Dravidian culture. **In** Smiraglia, Richard P. and Lee, Hur-Li. *Cultural Frames of knowledge*. – Wurzburg: Ergon Verlag, p. 19-61.

5 Neelameghan, A. and Raghavan, K.S. (2005) Semantics of relationships in knowledge organization: Lateral relationships. *SRELS Journal of Information Management*. 42(4): 361-382)

6 Neelameghan, A. and Raghavan, K.S. (2006) Semantics of relationships in knowledge organization – lateral relationships: update 1. *Information Studies*, 12(2); 115-122

7 Pratap Lingam. (1972) Use of seminal mnemonics in the presentation of ideas. *DRTC Annual Seminar*, 10, Paper AN.

8 Raghavan, K.S. (1985) General Theory of Classification as the basis for Structuring of Subject Headings. **In** *Classification and Communication: Proceedings of the second FID/CR Regional Conference*, New Delhi, p. 24-48.

9 Raghavan, K.S. and Hemalatha Iyer. (1978) Structuring of Compound and Complex Subjects in Social Sciences: A user's survey. **In:** *International Classification*, 5: 8-14.

10 Ranganathan, S.R. (1955) Heading and Canons: Comparative Study of Five Catalogue Codes. Madras: S. Viswanathan.

11 Ranganathan, S.R. (1967) Hidden roots of classification. *Information Storage and Retrieval*, 3, Sec. 7

12 Ranganathan, S.R. (1967) Prolegomena to library classification. (cf. *Prolegomena*, XB1 and XB2)

13 Roberts, Norman. (1969) An Examination of the Personality Concept and its relevance to the Colon Classification Scheme. *Journal of Librarianship and Information Science,* 1(3): 131-148.

14 Souza, Renato Rocha; Douglas Tudhope and Mauricio Barcellos Almeida. (2010) The KOS Spectra: A tentative typology of knowledge organization systems. **In** *Paradigms and conceptual systems in knowledge organization* / edited by Claudio Gnoli and Fulvio Mazzocchi. – Wurzburg: Ergon Verlag, p. 122-128.

15 Svenonius, Elaine. (2000) The intellectual foundation of information organization. Cambridge (Mass): The MIT Press.

16 Weinberger, David. (2013) Rediscovering Ranganathan (http://semanticstudios.com/publications/forrester.pdf - accessed 23rd October 2013

14

Tamil Classics: Categorization, Classification and Arrangement

A. Neelameghan and ***S.K. Lalitha***

Discusses different categorizations and classification of the 41 Tamil works of the Sangam period – first three centuries of the Common Era. The Tamil classics are (1) classified and arranged by Colon Classification, (3) organized into a thesaurus structure, and (3) arranged in the conventional list of these classics. Different search, retrieval and display facilities and hyper-linking within the schedules and with external files are demonstrated with examples. Greenstone Digital Library (GSDL) software has been used.

KEYWORDS: Classic works; Tamil classics; Categorization; Classification; Colon classification; Thesaurus structure; Organization; Presentation; GSDL

1 INTRODUCTION

1.1 Objectives

- To present different groupings / categorizations of the 41 Tamil classics (*see* Sec. 2).- (1). Conventional categorization into 8 groups; (2) Colon Classification (CC, ed. 6), and (3) Bilingual thesaurus of the 41 Tamil classics;
- To show different search, retrieval and display / presentation possibilities; and
- To demonstrate the use of hyper-linking within the groups and with external files.

1.2 Definitions

The following definitions are from the *Classified catalogue code* (Ranganathan, 1988, chapter FA*)* [2]

Expressed Thought: Thought expressed in a natural language, symbols, or in any other mode, usually embodied in a medium, and thereby made communicable. Also a picture, a mathematical formula, and chemical formula is each an Expressed Thought. So also is a gesture.

Work: Expressed thought.

Classic: Work usually having embodiments in several versions, adaptations, and translations, attracting other works on itself, and getting copied or brought out in print or other forms even long after its creation.

A classic is often treated as if it were a class or a subject. That is it is regarded as a quasi class.

Quasi-class: Work which is treated as a class in a classification scheme, or whose title is used as a subject-heading in cataloguing practice.

Classic Device: A Classic Device "brings together the different editions of a classic in a class, the different editions of each of its commentaries, the different editions of each of the sub-commentaries of each of its commentaries, and so on, and of securing that the group of sub-commentaries of a commentary is in juxtaposition to the commentary, that the group of commentaries of a classic is in juxtaposition to the classic, and that the group formed of each classic and its associated commentaries is in juxtaposition to the groups of the other classics of the same class.

"The Classic Device consists in suffixing the digit *x* to the number representing the ultimate class to which the classic should be otherwise assigned and adding after it an Author Facet and a Work Facet, if we cannot be certain that the Author wrote only one work, provided the classic is not a sacred book or a work belonging to the Main Class O Literature, as these are individualized otherwise."

....

"A Commentary Facet may be added after the Work Facet. The isolate in it may be determined by the Favoured Category Device for not more than 16 commentaries and by the Chronological Device for the others.

"Second Order Commentary, Third Order Commentary etc., Facets may be added successively after the Commentary Facet. The isolates in them may be determined as in the Commentary Facet."

2 TAMIL CLASSICS

The 41 works in Tamil created during the Sangam Period (first three centuries of the Common Era) are considered as Tamil classics. (*see* Why these forty one classics?, 2006)

In Ranganathan's *Colon Classification* (CC), ed. 6 (Ranganathan, 1960; 2006) [3] these Tamil works are treated as classics as defined in section 1.2 (quasi-class / quasi-subject), and assigned CC number to each work and its commentaries, sub-commentaries etc.

According to CC the Tamil classics are associated with two Main Classes: O Literature and P Linguistics.

The Facet structure for O Literature :

[P1] Language,
[P2] Form,
[P3] Author (derived by Chronological Device),
[P4] Work (derived by Enumeration)

Example:

O, Literature

O,31 Tamil literature
O,31,1 Poetry
O,31,1B ETTuttokai
O,31,1B9 PattuppATTu

The Facet structure for P Linguistics:

[P1] Language
[P2] Form
[P3] Author (derived by Chronological Device)
[P4] Work (derived by Enumeration)

Example:

P Linguistics
P31 Tamil
P31,J Modern Tamil
P31,Jx1,1 *NannUl* by Pava-nandi Munivar
P21,Jx1,1,1 *Urai* by Mayilai-nAthar

Thus, in CC the classics get arranged first by the ordinal value of' the digit(s) of the Main Class or Basic Facet with which the subject of the classic is associated;

then within this class by the original language of the work; then by the period in which the classic was created, etc.

In the CC classified list of classics, the 41 Tamil classics are distributed in the Main classes O Literature and P Linguistics. (*See* Ranganathan, 1960, Part 3)

In another categorization / classification, [4] the 41 Tamil classics are grouped into 8 broad categories; a category may have subclass(s) (*see* Fig. 2)

As a classic is treated as a subject in CC, we have generated a thesaurus-like structure for the 41 Tamil classics (*see* Table 1).

Table 1: Forty One Tamil Classics

சங்கனூல்	**P31,Dx1**	**Ca~ga~nUl**
NT: தொல்காப்பியம்	**P31,Dx1,1**	**tolkAppiyam**
NT1: இலம்பூரனர் (Commentary)	P31,Dx1,1,1	ilampUranar (Commentary)
NT2: கல்லாடனார் (Commentary)	P31,Dx1,1,1,2	kallATanAr (Commentary)
NT1: பெராசிரியர் (Commentary)	P31,Dx1,1,3	perAciriya r(Comemntary)
NT1: செனா-வரையர் (Commentary)	P31,Dx1,1,4	cenA-varaiyar (Comentary)
NT1: நச்சினார்க்கினியர் (Commentary)	P31,Dx1,1,5	naccinArkkiniyar (Comentary)
NT: எழுத்ததிகாரம்	P31,Dx1,11	ezhuttatikAram
NT: சொல்-அதிகாரம்	P31,Dx1,13	col-atikAram
NT: பொருள்அதிகாரம்	P31,Dx1,14	poruLatikAram
NT: இறையனார்	P31,Dx2	iRraiyanAr
NT1: அகப்பொருள்	P31,Dx2,1	akapporuL
NT2: நக்கீரர் (Comentary)	P31,Dx2,1,1	~nakkIrar (Comentary)
NT: பதினெண்மேல்கணக்கு	**031,1Az**	**patineNmElkaNakku**
NT: எட்டுத்தொகை	O31,1B	eTTuttokai
NT1: நற்றிணை	O31,1B1	~naRRiNai
NT1: குறுந்தொகை	O31,1B2	kuRu~ntokai
NT1: ஐங்குறுநூறு	O31,1B3	ai~gkuRu~gARu
NT1: பதிற்றுப்பத்து	O31,1B4	patiRRuppattu
NT1: பரிபாடல்	O31,1B5	paripATal
NT1: கலித்தொகை	O31,1B6	kalittokai
NT1: அகநானூறு	O31,1B7	aka~nAnURu
NT1: புறநானூறு	O31,1B8	puRa~nAnURu

NT: பத்துப்பாட்டு	**O31,1B9**	**pattuppATTu**
NT1: திருமுருகாற்றுப்படை	O31,1B911	tirumurukARRuppaTai
NT1: பொருநராற்றுப்படை	O31,1B912	poru~narARRuppaTai
NT1: சிறுபாணாற்றுப்படை	O31,1B921	ciRupANARRuppaTai
NT1: பெரும்பாணாற்றுப்படை	O31,1B922	perumpANARRuppaTai
NT1: முல்லைப்பாட்டு	O31,1B931	mullaippATTu
NT1: மதுரைக்காஞ்சி	O31,1B932	maturaikkA~jci
NT1: நெடுநல்வாடை	O31,1B941	~neTu~nalvATai
NT1: குறிஞ்சிப்பாட்டு	O31,1B942	kuRi~jcippATTu
NT1: பட்டினப்பாலை	O31,1B951	paTTinappAlai
NT1: மலைபடுகடாம்	O31,1B952	malaipaTukaTAm
NT: பதினெண் கீழ்க்கணக்கு	**O31,1C**	**patineN kIzhkkaNakku**
NT1: நாலடியார்	O31,1C21	~nAlaTiyAr
NT1: நான்மணிக்கடிகை	O31,1C22	~nAnmaNikkaTikai
NT1: இன்னாநாற்பது	O31,1C31	innA~nARpatu
NT1: இனியவைநாற்பது	O31,1C32	iniyavai~nARpatu
NT1: கார்நாற்பது	O31,1C33	kAr~nARpatu
NT1: களவழிநாற்பது	O31,1C34	kaLavazhi~nARpatu
NT1: ஐந்திணைஐம்பது	O31,1C41	ai~ntiNaiaimpatu
NT1: ஐந்திணைஎழுபது	O31,1C42	ai~ntiNaiezhupatu
NT1: திணைமொழிஐம்பது	O31,1C43	tiNaimozhiaimpatu
NT1: திணைமாலைநூற்றைம்பது	O31,1C44	tiNaimAlai~nURRaimpatu
NT1: பழமொழி	O31,1C63	pazhamozhi
NT1: சிறுபஞ்சமூலம்	O31,1C64	ciRupa~jcamUlam
NT1: திருக்குறள்	O31,1C5	tirukkuRaL
NT1: திரிகடுகம்	O31,1C61	tirikaTukam
NT1: ஆசாரக்கோவை	O31,1C62	AcArakkOvai
NT1: முதுமொழிக்காஞ்சி	O31,1C65	mutumozhikkA~jci
NT1: ஏலாதி	O31,1C66	ElAti
NT1: கைந்நிலை	O31,1C67	kai~n~nilai
NT: சிலப்பதிகாரம் / முத்தமிழ்க்காப்பியம்	**O31,1C92**	**cilappatikAram / muttamizhkkAppiyam**
NT: மணிமேகலை	**O31,1C93**	**maNimEkalai**
NT: முத்தொள்ளாயிரம்	**O31,1C94**	**muttoLLAyiram**
NT: இறையனார் களவியல்	**P31,Dx2**	**iRaiyanarar kaLaviyal**
NT1: *நக்கீரர் (Commentary)*	P31,Dx2,1;1	*~nakkIrar*

The Tamil classics file can be searched either by the Tamil name of the classic or by the CC number or by the name of the classic transliterated into Roman script. In any of these approaches the display will show the retrieved records in the other two corresponding lists also.

If the search term or CC number is that of a group, the system will retrieve all the hierarchically linked terms.

3 RETRIEVAL AND PRESENTATION

All displays present the descriptors / terms in Tamil script along with their corresponding Colon Class (CC) number and the transliterated descriptor in Roman script.

As mentioned in the Home Page the search can be by the Tamil term, or by the CC number or by the transliterated term. Return to the Home Page from any of the succeeding page is by clicking on the 'back' button at the top left of the page.

Fig. 1 displays "Tamil Classics Home Page.

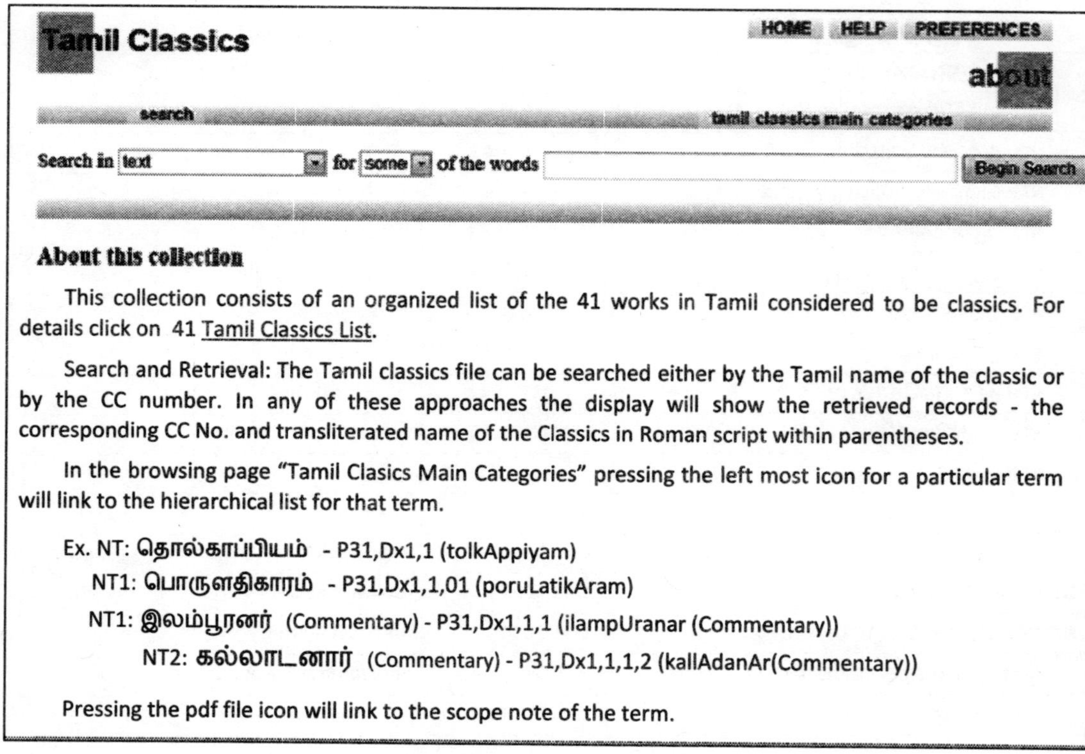

Tamil Classics

HOME HELP PREFERENCES

about

search | tamil classics main categories

Search in text for some of the words [Begin Search]

About this collection

This collection consists of an organized list of the 41 works in Tamil considered to be classics. For details click on 41 Tamil Classics List.

Search and Retrieval: The Tamil classics file can be searched either by the Tamil name of the classic or by the CC number. In any of these approaches the display will show the retrieved records - the corresponding CC No. and transliterated name of the Classics in Roman script within parentheses.

In the browsing page "Tamil Clasics Main Categories" pressing the left most icon for a particular term will link to the hierarchical list for that term.

Ex. NT: தொல்காப்பியம் - P31,Dx1,1 (tolkAppiyam)
NT1: பொருளதிகாரம் - P31,Dx1,1,01 (poruLatikAram)
NT1: இலம்பூரனர் (Commentary) - P31,Dx1,1,1 (ilampUranar (Commentary))
NT2: கல்லாடனார் (Commentary) - P31,Dx1,1,1,2 (kallAdanAr(Commentary))

Pressing the pdf file icon will link to the scope note of the term.

Fig. 1: Tamil Classics Home page (Partial)

Clicking on **'41 Tamil Classics List'** in Tamil Classics Home Page (Fig. 1) will link to a list of the 41 Tamil classics (a MSWORD file) as shown in Fig, 2 right panel.

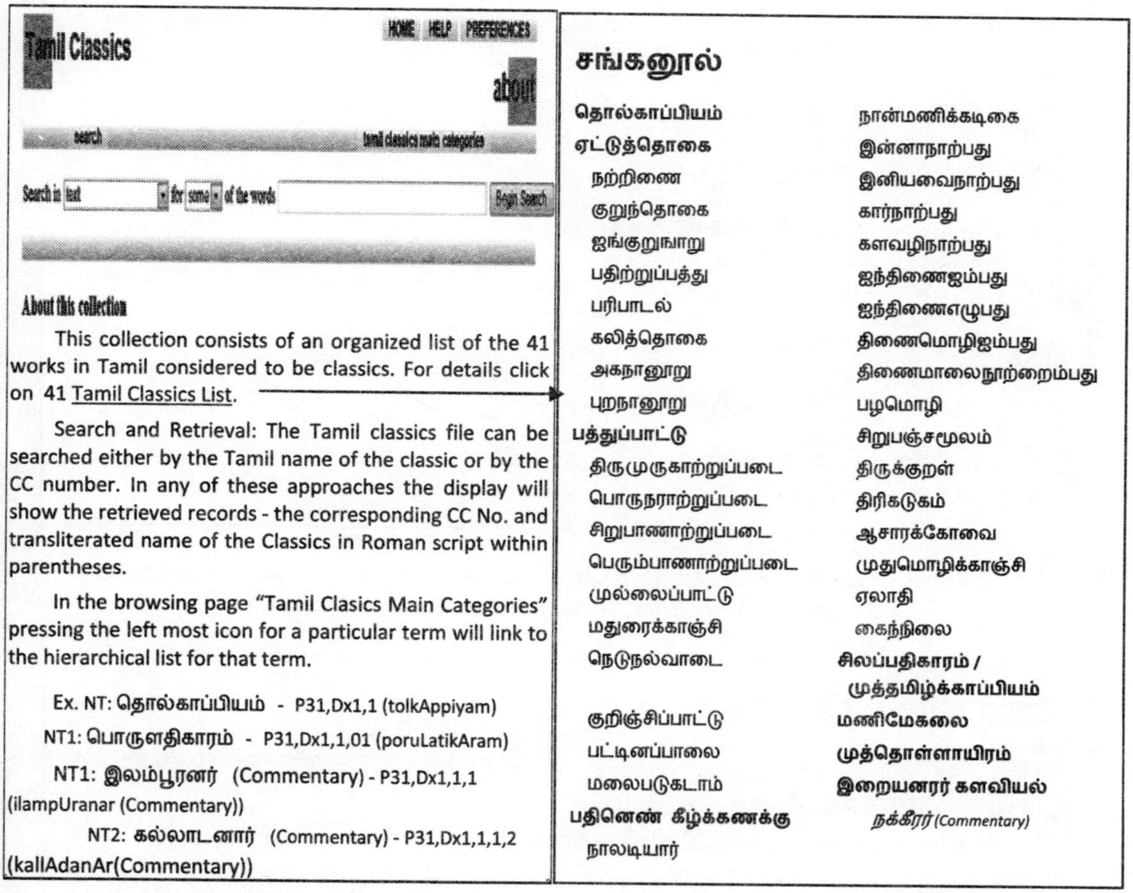

Fig. 2: Clicking on hyperlink "Tamil Classics Main Categories" – shows all 8 categories (Partial)

Clicking on "Tamil Classic Main Category" in the Home page (Fig. 1) will display a list of the 8 main categories of the Tamil classics (Fig.3). There are two icons against each category name. Clicking on an icon in the first column (say the descriptor **'தொல்காப்பியம்** (TolkAppiam)') will link the descriptor to its hierarchically related term(s) as shown in Fig. 4. The CC number and the transliterated term (in Roman script) are also shown.

Clicking on the pdf icon in the second column against a descriptor, say **'மணிமேகலை (maNimEkalai)'** (in the list in Fig. 3) will link it to a brief description (scope note) about the descriptor as shown in Fig. 5

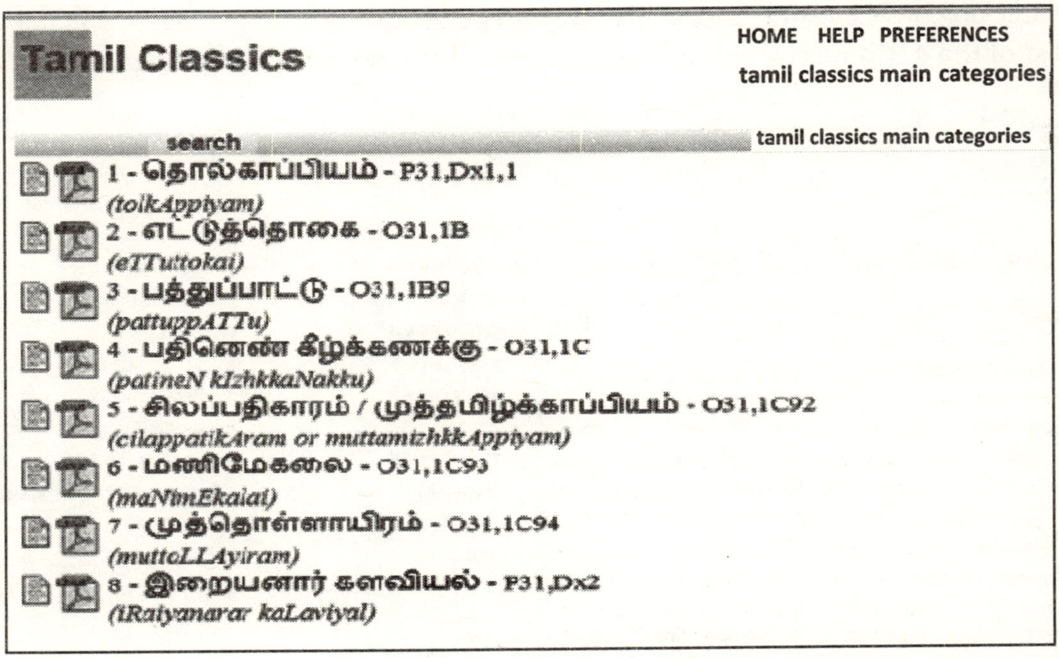

Fig. 3: Browsing the "Tamil Classics Main Categories Classifier" – Shows list of main 8 Tamil categories with two icons, CC No. and transliterated descriptors

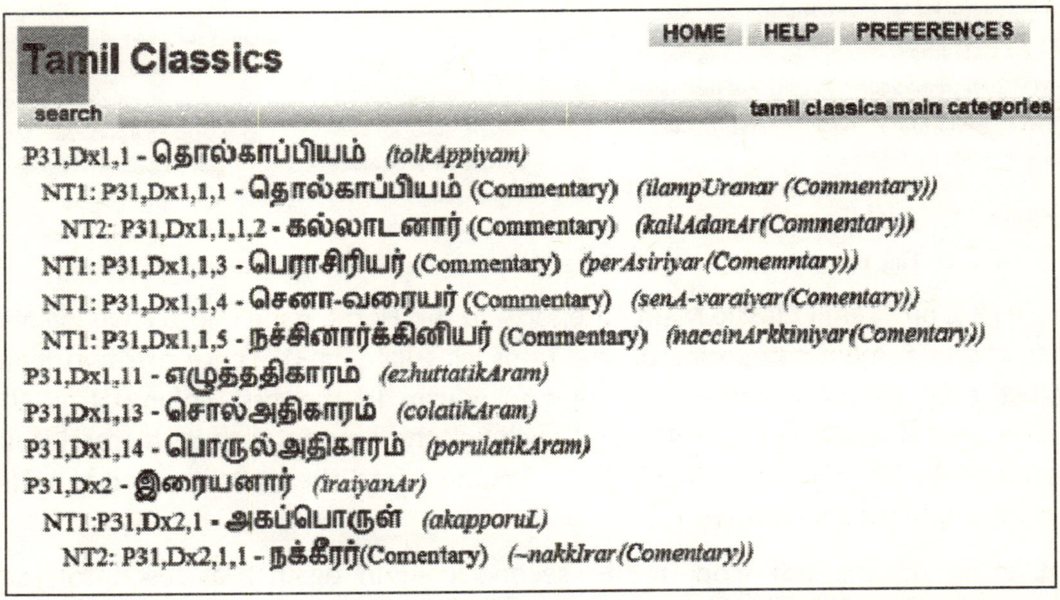

Fig. 4: Clicking the icon in the first column for "தொல்காப்பியம் (tolkApiyam)" (in Fig. 3) - shows Hierarchical list of descriptors

The twin epics, Cilappatikaram and Manimekalai, commonly assigned to the second century A.D., tell the stories of two great women, Kannaki and Manimekalai respectively. The first one, also known as Muttamilkkappiyam (three-fold epic) because of the blending of poetry, music and dance, has its important scenes set in the capitals of the three major kingdoms of Tamilnatu. It celebrates the achievement of a chaste woman who exposes the injustice done to her by the king and burns his capital city, Madurai. The poem is known for its remarkable structure and texture and the poet for his narrative skill and humanism. Manimekalai, narrating the life of a danseuse turned nun, has a clear religious motive, the propagation of Buddhism.

(Source: Why these forty one classics?" *Chemmozhi*, v.1(1), Oct-Dec., 2006)

Fig. 5: Clicking pdf icon for "மணிமேகலை (maNimEkalai)" in the second column (in Fig. 3) - shows scope note for the descriptor

For search by a transliterated term, say, paTTinappAlai in the "serch box" will retrive and display the descriptor and its two icons as in Fig. 6.

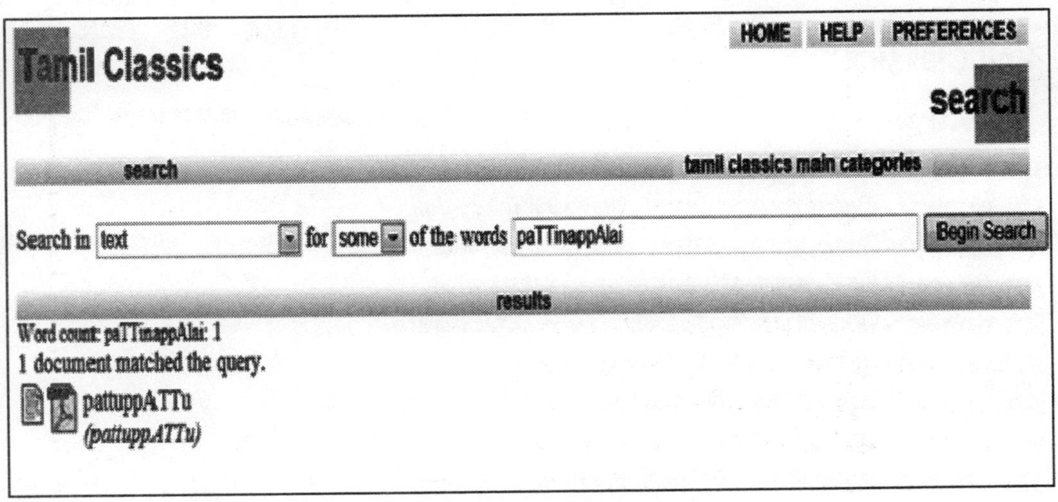

Fig. 6: Shows the result of search by transliterated term "paTTinappAlai"

The result of clicking the icon in first column for the transliterate term "paTTinappAlai" (in Fig. 6) shows the term highlighted as in Fig. 7

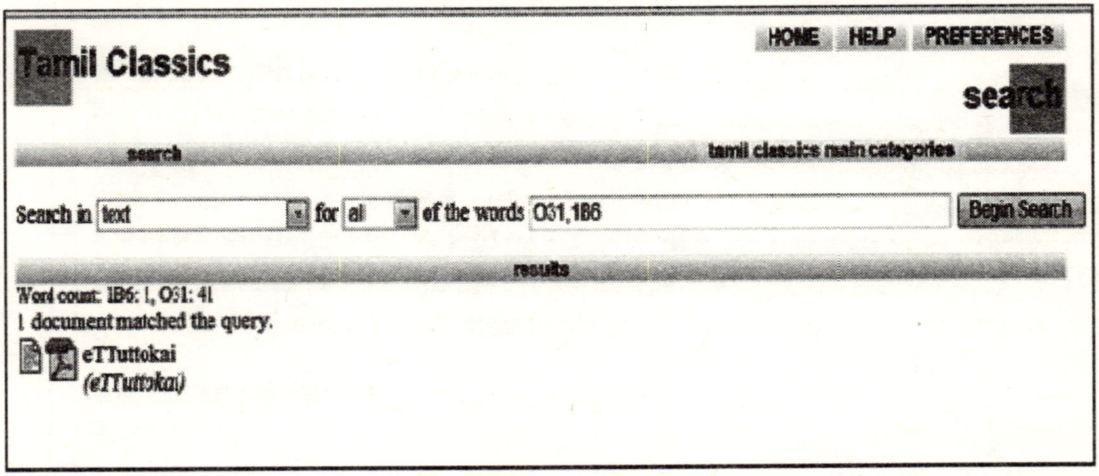

Fig. 7: The result of clicking the icon in the first column for transliterate term "paTTinappAlai" (in Fig. 6) shows the term highlighted here (Fig. 7)

Similarly, search by a CC number say, "O31,1B6" will retrive and display the descriptor and its two icons as in Fig. 8.

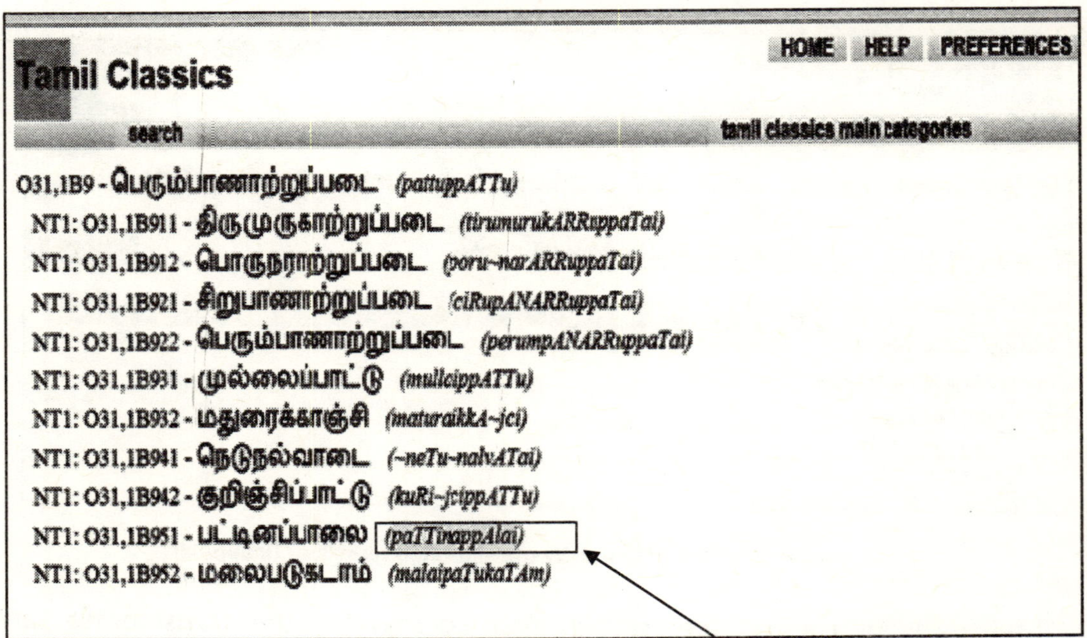

Fig. 8: Shows the result of search by CC No. "O31,1B6"

The result of clicking the icon in the first column for the transliterated term "eTTuttokai" (in Fig. 8) shows the CC No. highlighted as in Fig. 9

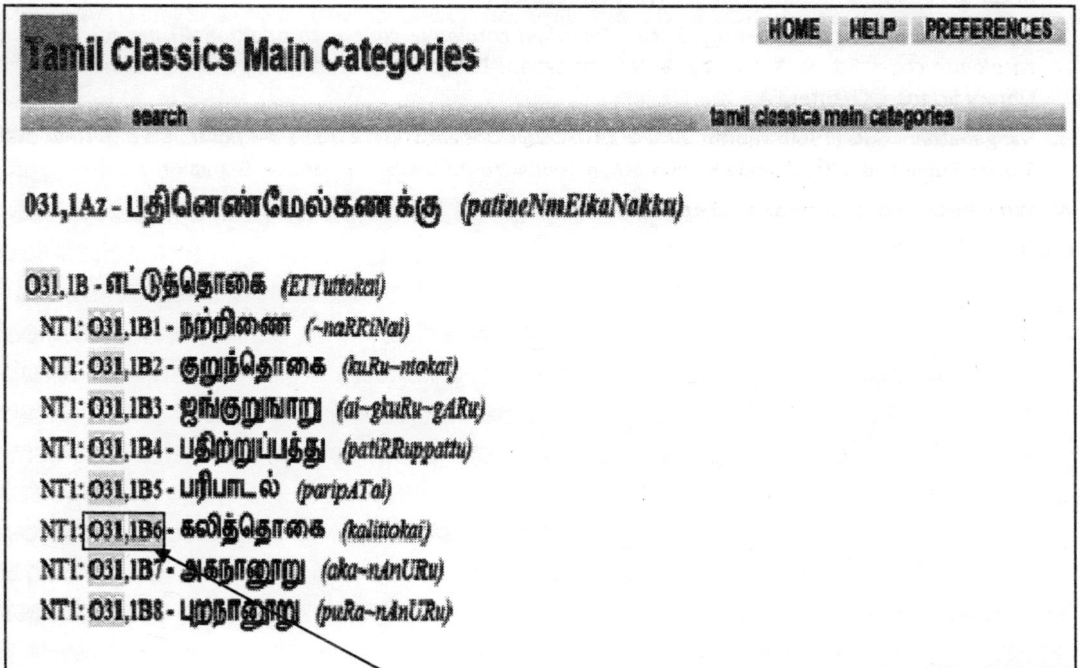

Fig. 9: The result of clicking the icon in the first column for CC No. "O31,1B6" (in Fig. 8) shows the descriptors highlighted here (Fig. 9)

4 CONCLUDING REMARKS

In this paper we described the categorization and classification of the 41 Tamil classics of the Sangam period. A bilingual (Tamil English) thesaurus structure based on the classified list of the classics (CC, ed. 6) is presented. Search and retrieval in the list of classics either by the name of the classic in Tamil script or by the CC number or by the transliterated name of the descriptor in Roman script is demonstrated. The advantages of using a class code (e.g. CC number in our work) in multilingual thesaurus have been discussed in another paper (Neelameghan and Lalitha, 2013) [1].

REFERENCES

1. Neelameghan, A. and Lalitha, S.K. (2013). Multilingual thesaurus and interoperability. *DESIDOC Journal of Library and Information Technology*, 33(4): 290-295.
2. Ranganathan, S.R. (1964; reprint 1988). *Classified catalogue code with additional rules for dictionary catalogue code*. Ed. 5. Assist. by A. Neelameghan. Bangalore: Sarada Ranganathan Endowment for Library Science; Chapter FA.
3. Ranganathan, S.R. (1960; reprint 27th, 2006). *Colon classification. Basic classification.* Ed. 6 New Delhi: Ess Ess Publications for Sarada Ranganathan Endowment for Library Science, Bangalore.
4. Why these forty one classics? *Chemmozhi,* 1(1): Oct-Dec., 2006.

15

Methodology for Designing a Conceptual Model of Knowledge Mapping in the Field of Liquid Rocket Propulsion System

C. Sugumaran

"Knowledge mapping is a process of surveying, assessing and linking the information, knowledge, competencies and proficiencies held by individuals and groups with in an organization and in the subject domain." Components that can be found on a knowledge map are primarily the organization's knowledge assets, also it will reflect, where the subject experts are lagging and its importance. The map will also include information as to their source, their format, the meta-data as well as stakeholders.

Liquid Propulsion Rocket Systems (LPRS) is a subject domain, which deals with the Liquid Propulsion systems for Space Launch Vehicles and Satellites. By analyzing the literature published all over the world and also the internal reports published in the organization, extracting the concepts, it is proposed to build the knowledge map, by linking various concepts to model the LPRS domain.

By mapping the above domain, one can visualize how the concepts are evolved to form new concepts. This paper explains the design methodology to develop the Conceptual model of Knowledge Mapping in the LPRS domain.

Keywords; Domain mapping; Liquid Rocket Propulsion System; Concept maps

1 INTRODUCTION

Knowledge Map is a navigation aid to explicit (codified) information and tacit knowledge, showing the importance and the relationships between knowledge stores and dynamics [1].

Knowledge Map is the diagram of captured information and relationships which enables the efficient communications and learning of knowledge by observers with differing background at multiple levels of details [4].

2 CLASSIFICATIONS OF KNOWLEDGE MAP

As described by [3], there are five types of Knowledge maps:

1. Knowledge Source Maps: these maps structure a population of company experts;
2. Knowledge Asset Maps: this map visually presents the existing stock of knowledge;
3. Knowledge Structure Maps: these maps outline the global architecture of the knowledge domain and relationships;
4. Knowledge Application Maps: these maps show which type of knowledge to be applied at a certain process stage; and
5. Knowledge Development Maps: these maps can be used to depict the necessary stages to develop a certain competence.

3 LPRS CONCEPT

Liquid Propulsion Rocket System (LPRS) is a multidisciplinary subject; its applications are varied and many. It deals with aspects that range from basic principles of engineering to advanced cryogenic technology. It also comprises such aspects as: Material, Manufacturing, Quality Control, Test Facilities, Propellant Storage, Test Facilities, Safety, etc. With the growth and evolution of an organization it becomes necessary and important to manage multidisciplinary and large volumes of knowledge. Thus there is need for a method to classify and categorize knowledge artifacts generated and stored in the organization. From this point of view, a knowledge map which is a representation tool to visualize knowledge sources and relationships among knowledge artifacts is an important tool for both practitioners and academicians.

Construction of a knowledge map is generally composed of various phases, building up map structure and mapping knowledge artifacts into it. First in accordance with necessities of an organization, the structure of knowledge map can be organized by various criteria. For example knowledge map can take the form of a business model, workflow, technology tree, etc. Once the structure of a knowledge map is established, we need to identify into which location knowledge artifacts are to be mapped. In other words, we should assign each knowledge artifact to a specific category of knowledge map previously defined.

4 KNOWLEDGE MAPPING PROCESS

The process consists of the following steps [2]:

- Acquire data (through e.g., Text mining, Survey etc);
- Manipulation data (to produce first order data);
- Store data (to form knowledge mapping database);
- Process data (analysis, aggregation and contextualization to produce higher order data); and
- Visualize data (to produce knowledge maps).

Issues on Knowledge Mapping:

- Scope
- Timeliness – A one-time initiative or requiring on-going updating efforts?
- Completeness and level of granularity – can all concerned knowledge be completely mapped? How comprehensive?
- Design issues – to reduce miscommunication and increase communication.
- Dissemination of deliverables – in the form of written reports / documents, websites, databases? Navigation interfaces for users?

5 METHODOLOGY

As ISRO is already having the database of published literatures on LPRS, the subject heading, keywords assigned by the database creators are extracted. Also the database of internal technical reports is analyzed. By text mining of the literature, about 3000 (knowledge artifacts) concept terms are extracted. These concepts terms are arranged and the linkages between these concepts are being established.

6 MODEL OF KNOWLEDGE MAP IN LPRS

The model concept map of the domain of Liquid Propulsion in is given the Figure 1. From this one can visualize, the place of LPRS domain in the universe of knowledge.

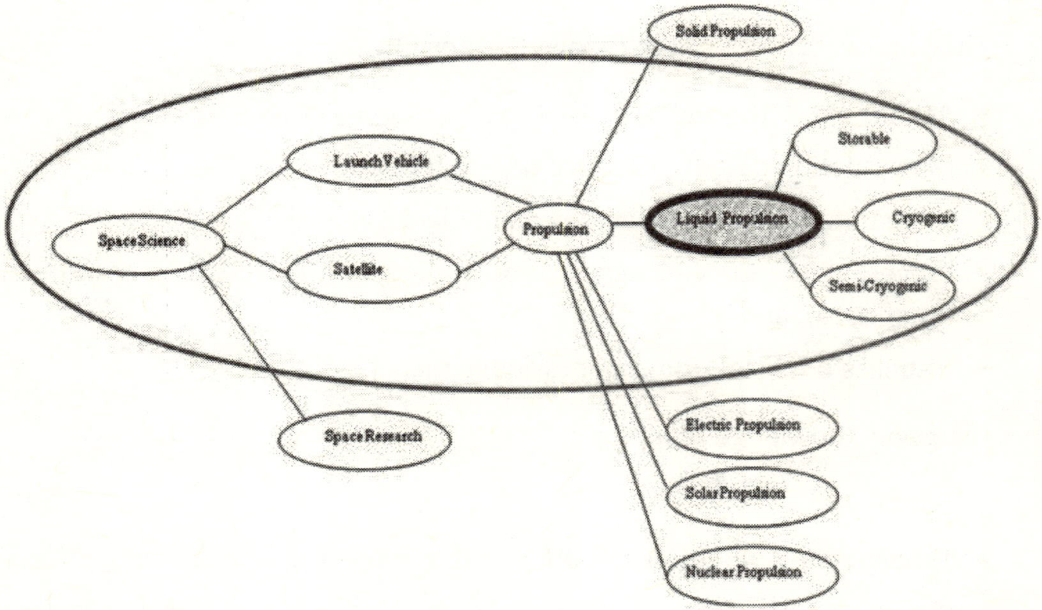

Fig. 1: Liquid propulsion concept in the Universe of knowledge

In Fig. 2, a simple concept model for Liquid Rocket Propulsion and its sub-systems is given. Here one can see that, 'Test Facilities' itself is one another concept model. Like this so many minor concept models are formed. Then finally the total LPRS- knowledge map is created, by combining all the smaller concept maps. As it is multidisciplinary in nature the concept maps are linked in many ways.

The process of creating a database of experts by collecting the information from all the technical employees of the organization has also been initiated. A questionnaire has been prepared in order to collect the meta-data as given in Figure 3.

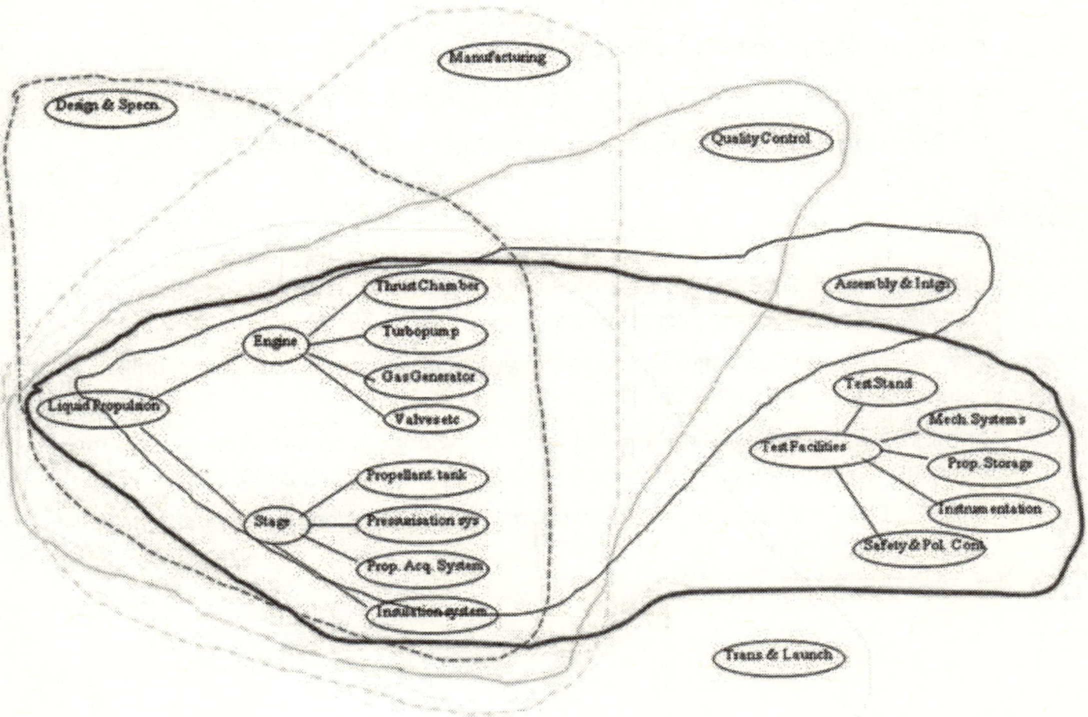

Fig. 2: Simple concept model for liquid rocket propulsion and its sub-system

Name	Designation (Present)	Division (Present)	Academic field / Area	Academic Project	Special / Own Area of Interest	Internal Technical Reports	Previous Projects / Sub. Area	Current Projects / Sub. Area

Fig. 3: Knowledge holders databases

7 CONCLUSION

Knowledge mapping looks at how knowledge flows and identifies where knowledge assets and gaps exist. This includes mapping explicit and tacit knowledge. Applying knowledge mapping allows decision-makers to understand the processes and gaps in knowledge translation. This technique can identify gaps in knowledge translation processes, including

- Setting research priorities;
- Monitoring research in progress;
- Policy making and the use of evidence in policy making; and
- Mechanisms for capturing knowledge from practice.

REFERENCE

1 Eppler, J. Martin. (2008) A process-based classification of knowledge maps and application examples. *Knowledge and process Management*. 15(1): 59 -71.

2 Grey, D. (1999) Knowledge mapping: a practical overview. Available online at http://kmguru.tblog.com/post/98920.

3 Karimi, B. and Saeedikia M. (2009) Bulding a Knowledge Map based on process mapping for R&D centers. *Australian Jl. of Basic and Applied Sciences*, 3(3): 2405-2409,

4 Vail, E.F. (1999) Mapping organizational Knowledge. *Knowledge Management Review,* 2(8): 10-15.

16

Spatial Information System for Socio-economic Development Planning: Categorization, Organization, Integration, Representation and Presentation of Data

A. Neelameghan

A Spatial Information System (SIS) = Geographic Information System (GIS) is an important data support component of the socio-economic development planning system. Socio-economic development planning being oriented towards the future, it has to rely on knowledge, as complete as possible, of the attributes of the components of the society the plan covers. The planner needs data / info on all the present aspects of the society and their environment, and of the recent past that created the conditions for development. It implies data on the state and trend in all sectors of economic activity – agriculture, industry, commerce, transportation, business, finance, human resources, etc.; also data / info on and from the supporting infrastructure in all these sectors – the land, fauna, flora, population, housing, nutrition, public health, education, cultural activities, and so on. A range of different categories of data / info constituting components and services – stable and dynamic – from the national , down to the village level - to be used in an integrated manner. Briefly discusses what is SIS, what support facilities it can provide, the categories of users and uses, the components of SIS – thematic cartography, inventorial cartography, different sources of data input, integration of different types of data; the different types of outputs, etc. Several illustrative examples are given

Keywords: Spatial information system, SIS, Categories of data, users, Uses; Categories data sources; Components: thematic cartography, Inventorial cartography, Synthetic cartography; Illustrations

1 INTRODUCTION: SOCIO-ECONOMIC DEVELOPMENT PLANNING

Socio-economic development and its planning focused on achievement of social goals involves using the products, processes and practices of science and technology, both within and outside the country . This needs to be supported by the formulation and implementation of legislative, administrative, political and institutional policies, programmes and projects. Development planning touches every sector of societal life. Planning being oriented towards the future, it has to rely on knowledge, as complete as possible, of the attributes of the components of the society the plan attempts top cover. Therefore, the planner needs data / info on all the present aspects of the society and their environment, and of the recent past that created the conditions for development. That is data / info on the state and trend in all sectors of economic activity – agriculture, industry, commerce, transportation, business, finance, human resources, etc. Also data / info on and from the supporting infrastructure in all these sectors – the land, fauna, flora, population, housing, nutrition, public health, education, cultural activities, and so on; a range of different categories of data / info providing components and services – stable and dynamic - at different levels - national and sub-national, down to the village level - to be used in an integrated manner. In this context, Spatial Information System (SIS) is an important data / info support component of the national development planning system[1,2,3]

2 SPATIAL INFORMATION SYSTEM

2.1 What is SIS?

- A SIS is a computer-based information system that captures, integrates, stores, processes data e.g edits, analyzes, organizes, and presents data related or linked to location(s);
- Describes and displays geographic / spatial information in different forms and format; and
- SIS applications provide tools to create interactive queries (i.e. user created searches), analyze spatial information, edit data, maps, and present the results of these operations.

2.2 What SIS does?

- SIS collects and provides data about objects below the earth surface (undeground), under water, on the ground, above the ground (atmosphere).

---

[1] Neelameghan, A. (1997). *Information support for socioeconomic development planning.* Bangalore, SRELS. Especially chapter 4 Geographical information systems: an overview.

[2] USGS Science for a changing world. Geographic information system

[3] Cohen, Jean-Claude and Chappuis, Anne (1988). *Government information systems and socio-economic data: training package.* Pilot version. V.1 – *Instructors' manual.* Paris: UNESCO. (referred here as UNESCO Training manual)

- **Data Capture**: If the data to be used are not already in digital form, there are various techniques to capture the information. "Maps can be digitized by hand-tracing with a computer mouse on the screen or on a digitizing tablet to collect the coordinates of various features. Electronic scanners can also be used to convert maps to digitized form. Coordinates from Global Positioning System (GPS) receivers can be entered into a SIS.
- Data capture involves identifying the objects on the map, their exact location on the Earth's surface, and their spatial relationships. Software tools automatically extract features from satellite images or aerial photographs. Objects are identified in a series of attribute tables—the "information" part of a GIS. Spatial relationships, such as whether features intersect or whether they are adjacent, are the key to all SIS-based analysis
- A GPS (global positioning system) - a seeing eye in the sky (aerial photography, satellites with cameras, digital imaging systems, remote sensing devices IR cameras, etc.) and a data receiving system that can process, analyze, organize and present the data in various forms and formats (photographs, other images, 3Ds, maps, tables, texts, etc.); and hand-held devices, showing road-maps and other sites / locations.
- Statistical analysis, pattern analysis, modeling and interpretation relating to societal needs and characteristics.
- **Data Conversion and Analysis**: Computer databases from different sources can be directly entered into a SIS; so also different kinds of data in map form. SIS can also convert existing non-map digital data, into forms that the SIS can recognize and use. For example, "digital satellite images can be analyzed to produce a map of digital information about land use and land cover (figs. 3 and 4). Similarly, census data or hydrologic tabular data can be converted to a map-like form and serve as layers of thematic information in a SIS."
- **Networking**: SIS may be networked with other SISs and other data information system to facilitate collaborative work and exchange of information.

2.3 What the Data Describe?

- The data describes the objects in terms of their position with respect to a known coordinate system;

- their attributes not related to position, e.g. colour, incidence of disease, population density, location of roads, bus stations, etc.; and
- their spatial inter-relation with each other (topographical relationships) - how they are linked together or how one can move between them.

Thus, SIS enables relating different information and data in a spatial context and to identify this relationship and derive inferences. For instance, by comparing rainfall information in an area with other information, such as the location of dry lands across the area, may indicate that certain locations receive little rainfall. Such inference can help making appropriate decisions about actions to be taken by the concerned people / authorities. A SIS, therefore, helps discovery of new information that assists better decision making.

SIS can emphasize the spatial relationships among the objects being mapped. Compared to a computer-aided mapping system that represents a road simply as a line, a SIS can also recognize that road as the boundary between wetland and urban development, etc. (*see also* topological relationship modeling below).

Data Integration: SIS enables the linking, or integration of data / information. For example, by combining mapped variables SIS can construct and analyze new variables –"by combining agricultural records with hydrographic data enables identification of which streams will carry certain levels of fertilizer runoff. Agricultural records can indicate how much pesticide has been applied to a piece of land. By locating these areas and intersecting them with streams, the SIS enables prediction of the amount of nutrient runoff in each stream. Then as streams converge, the total loads can be calculated downstream where the stream enters a lake".

Data Structures, Projection and Registration: Map information in a SIS needs to be processed so that it fits with information collected from other maps before analysis. The digital data may have to undergo such manipulations as projection conversions that integrate them into a SIS. A projection is a mathematical mode of transferring information from the Earth's three-dimensional, curved surface to a two-dimensional medium - paper or a computer screen. Different projections are used for different types of maps; computers can transform digital information, gathered from sources with different projections, to a common projection (Figs. 10a and b).

As digital data collected are stored in different ways, two data sources may not be fully compatible. Hence, a SIS must be able to convert data from one structure to another. Satellite image data that have been interpreted by a computer to produce a land use map can be "read into" the SIS in raster format. Raster files can be manipulated by the computer, though often less detailed and may be less visually appealing than vector data files, which can approximate the appearance of more traditional hand-drafted maps. Data restructuring can be done by a SIS to convert data between different formats - a SIS can convert a satellite image map to a vector structure by generating lines around all cells with the same classification, while determining the spatial relationships of the cell, such as adjacency or inclusion. Vector digital data can be captured as points, lines (a series of point coordinates), or areas (shapes bounded by lines).

Data Modeling: As it is impossible to collect data over every square foot of the Earth's surface, samples are taken at carefully selected locations. SIS can then show two- and three-dimensional characteristics of the Earth's surface, subsurface, and atmosphere from points where samples have been collected. There are several methods of estimating the characteristics of surfaces from a few point measurements. Two- and three-dimensional contour maps created from the surface modeling of sample points from pH measurements can be analyzed together with any other map in a SIS covering the area.

A SIS can recognize and analyze the spatial relationships among mapped phenomena or entities. Conditions of adjacency (what is next to what), containment (what is enclosed by what), and proximity (how close something is to something else) can be determined with a SIS. This process is called topological relationship modeling.

3 THREE TOPOLOGICAL COMPONENTS

Spatial data can be reduced or categorized into 3 topological concepts: The Point, the Line, and the Area. It means that a spatial phenomenon can be represented by a combination of these concepts, plus a label or name indicating what it is.

4 CATEGORIES OF USERS AND USES OF SIS

In designing and developing an information system for socio-economic development planning and implementation, knowing about the already existing categories of users and potential future users and the types of use of the different categories is a prerequisite. Some of the categories are:

- Earth Scientists
- Urban Planners
- Cadastral Agencies
    - *Distribution of Land*
    - *Distribution of Resources*

      Example: Sharing of river water (between districts, between countries)
- Civil Engineers
    - *Road Systems*
    - *Waterways*

      Example: For estimation of construction costs, including cutting away hillsides and filling valleys, forests, etc.
- Health Service Agencies

  Example: Pattern of spread of diseases, epidemics. Spread of pollution, waste
- Environment Monitoring Agencies

  Example: Pollution, waste disposal, oil spills, etc.
    - *Biodiversity interests*

      Example: Study of life cycle, movements, and migration patterns of microorganisms, plants, animals, etc

4.1 Development Planning Applications

According to UN FAO / UNEP **"Land and Land Resources** refer to a delineable area of the earth's terrestrial surface, encompassing all attributes of the biosphere immediately above or below this surface, including those of the near-surface, climate, the soil and terrain forms, the surface hydrology (including shallow lakes, rivers, marshes and swamps), the near-surface sedimentary layers and associated groundwater and geo-hydrological reserve, the plant and animal populations, the human settlement pattern and physical results of past and present human activity (terracing, water storage or drainage structures, roads, buildings, etc.)" Application areas include:

- River management;
- Groundwater movements, aquifer conditions;
- Coastal wetlands planning;
- Urban wetlands management;
- Land evaluation and planning;
- Land use changes monitoring;
- Wasteland development;

- Location of industries (water, power, market access, etc);
- Environment impact analysis;
- Air quality assessment, water quality analysis;
- Agro-climatic planning;
- Mining and quarrying sites, landslides – impact, changes, etc...; and
- Island eco-system studies.

The databases and information systems of the UN FAO and associated organizations to support agriculture development, include a number of spatial map systems, databases, and networks as indicated in the following figure:

Source: http://www.fao.org/nr/land/databasesinformation-systems/en/ Similarly, there are many Aquatic Species Distribution Maps.

Other SIS application areas: Scientific investigations; Criminology, Archaeology, Vehicle guidance; Toll collection, Education, Text and Image transfer, etc

5 SPECIAL ADVANTAGES OF SIS

- Large amount of information /data can be viewed in a small space as compared to e.g presentation in tabular form;
- Focus attention on particular functions;
- Draw attention to unreliable data;
- Easier identification of areas with development potential;
- Identification of underutilized development potential;
- Superimposition of indicators;
- Identification of gaps in data collection / reporting;
- Representation of qualitative information;
- Inventorial cartography;
- Locating areas of high production / low production e.g. crops; and
- Regional comparisons.

6 SIS COMPONENTS

6.1 Thematic Cartography

- Land information system;
- Soil, ground water etc.;
- Cadastre--a public register showing the details of ownership and value of land; made for the purpose of taxation;
- Natural resources (environment...); and
- Infrastructure (buildings, roads, etc.).

Socio-economic data / info

- Population (location, density, groups...)
- Economic activities (agriculture, industries...)
- Administrative services (education, health, transport...)

6.2 Inventorial Cartography

Physical

Topographic maps

Administrative

- Cadastral maps
- Land use plans
- Census maps

6.3 Synthetic Cartography

7 CONCLUDING REMARKS

This paper emphasizes the importance of Spatial Information System (SIS) as a component of the set of information systems that are required to support national socio-economic development planning and plan implementation. The different categories of information / data inputs to and the variety of outputs from a SIS are discussed. The special features and advantages of SIS over conventional / traditional information systems are mentioned. The selected illustrations of output photographs and images, separately and /or integrated or superimposed provide clarification of the textual descriptions.

8 ACKNOWKLEDGEMENT

Thanks are due to Smt. S.K. Lalitha of the Sarada Ranganathan Endowment for Library science for her assistance in organizing the illustrative pictures presented in the Annexes.

Annex 1:

Fig. 1: illustrates integration / superimposition of different types of data derived from different sources – satellite images, aerial photography, remote sensing, digitized maps, tabulated data – to create a SIS / GIS map of the road system in a State together with location of cities and towns in the state, marking borders of neighbouring states, and legend, etc. state boundary, major roads and national highways. (Modified US Geological Survey picture)

Fig. 2: shows the broad data categories constituting components of a thematic map in a SIS to support national development planning (from UNESCO Training manual)

Fig. 3: mentions the broad data categories constituting components of an inventorial map in SIS to support national development planning (from UNESCO Training manual)

Annex 2:

Figures show different categories of presentation of data about a spatial entity. The pictures 1 to 5 are selected from USGS pictures; and pictures 6 to 9 are from UNESCO Training manual.

Annex 1

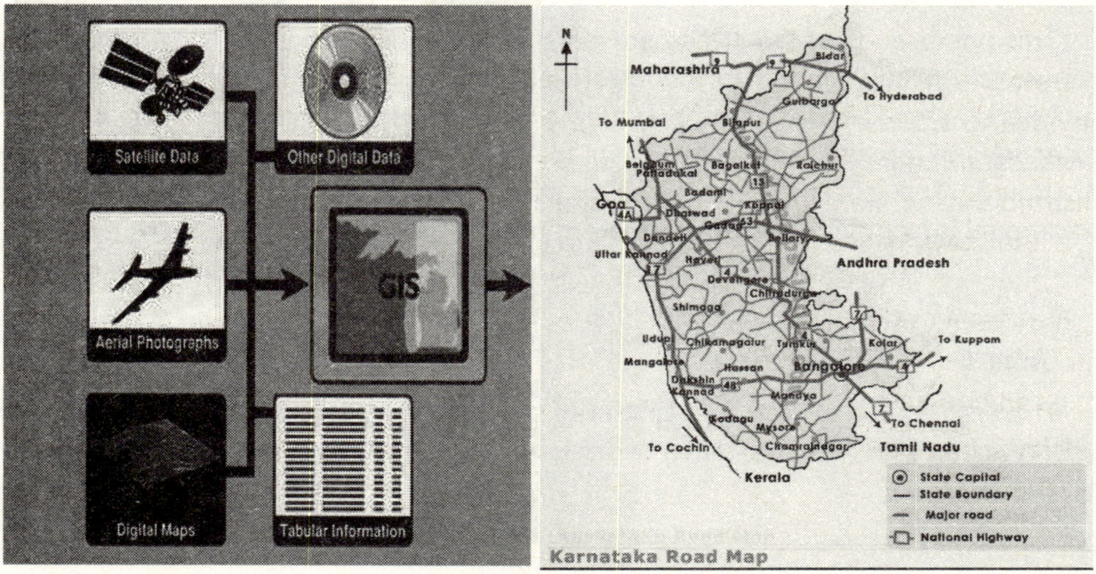

Fig. 1: Integration of Files

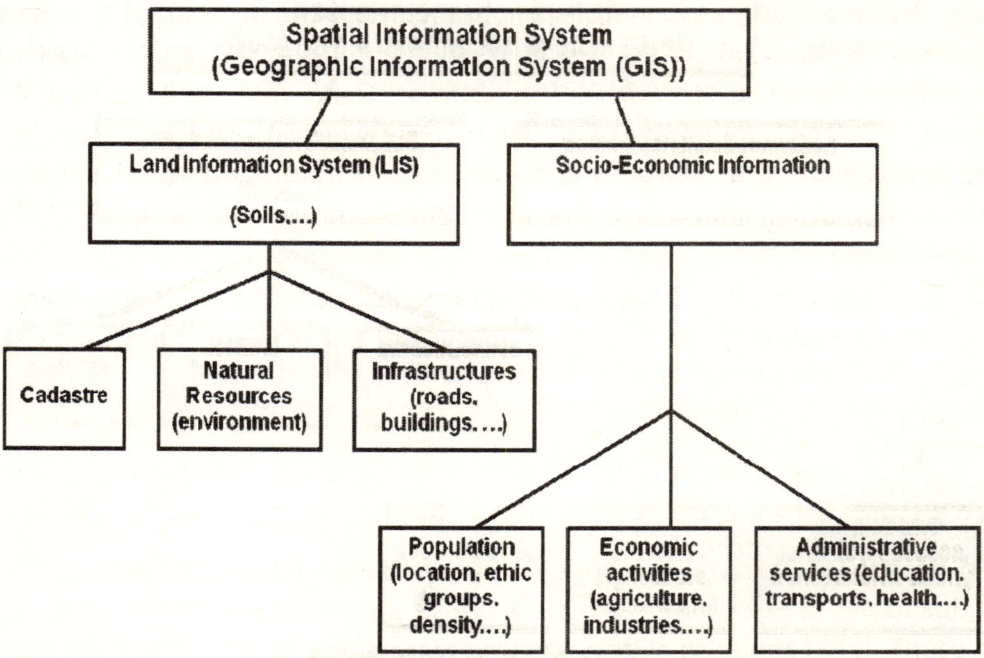

Fig. 2: Parts of Thematic Cartography

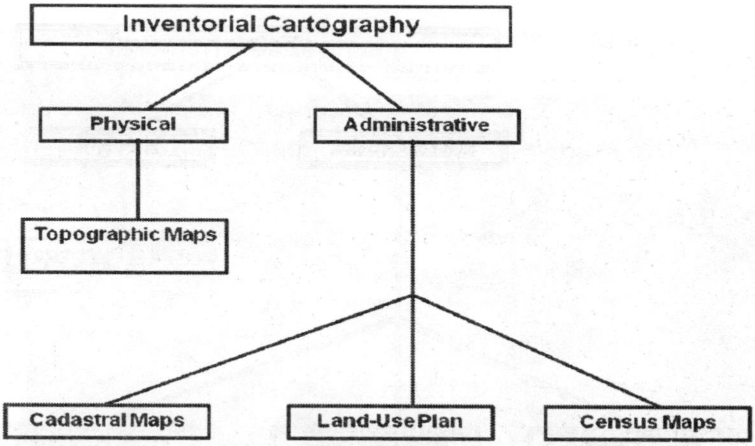

Fig. 3: Parts of Inventorial Cartography

Annex 2

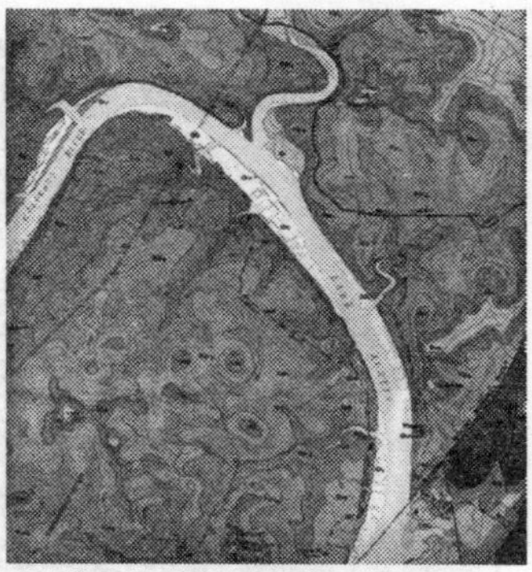

Fig. 1a: Geologic map.

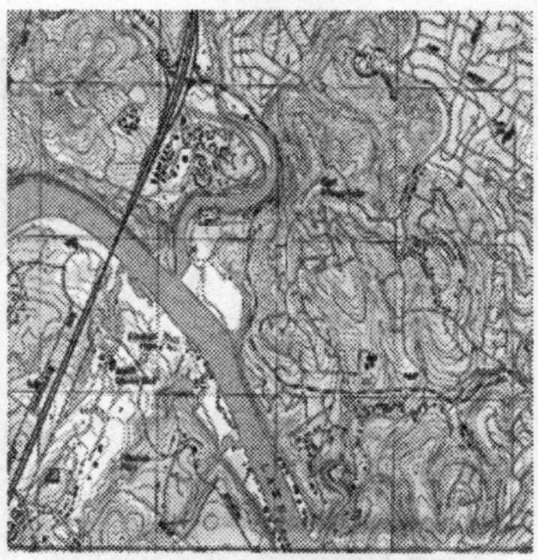

Fig. 1b: Scanned, rectified topographic map – digital raster graphic

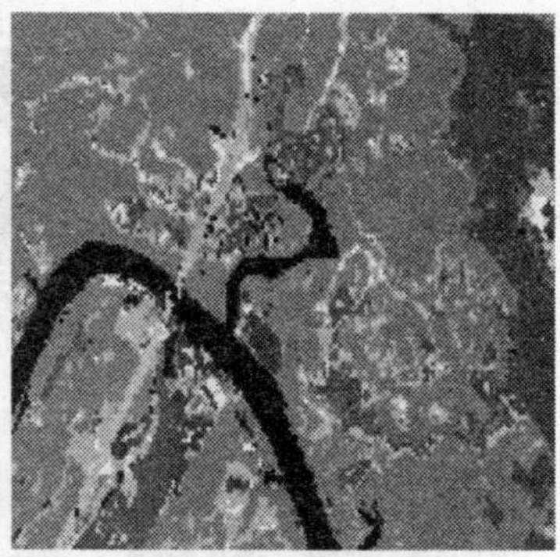

Fig. 1c: Satellite image data in figure 4d analyzed to indicate classes of land uses and cover

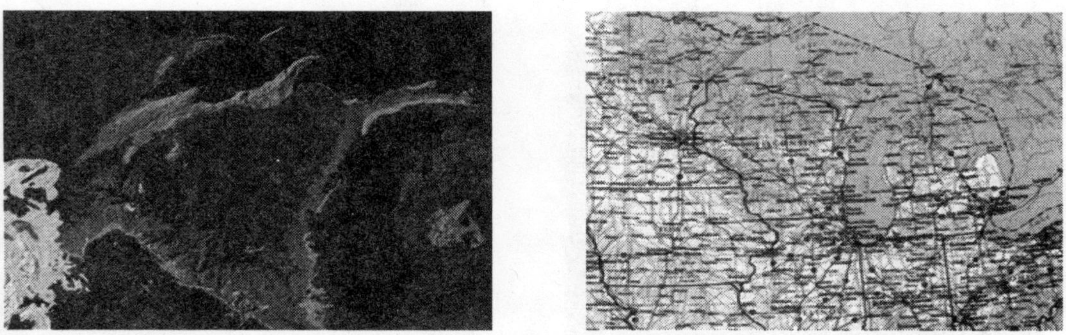

Fig. 2: Examples of finished maps that can be generated using a SIS, showing landforms and geology (left) and human-built and physical features (right).

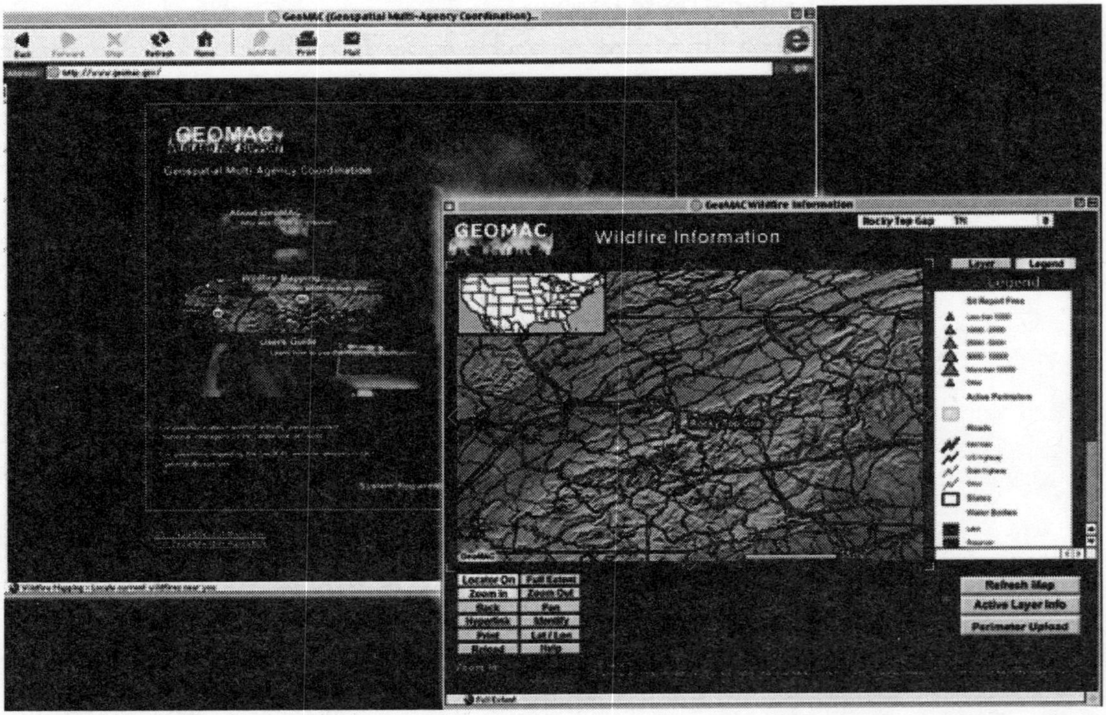

Fig. 3: Superimposed maps of wild fires

Fig. 4a: Digital line graph data of roads

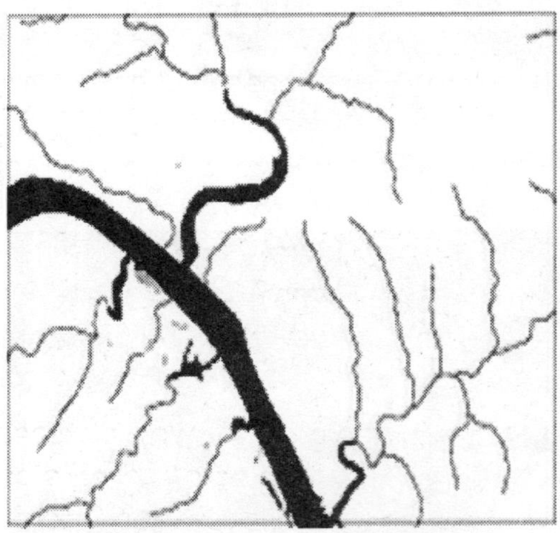

Fig. 4b: Digital line graph data of rivers

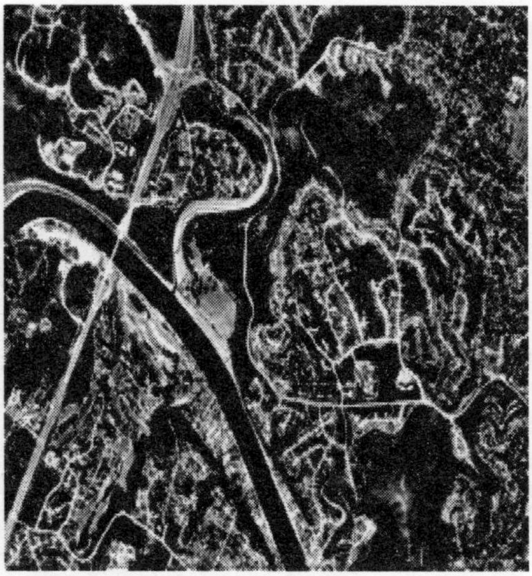

Fig. 4c: Digital orthophoto quadrangle

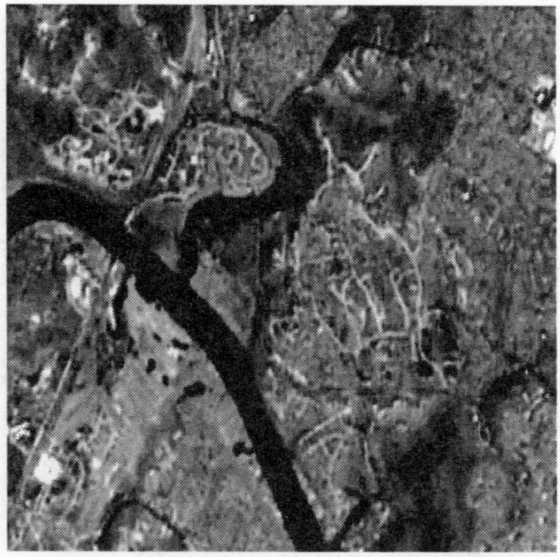

Fig. 4d: Satellite image from which land cover information can be derived

Fig. 5a: Flow superimposed on a digital orthophoquad of the area

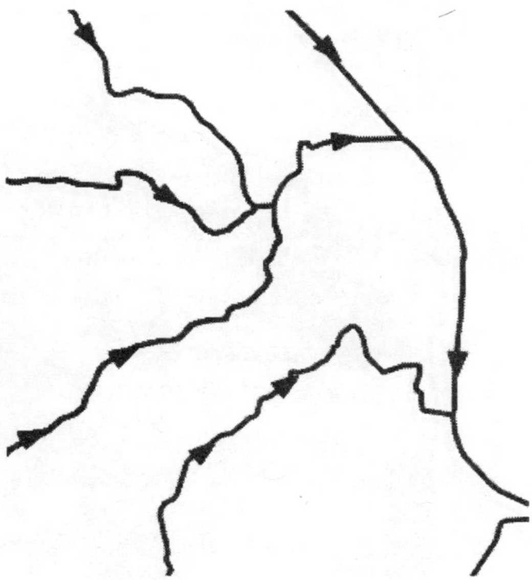

Fig. 5b: Simulation of the movement of materials along a network of lines, showing the route of pollutants through a stream system. Arrows indicate flow directions

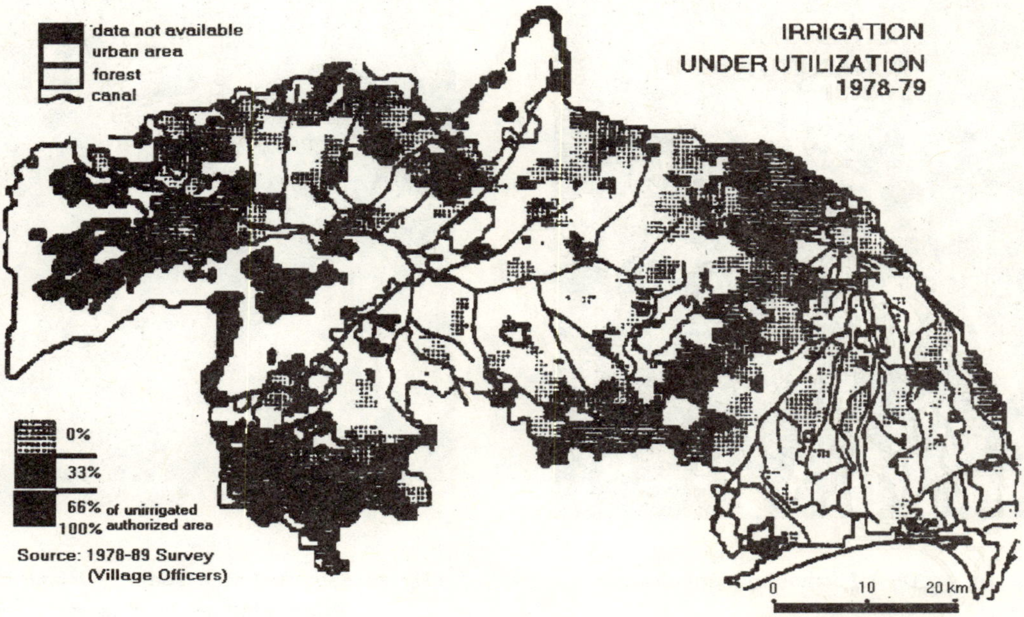

Fig. 6a: Irrigation - under-utilization 1978-79

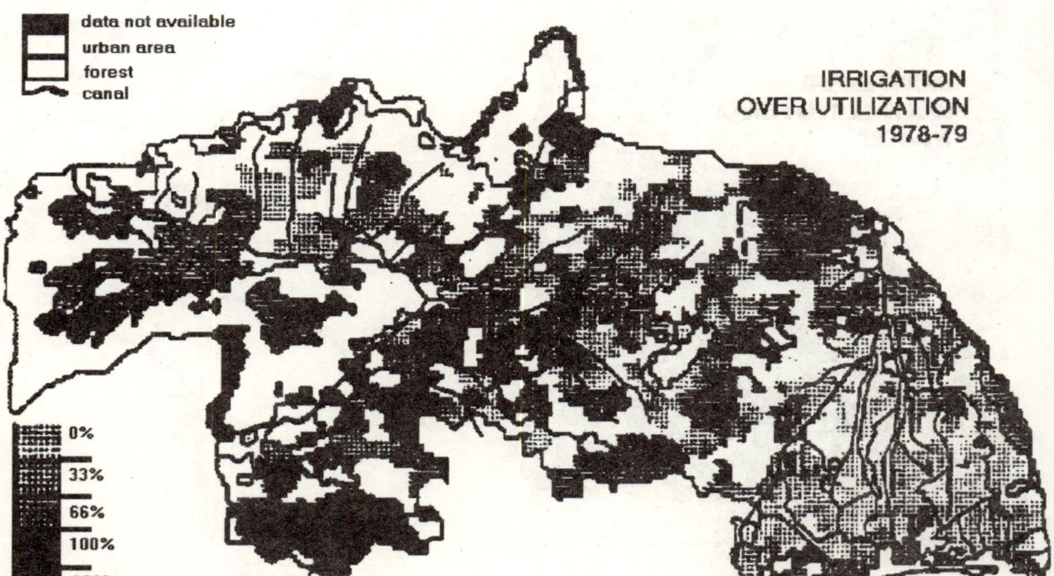

Fig. 6b: Over-utilization of Irrigation

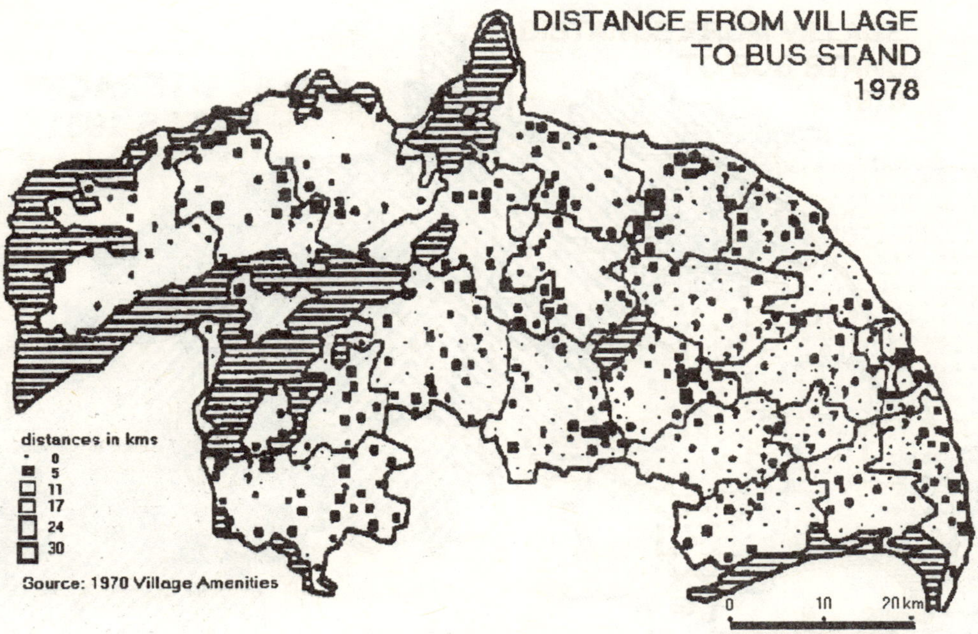

Fig. 7: Identification of Gaps in the Infrastructure

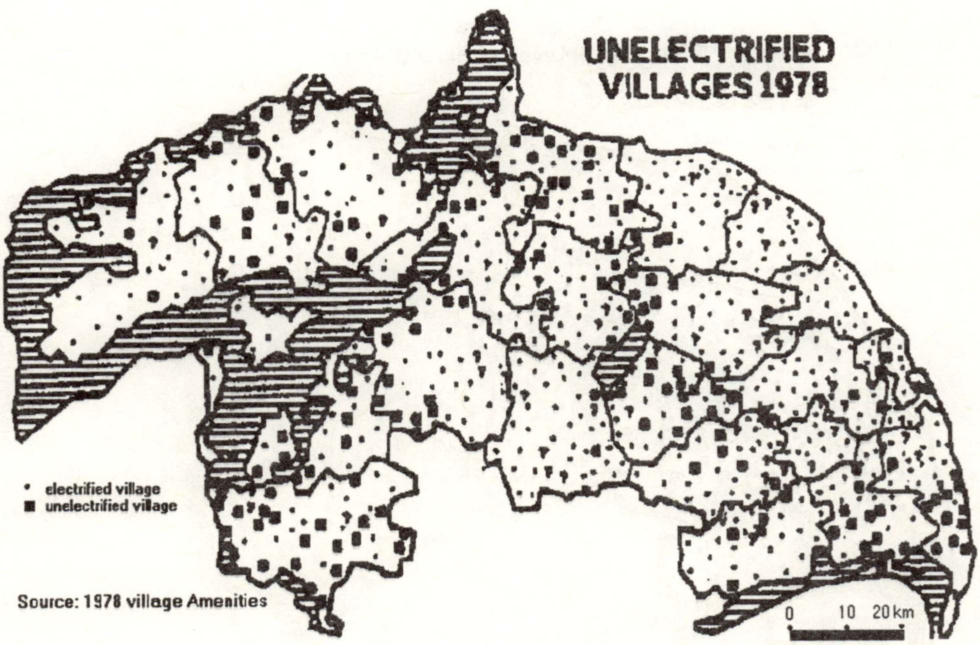

Fig. 8: Representation of Qualitative Data

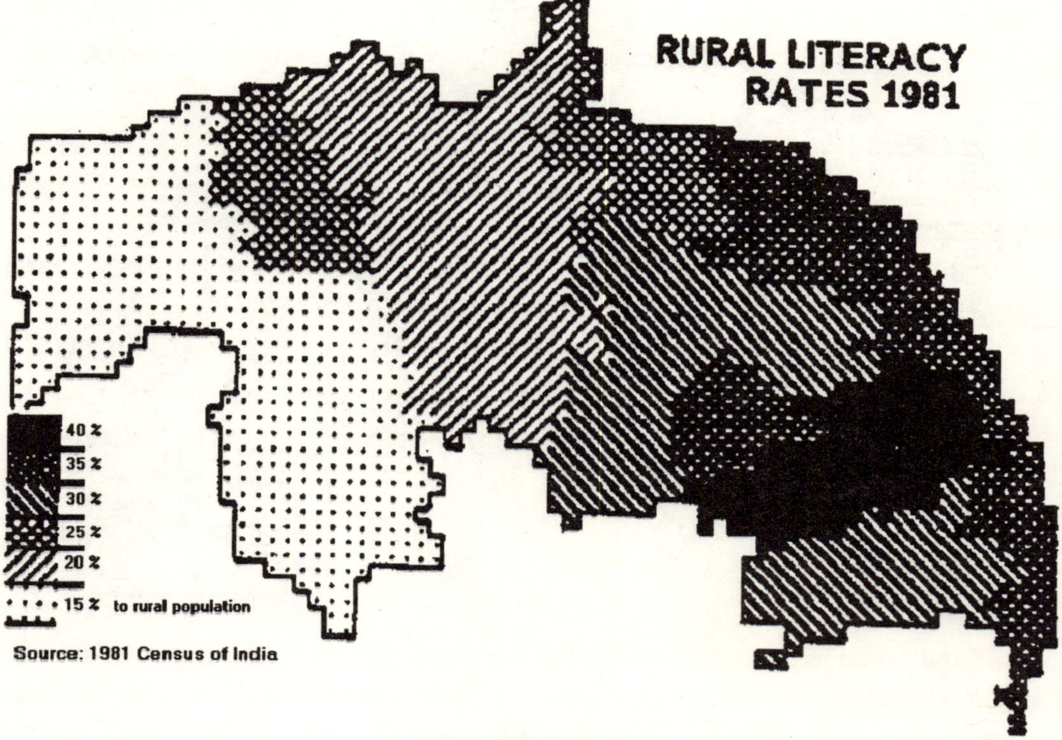

Fig. 9: Levels of Rural Literacy

List of Contributors

Bean, Carol

U.S. Department of Health and Human Services - 200 Independence Avenue, S.W. - WASHINGTON, D.C. 20201, USA. E-mail: Carol.Bean@hhs.gov.

Broughton, Vanda

Professor of Library & Information Studies, University College London, UNITED KINGDOM. E-mail: v.broughton@ucl.ac.uk

D'Ambrosio, Amber J.

Special Collections Librarian and Archivist, Dixie State University Library, 225 South 700 East, St. George, UT 84790, USA. E-mail: dambrosio@dixie.edu

Gnoli, Claudio

University of Pavia. Science and Technology Library, via Ferrata 1, 27100 Pavia, ITALY. E-mail: claudio.gnoli@unipv.it

Green, Rebecca

OCLC, Dublin, Ohio, USA. E-mail: greenre@oclc.org

Iyer, Hemalata

Department of Information Studies, College of Computing and Information, University at Albany, State University of New York, 135 Western Avenue, Albany, NY 12222. USA. E-mail: hi651@albany.edu

Karanth, Pallavi

Centre for Knowledge Analytics and Ontological Engineering – KAnOE, Department of Computer Science and Engineering, PES Institute of Technology, Bangalore 560085, INDIA, E-mail: karanthpallavi@gmail.com

La Barre, Kathryn

Graduate School of Library and Information Science, University of Illinois at Urbana-Champaign 501 E. Daniel Street, MC-493, Champaign, IL 61820-6211 USA. E-mail: klabarre@illinois.edu

Lalitha, S. K
Sarada Ranganathan Endowment for Library Science, 702, Upstairs, 42nd Cross, Rajajinagar 3rd Block, Bangalore 560010, INDIA. E-mail: sklalitha60@gmail.com

Mahesh, Kavi
Centre for Knowledge Analytics and Ontological Engineering – KAnOE,
Department of Computer Science and Engineering, PES Institute of Technology,
Bangalore 560085, INDIA, E-mail: drkavimahesh@gmail.com

Mazzochi, Fulvio
CNR-Institute for Complex Systems, Via Salaria Km 29,300 - C.P. 1000015 Monterotondo St. (RM), ITALY, E-mail: fulvio.mazzocchi@isc.cnr.it

Mustafa El Hadi, Widad, University of Lille 3- Laboratoire, GERIICO- France. E-mail: widad.mustafa@univ-lille3.fr

Neelameghan, A.
Sarada Ranganathan Endowment for Library Science, 702, Upstairs, 42nd Cross,
Rajajinagar 3rd Block, Bangalore 560010, INDIA. E-mail: anm2002@vsnl.net

Ohly, H.Peter
President, International Society for Knowledge Organization, Prinzen Str. 179, 53175 Bonn, GERMANY E-mail: peter.ohly@gmx.de

Raghavan, K.S.
Centre for Knowledge Analytics and Ontological Engineering – KAnOE,
PES Institute of Technology, Bangalore 560085, INDIA. E-mail: ksragav@hotmail.com

Shepherd, Mike
Dalhousie University, Halifax, Nova Scotia, CANADA. E-mail: Michael.Shepherd@dal.ca

Smiraglia, Richard P.
School of Information Studies, University of Wisconsin – Milwaukee, Milwaukee, USA.
E-mail: smiragli@uwm.edu

Sugumaran, C.
Scientist / Engr 'SF', Documentation Officer, LPSC / ISRO, Thiruvananthaturam 695 547, INDIA. E-mail: c_sugumaran@yahoo.co.in

Tennis, Joseph T..
Information School, University of Washington, Seattle, USA,
E-mail: jtennis@u.washington.edu

Watters, Carolyn
Dalhousie University, Halifax, Nova Scotia, CANADA, E-mail: Carolyn.Watters@dal.ca

Index